# Defence Relation

*An overview*

# Defence Relation

## *An overview*

**Col. (Retd.) S. C. Narang**

**Prashant Publishing House**
**DELHI - 110094 (INDIA)**

**PRASHANT PUBLISHING HOUSE**
C-34, 28 Foota Road, Gali No. 3
West Karawal Nagar, Delhi-110094
Phone : 9810396373, 22963970

*Defence Relation : An Overview*



First Published : 2010

ISBN : 978-93-80565-09-5



PRINTED IN INDIA

---

Published by Mr. R. K. Jha M/s. Prashant Publishing House, Delhi and Printed at H.S. Offset Press, Delhi.

# Preface

India's strategic interests in Asia are two-fold: ensuring security in its immediate neighborhood and protecting India's interests, including its economic and energy needs, in the rest of Asia and the Middle East.

Indian officials believe that the most likely military contingencies they face in the medium term are "Kargils and Tsunamis"—sharp, limited land engagements on their borders and broader humanitarian problems in the extended region. They seek capabilities that would equip India to make its presence felt in the area, from the Persian Gulf to Southeast Asia, and to respond if necessary to other kinds of contingencies.

India's national security policy is based on the premise that its immediate neighborhood is dangerous and that regional instability from neighboring countries fuels India's internal insurgencies. India's relationship with Pakistan has been troubled from the start and has often been a sticking point for the United States.

Insurgents in Kashmir have close ties with counterparts in Pakistan. Central India's "Naxalite" revolutionaries are said to have loose ties with Maoists in Nepal. India has traditionally discouraged any direct U.S. involvement in the region's geopolitics. Improved relations with the United States, however, have brought Indian and U.S. policies into closer alignment on problems in Nepal, Bangladesh, and Sri Lanka.

*—Author*

# Contents

# 1

# Introduction to Defence Relations

The historical commitment of Australian and French troops fighting side by side in major conflicts over the last century is one of the founding elements of our defence cooperation. Remembrance of the common sacrifices has led to the establishment of a strong bilateral relationship between France and Australia.

Australian-French defence cooperation is multifaceted and takes place within a bilateral framework as well as through international organisations.

It is based on a regional commitment to security and stability as well as on regular exchanges on a strategic, operational and tactical level. Regional cooperation is a good example of the high level of our relationship. The presence of French troops in the Pacific facilitates regular and high-quality contacts between the French and Australian defence forces. This involves disaster relieve (FRANZ agreement) and fishery surveillance operations, joint exercises in New Caledonia (Croix du Sud) as well as participation of French forces in regional Australian exercises (Pitch Black and Kakadu).

Defence cooperation is based on the organisation of regular meetings between headquarters and between Foreign Affairs and Defence officials. These regular consultations are complemented by visits from military, civilian and industrial authorities within the defence domain, and also frequent calls from French naval vessels in Australian ports.

A defence cooperation agreement facilitating our reciprocal activities will form the framework for a strengthening of our bilateral relationships in the field of defence.

Finally, the signing in December 2005 of contracts between the Australian Defence Force and French industrials to provide defence equipment bears witness to the promising commercial perspectives in this field for companies which are able to establish local subsidiaries, as well as the renowned quality of French defence equipment.

A relationship of trust has developed between the Délégation Générale pour l'Armement (DGA) and the Defence Materiel Organisation (DMO) which cooperate efficiently in the management of programs aimed at equipping the armed forces of two countries with similar materiel, in particular helicopters (Tiger, NH/MRH 90).

## Security, Defence and International Relations

This section is concerned with providing strong protections for records whose disclosure could reasonably be expected to damage

- the security of the State
- the defence of the State
- international relations, or
- matters relating to Northern Ireland.

Traditionally the area of security, defence and international relations has attracted a high level of protection in Freedom of Information legislation. This level of protection is reflected in the following aspects of the section:

- no public interest test
- refusal to confirm or deny provision
- ministerial certificate (section 25)
- mandatory exemption for classes of records (subsection (2))

The strength of these protections do not relieve the decision maker of the obligation to assess the effects of disclosure in cases to which section 24(1) applies and to explain, where appropriate, how release of the records in question will adversely affect one of the interests outlined in that subsection. It is to be expected that decisions on FOI requests relating to such material will only be taken at a senior level.

## Elements of the Section

24.-(1) A head may refuse to grant a request under *section 7* in relation to a record if, in the opinion of the head, access to it could reasonably be expected to affect adversely-

(*a*) the security of the State,

(*b*) the defence of the State,

(*c*) the international relations of the State,

(*d*) matters relating to Northern Ireland, or

(e) matters relating to the functions of the Independent Commission for the Location of Victims' Remains (within the meaning of the Criminal Justice (Location of Victims' Remains) Act, 1999). Subsection (1) provides that information may be protected if could reasonably be expected to affect adversely the security of the State, defence of the State, international relations of the State, matters relating to Northern Ireland or matters relating to the functions of the Independent Commission for the Location of Victims' remains (within the meaning of the Criminal Justice (Location of remains) Act, 1999).

There is no separate requirement to consider public interest in relation to a record to which subsection (1) applies.

24. (2) A head shall refuse to grant a request under section 7 if the request concerned contains specified classes of information or relates to certain records concerning security, defence or international relations or contains information that relates to the functions of the Independent Commission for the Location of Victims Remains.

A record falling within subsection (2) must be considered exempt. There is no requirement to consider harm or public interest in relation to records falling within this subsection.

## The Security of the State and Defence of the State

The following classes of record must be considered exempt in accordance with paragraph (a) of subsection (2):

- A record containing information that was obtained or prepared for the purposes of intelligence or the security or defence of the State;

- A record that relates to the tactics, strategy or operations of the Defence Forces in or outside the State;
- A record that relates to the detection, prevention, or suppression of activities calculated or tending to undermine the public order or authority of the State (which expression has the same meaning as in section 2 of the Offences against the State Act 1939).

In relation to other records which may impact on the security or defence of the state, where the risk or damage may not be obvious to those who work outside of the security area, a decision maker must take care to identify what particular interests would be put at risk by disclosure. Of course it may not be feasible on occasion to disclose such interests to the requester. Nevertheless, such factors must always be clearly recorded, if only for the purposes of any subsequent review.

The importance of balancing the security interests of the State and the interests of the individual has been considered by the Supreme Court.

In Heaney-v-Ireland, which dealt with the curtailment of the right to silence, the Supreme Court said "on the one hand constitutional rights must be construed in such a way as to give life and reality to what is being guaranteed. On the other hand, the interest of the State in maintaining public order must be respected and protected". This balancing of rights has also been considered by the Courts abroad which have held that it was 'the essence of a free society that a balance is struck between the security that is desirable to protect society as a whole and the safeguards that are necessary to ensure individual liberty'.

## International Relations of the State and Matters relating to Northern Ireland

In assessing adverse affect to the international relations of the State, one should firstly consider whether any of the records fall within paragraphs (b)-(f) of subsection (2), in which case the record or records concerned must be considered exempt. Each of these provisions is described in more detail below.

In relation to other records, the decision maker should consider whether disclosure could:

- create difficulty in the conduct of relations between this country and other States
- disclose positions or plans which could impede or weaken its negotiating strategy with other States or organisations of States.
- substantially impair good working relationships between this country and another State, thereby prejudicing the future supply of information required for the effective conduct of our foreign policy.

As regards matters relating to Northern Ireland, the purpose of Section 24 is to carefully protect information which could, if released, adversely affect such matters. The section is designed to protect information of the following type:

- material relating to negotiations, positions or plans
- contacts between the Government or its representatives and parties or persons either within or outside of Northern Ireland on matters relating to Northern Ireland
- confidential information received
- intelligence information relating to security and defence matters

Section 24(2)(b)-(f) specifies the type of record likely to come within the meaning of international relations or matters relating to Northern Ireland. While a record falling within one or other category attracts mandatory exemption, it must be remembered that this list is not exhaustive and that subsection (1) may apply to other records.

(b) contains a communication between a Minister of the Government and a diplomatic mission or consular post in the State [Section 24(2)(b)]

This would include correspondence or communications between the Government and the diplomatic representatives of another country in this State e.g. a foreign embassy or consular post.

(b) contains a communication between the Government or a person acting on behalf of the Government and another government or a person acting on behalf of another government [Section 24(2)(b)]

This refers to the most commonly understood meaning of international relations and concerns communications between Governments and their representatives

(c) contains a communication between a Minister of the Government and a diplomatic mission or consular post of the State [24(2)(c)]

This provision refers to communication between the Government and its own embassies and consular posts abroad.

(d) contains information communicated in confidence to any person in or outside the State from any person in or outside the State and relating to a matter referred to in subsection (1) or to the protection of human rights and expressed by the latter person to be confidential or to be communicated in confidence [24(2)(d)]

This provision protects information communicated in confidence whose disclosure would adversely affect any of the interests referred to in subsection (1). The information must be inherently confidential and imparted in circumstances importing an obligation of confidence (please refer to section 26 for a more detailed discussion on the obligation of confidence).

In addition, this section also protects information communicated in confidence relating to the protection of human rights.

(e) contains information communicated in confidence from, to or within an international organisation of states or a subsidiary organ of such an organisation or an institution or body of the European Union or relates to negotiations between the State and such an organisation, organ, institution or body or within or in relation to such an organisation, organ, institution or body, [24(2)(e)]

This provision applies to information:

- communicated in confidence to or within an international organisation of states or a subsidiary organ of such an organisation,
- communicated in confidence to or within an institution or body of the European Union, or
- relates to negotiations between the State and such an organisation, organ, institution or body or within or in relation to such an organisation, organ, institution or body

The elements of confidence referred to above in relation to paragraph (d) also apply to confidential information coming within this subsection.

### *International Organisation of States*

The phrase suggests that the participants are representing their Governments and would include such international organisations of States as the UN and its subsidiaries. Transnational federations, sporting, cultural or educational organisations may not come within this definition unless all the members are representative of and appointed by the Governments of the various States involved.

(f) is a record of an organisation, organ, institution or body referred to in paragraph (e) containing information the disclosure of which is prohibited by the organisation, organ, institution or body [24(2)(f)]

This provision refers to information which is prohibited from disclosure by any of the international organisations referred to above

### *Information Relating to the EU*

As indicated above, information relating to the EU must be protected in accordance with section 24(2)(e) and (f). Where the information in question is a record of the EU, and is being withheld on these grounds, the person in question should be advised of his or her right to seek access to EU information directly from the EU Commission, Council or Parliament.

## Information Commissioner in Relation to Sensitive Records

Section 43 specifically requires the Commissioner and the Courts to take appropriate precautions to guard against any disclosure of sensitive information during the course of an investigation or proceedings.

### *Refusal to Confirm or Deny Provision*

*(3) Where a request under section 7 relates to a record to which subsection (1) applies, or would, if the record, existed, apply, and the*

*head concerned is satisfied that the disclosure of the existence or non-existence of the record would prejudice a matter referred to in that subsection, he or she shall refuse to grant the request and shall not disclose to the requester concerned whether or not the record exists.*

In seven exemptions, provisions exist that allow a public body to respond to requests or parts of requests on the basis of refusing to confirm or deny the existence of records-sections 19, 22, 23, 26, 27, 28, and subsection (3) above refer. These provisions are necessary because, in some instances, merely confirming the existence of information will directly or implicitly disclose sensitive information. The following points should be noted in relation to such provisions:

- Their use will be justified only in rare situations
- It is not appropriate where it is the contents of the record rather than its existence that warrants protection
- Persons should always be advised of their rights of appeal when notifying them of such a decision

This refusal to confirm or deny provision, which is subject to particular criteria, gives the public body the option of responding to a request in an equivocal fashion and thus not "giving the game away". By not confirming that a record exists or does not exist, a requester can be prevented from drawing inferences which might otherwise be available. Such a response is justifiable in this section on the grounds that disclosure of the existence or non-existence of the record would have the precise adverse effect which this exemption seeks to avoid.

A difficulty with these provisions is that their use can convey a signal that the body is alarmed about the request. There is also a danger that inferences may be drawn and the response could lose some or all of its value. However, experience suggests that this can be tackled through a number of approaches.

### *A Mix of Records is Sought*

A requester seeks material which is a mix of records, some of which may be subject to the "confirm or deny" provision, and others which may not. For example a taxpayer seeks access to her tax files. Unknown to her these include records relating to an ongoing highly confidential investigation of a serious criminal matter. In an instance such as this the public body may need to consider remaining entirely silent about the investigation.. This is justified by section 8(5) of the Act which states that a statement of reasons need not include any information which is itself exempt. The approach should be employed only in cases of extreme sensitivity.

### *The Request is Purely*

A requester directly asks for extremely sensitive material the disclosure of which would have the effect of causing damage to matters which the exemption seeks to protect. The options here are either the direct use, or a refusal to confirm or deny response in relation to the request, or a response on the lines of "the department has no records which fall within the ambit of the Act". Depending on the circumstances, it may be equally beneficial to invoke upfront the neither confirm or deny provision e.g. a request for records which seeks to ascertain whether a meeting between certain parties has taken place.

### *Circumstances Carry Danger*

A significant criminal investigation is underway and at a particularly sensitive stage. The subject matter suspects that an investigation is underway. She asks for the records and other matters relating to herself. Here the request for the other material should be treated as per normal. The refusal to confirm provision or a variation thereof, as set out at scenarios (1) and (2) above, should be used to refuse a request for the investigation records.

### *General Comments*

This provision lessens the duty to provide reasons for the decision to the requester. There is for example no obligation to provide details of the provision of the Act pursuant to which the request is refused. Also excluded is the obligation to provide findings on material issues of fact and particulars of the public interest in cases where a refusal to confirm or deny provision is invoked (s 8(2)(d)(ii)). However unless the material is such that it requires no acknowledgement whatever as to its existence, the relevant provision, in this case section 24(3), may be quoted in the statement of reasons required by the Act (section 8(2)(d), 13(3) and 14(5)(c)).

This means that while the statement of reasons can be relatively more cursory it should usually refer at least to the refuse to confirm or deny provision itself and to the criteria considered by the decision maker and the reason for the conclusion reached.

Otherwise, the decision making process described in Part 1 of this manual must be followed. Decisions to refuse to confirm or deny constitute a refusal to give access to a record under the Act. Such decisions can of course be reviewed through internal and external review. The reviewer will be able to look at the documents involved (if they exist) and form his or her own view about whether the invoking of the refusal to confirm or deny provision was appropriate.

## *Central Policy Unit Advises*

·Section 4 provides for delegation of decision-making on FOI requests. It is strongly recommended that FOI decisions on sensitive material likely to fall under this section should be taken only at a senior level. Delegations under section 4 should provide accordingly.

- This section should be read in conjunction with section 46 which excludes from the Act material which discloses the identity of a confidential source of information re. criminal law.
- Where release of information is likely to have consequences for State security, defence or international relations or Northern Ireland matters or where a decision maker is unsure if a record is one to which subsection (2) applies, informal consultations with the public body having principal responsibility in that area should be undertaken e.g. if disclosure of a document is likely to affect international relations, the decision maker should learn the views of the Department of Foreign Affairs.
- Section 25 outlines a Ministerial Certificate procedure which may be considered where the records in question are of such seriousness or sensitivity to warrant doing so.
- Where sensitive information requires protection, consideration should be given to invoking the 'refusal to confirm or deny' provision in preference to a Certificate.

The issue of a Certificate may attract attention to the existence of sensitive material.

- Section 24 should be read in conjunction with section 26 (Information obtained in confidence).

## Secretary of Defence's Overview

The roles of the Ministry of Defence are set out in section 24 of the Defence Act 1990. They are:

- to assist the Government make well-informed decisions about the defence of New Zealand and its interests through the provision of timely, high quality advice;
- to conduct audits and assessments of the New Zealand Defence Force and the acquisition activities of the Ministry; and
- to procure, upgrade, or repair significant items of military equipment.

These roles are reflected in the Ministry's Statement of Intent and contribute to the high-level outcome of supporting New Zealand's security objectives and contributing to the security of other countries.

This high-level outcome is based on a simple, but fundamental principle that a secure New Zealand is critical to our economic and social well-being. Achieving this has both domestic and international dimensions. At home, a strong economy and a prosperous workforce are predicated on securing our borders and our Exclusive Economic Zone, as well as assisting our South Pacific neighbours do the same. Further afield, New Zealand's present and future prosperity is closely linked to a stable and peaceful international security environment, in which all nations are encouraged to play by the rules. Our active participation in international security operations ensures our own security.

How well the Ministry does in meeting the high-level outcome is measured against an intermediate-level outcome of ensuring that our advice and actions are credible and respected, and the Government's defence policy objectives are achieved.

The Government's defence policy objectives are set out in *The Government's Defence Policy Framework* (June 2000). They are: to defend New Zealand and to protect its people and territorial waters; to meet our alliance commitments to Australia; to assist in the maintenance of security in the South Pacific; to play an appropriate role in the security of the Asia Pacific region; and contribute to global security. A second document, the *Government Defence Statement: A Sustainable Defence Force Matched to New Zealand's Needs* (May 2001), identifies the military capabilities the Government needs to meet these five objectives.

In the last year, the Ministry has continued to implement the Government's *Defence Long-term Development Plan* (LTDP) to update and replace a range of obsolete equipment. Committing $3 billion over ten years, the plan links the Government's defence policy objectives, as set out in the *Defence Policy Framework*, with the capability requirements announced in the May 2001 Statement. Since the plan's release in 2002, Defence has progressed twenty-seven re-equipment projects. A highlight of the work undertaken during this reporting period was the Government's decision to purchase eight NH90 medium utility helicopters to replace the Royal New Zealand Air Force's aging Iroquois fleet. Ensuring that LTDP projects remain on track is a key focus for the Ministry.

Investment in new capabilities is being matched by investment in people and infrastructure. Many of the priorities for this reporting period flowed from the Government's Defence Sustainability Initiative and the defence funding programme of $4.6 billion over ten years attached to it. The aim of the initiative is to achieve long-term sustainability for Defence by building personnel levels, bringing new and upgraded equipment into service, and strengthening defence planning and management systems. Key priorities included addressing the gaps in the Ministry's policy capability, particularly where it lacked specialist technical and financial analysis skills, and working with the New Zealand Defence Force to strengthen organisational and corporate planning, policy, and governance capabilities.

The Government has indicated the importance of prioritising policies that will contribute to a strong sense of national identity. Ministers recognise that as New Zealanders we take great pride in who we are, what we do, and how we are seen, expressed in part through our stance on international issues and our willingness to assist in maintaining peace in various trouble spots around the world and in responding to humanitarian crises. An important focus for the Ministry is to provide the Government with sound policy advice on security risk management, military deployments, and purchasing equipment, the aim of which is to ensure that our Defence Force personnel are appropriately trained and equipped to undertake the wide-ranging tasks New Zealanders expect them to perform, often under very difficult conditions.

The deployment of New Zealand Defence Force personnel to restore order in the Solomon Islands and Timor-Leste are the most recent examples of this willingness to become involved in order to resolve conflict and prevent bloodshed. In both cases, New Zealand, working alongside our alliance partner Australia, responded quickly and appropriately to the requests for assistance from Solomon Islands and the Timor-Leste Governments, providing a meaningful military presence and allowing space for a political solution to evolve in both countries.

In Afghanistan, the work of New Zealand's Provincial Reconstruction Team, now in its fourth year, is a further example of how our Defence Force personnel can put their military skills to practical use, both in securing a troubled country and in helping to build the infrastructure and institutions of a viable Afghan state. This work, in helping to ensure that Afghanistan does not again become a haven for terrorists, underlines the seriousness in which New Zealand takes its international responsibilities, including in countries far from home.

## *Policy and Planning*

The Secretary of Defence is the principal civilian adviser on defence matters to the Minister of Defence and to the Government. The Chief of Defence Force, who commands the New Zealand Defence Force, is the principal military adviser.

A strong and mutually reinforcing relationship between the Ministry and the New Zealand Defence Force is critical to Defence's strategic-level interaction with the Government and with other central government agencies. This cooperation is facilitated through the Office of Chief Executives, which brings the Secretary of Defence and the Chief of Defence Force together to discuss policy issues of mutual interest; the Executive Capability Board, through which senior military and civilian officials oversee major capital acquisition projects; and a range of joint engagements, formal and informal, between the Vice Chief of Defence Force and the Deputy Secretary (Policy and Planning), and their staff, that are designed to exchange information and improve collaboration within the Defence establishment.

The Defence Policy and Planning Unit is made up of staff from both the Ministry and the New Zealand Defence Force. It consists of the Strategic Policy Branch, the International Defence Relations Branch, and the new Strategy and Capability Analysis Branch. The principal role of the Unit is to provide consistent information and policy advice to both the Secretary of Defence and the Chief of Defence Force, and through them to the Minister of Defence and the Government.

## Policy Development

### *Defence Sustainability Initiative*

In the past year, the Ministry has worked closely with the New Zealand Defence Force in continuing to implement the Defence Sustainability Initiative (DSI). The DSI is a ten-year defence funding package to enable the New Zealand Defence Force and the Ministry to rebuild capacity, and to fulfil the Government's goal of achieving a modern sustainable defence force matched to New Zealand's needs. A total of $4.6 billion over a ten-year period was allocated by the Government in 2005/06, to be directed towards:

- personnel issues, including additional recruitment, improving retention, conditions of service, allowances and developing special training (including trades training) in all three services;
- implementing Government capability plans in the *Defence Long-term Development Plan* (LTDP);
- reviewing the Army's configuration;
- developing a real estate strategy, accommodation policy, and a policy on maintenance of the New Zealand Defence Force's property portfolio;
- addressing the backlog in minor capital projects, for example, in infrastructure, equipment and information technology; and

- expanding the Ministry's policy and purchase advice functions.

To manage this additional funding and the associated remedial work programme, the Government has directed the New Zealand Defence Force and the Ministry to enhance their management and organisational processes. To this end, a considerable work programme of eighteen separate projects was undertaken during this reporting period by the New Zealand Defence Force and the Ministry, with input from Treasury and the State Services Commission. As at 30 June 2006, these projects had either been completed or were well-advanced towards completion.

The projects in this programme addressed a wide range of governance and management issues, largely within the New Zealand Defence Force. The Ministry, however, also received additional funding to strengthen its policy advice capability, with specific emphasis on technical analysis. This has been achieved through the establishment of the Strategy and Capability Analysis Branch.

## Defence Capital Asset Management

On 15 May 2006, Cabinet approved the Terms of Reference of the Defence Capital Asset Management Practice Review (DCAMP). This important review is part of an over-arching review of public sector capital asset management, which in turn is one of a number of public sector expenditure reviews that address a range of departments and functional activities. The objective of these reviews is to achieve better value for money from public expenditure. A project team of senior personnel drawn from both the Ministry and the New Zealand Defence Force is undertaking the review. Meeting the report back date of September 2006 will be a priority for the Defence establishment over the next reporting period.

### *Strategic Policy Advice*

Defence policy needs to have a solid empirical basis. As defence-policy makers we seek to comprehend the risks and challenges in our strategic environment and how they affect New Zealand's defence and security interests. A key function of the Ministry is to prepare periodic assessments for the Minister of

Defence on the strategic environment, including the implications any changes may have for defence policy. In the last year, the Strategic Policy Branch prepared a geopolitical scan assessing the influences which are likely to shape our security interests over the next five years. Work on the scan informed a series of briefings prepared for the Minister of Defence on a number of defence-related issues, including:

- defence policies of Australia and Japan;
- defence transformation in the United States;
- the implications for New Zealand's defence policy of natural disasters; and
- Defence's role in contributing to the Government's disarmament and arms control policies.

## Capability Development

First released on 11 June 2002, the LTDP is the key capital project-planning document covering the ten-year period out to 2012. Regularly updated, the plan enables decisions on major defence acquisitions (projects over $7 million) to be prioritised and taken in the context of the Government's defence policy objectives and the project's fiscal affordability. During the reporting period, work commenced on a third LTDP update. Due to be released shortly, the 2006 update will provide a current list of projects, as well as their associated preliminary costings, timings and priorities.

The Strategic Policy Branch has provided policy advice on a number of capability development issues over the past twelve months, including:

- Helicopter replacement: The Government selected the NATO Helicopter Industries' NH90 medium utility helicopter as the replacement for the Air Force's Iroquois fleet. Aside from a considerably greater carrying capacity, the new helicopters will be more appropriately configured to support the Army's enhanced mobility and firepower, as well as provide greater assistance to civil agencies during both national and international emergencies. The NH90 will also be able to operate from the helicopter decks of the Navy's ANZAC class frigates, the new multi-role vessel, and the new offshore patrol vessels.

Advice has also been provided on the next stage of the training/ light utility helicopter project.

- Improvised explosive device disposal: Approval was given for the establishment of a radiological improvised explosive device disposal (IEDD) capability alongside the newly enhanced chemical, biological and conventional IEDD capability.
- Boeing 757 modification: Final proposals were approved for the programme to modify the Air Force's two Boeing 757 aircraft to a combined passenger/freight configuration. A decision was also taken not to modify the aircraft for use in supporting operations to Antarctica. This project is now in the equipment procurement phase.
- Joint Command and Control System: The project will provide Defence Force commanders with the means to command and control their forces individually, in groups, within a combined force, and in coalition environments. The Strategic Policy Branch has been involved in determining the options for operating and supporting the system throughout its life.
- Land intelligence, surveillance, and reconnaissance: The project addresses the gaps in the New Zealand Army's intelligence, surveillance, and reconnaissance capabilities. It aims to provide Army commanders with the ability to detect threats at greater distances and with greater certainty. The Strategic Policy Branch has been involved in determining the project's requirements.

### *Other Projects*

The Strategic Policy Branch has also been involved in reviewing the Capability Management Framework and has provided advice on navy projects and inter-agency preparedness for the introduction of the Project Protector fleet into service.

## International Defence Relations

The trans-Tasman defence relationship is a uniquely close one. We share a common interest in a stable region and we work closely together to promote this. Our combined response to the civil unrest in the Solomon Islands in April and Timor-Leste in

May 2006 underlined the close cooperation which exists between our two defence forces. Regular high-level discussions between officials ensure a deep, practical understanding of each other's policies and enhance our ability to cooperate effectively.

In the past year, New Zealand and Australia have continued to collaborate and share information over a range of areas, including logistics, communications, personnel and capability development. Both countries are undertaking major capability renewal and acquisition programmes, which offer prospects for project cooperation and greater interoperability. A range of bilateral and multilateral exercises assist in maintaining the complementary skills and capabilities necessary to operate together.

The Minister of Defence met Dr Brendan Nelson, his Australian counterpart in May 2006 for the annual defence Ministerial talks. The Ministers reaffirmed the importance of New Zealand and Australia staying closely engaged on regional security issues. They noted that recent developments emphasised the importance of the two countries working together with their Pacific neighbours to achieve security and stability in the region.

The Ministers also agreed that Australia and New Zealand would continue to look to develop further areas of collaboration and information sharing. This includes the logistics and communications fields, as well as key areas of capability development including the acquisition of medium utility helicopters, ANZAC ship upgrades, and the replacement of Army vehicle transport fleets and artillery and small arms replacement projects.

## *South Pacific*

In the past year, developments in the South Pacific have continued to shape defence policy, outputs, and decisions on defence capabilities. This is indicative of New Zealand's enduring strategic interests in the region and the strong bonds of geography, history, and culture which link us closely to it. We have special obligations to assist our South Pacific neighbours in maintaining peace, promoting good governance and helping achieve economic well-being. The need for this assistance is increasing, including in the defence and security arena. The region faces cumulative stresses arising from ethnic tensions, governance failures, and fragile economies which make it susceptible to debilitating trans-national security challenges.

A wide range of defence activities in the Pacific support New Zealand's interests. Principal areas of engagement include assistance with maritime surveillance, disaster relief, maritime search and rescue, strengthening peacekeeping capabilities and developing the professionalism of defence and police forces through the Mutual Assistance Programme (MAP). Major developments over the last twelve months in New Zealand's defence engagement in the South Pacific particularly covered Solomon Islands, Fiji, Tonga, Papua New Guinea, Vanuatu, Cook Islands, and Samoa.

### *Solomon Islands*

The Regional Assistance Mission to Solomon Islands (RAMSI) has been in place for three years. It has achieved progress in restoring law and order, governance reforms, and economic development. The mission remains popular with Solomon Islanders.

RAMSI experienced a serious set back in April when rioting broke out in Honiara following the election of a new Prime Minister. Order was quickly restored with the assistance of additional military and police forces from New Zealand, Australia, and South Pacific nations. As the security situation stabilised, some of the additional forces were withdrawn. Despite the restoration of order, RAMSI is likely to require continuous New Zealand military support for some time to come.

### *Fiji*

Fiji is an important South Pacific neighbour and a key partner in RAMSI. Our objectives for Fiji are to rebuild professionalism in, and strengthen the peacekeeping capacity of, the Republic of Fiji Military Forces. In the last year, bilateral defence activities have included New Zealand military exercises in Fiji, training courses for Fijian military personnel, and visits to Fiji by the Minister of Defence and the New Zealand Chief of Defence Force.

### *Tonga*

The deployment of Tongan Defence Services (TDS) personnel to Solomon Islands as part of RAMSI is a recent and significant development. The TDS is likely to contribute more actively to regional peace support operations such as RAMSI, where they performed very credibly. The New Zealand Defence Force's engagement with the TDS will therefore be broadened beyond the traditional focus on trade training, band and officer training to assist them to continue to participate meaningfully in regional operations.

### *Papua New Guinea*

We continue to enjoy good defence relations with the Papua New Guinea Defence Force (PNGDF) which, like the military forces of Fiji and Tonga, has made a valued contribution to RAMSI. A key feature of New Zealand's defence engagement with Papua New Guinea is the ongoing support provided to the Commercial Support Programme (CSP), which has made significant progress over the last two years. The way the New Zealand Defence Force has provided support to the CSP is regarded as a model for New Zealand assistance to other Mutual Assistance Programme partners. After initially providing a New Zealand officer to the PNGDF to implement and oversee the CSP project, responsibility for managing the project has been shifted to the PNGDF. The New Zealand Defence Force role is now confined to providing ongoing advice and support from New Zealand.

### *Vanuatu*

Our focus is to help the Vanuatu Police develop skill sets relevant to their policing work, and to strengthen the Vanuatu Mobile Force's national engineering capacity, while emphasising the latter's role as an integral component of the Police Force. In cooperation with the Vanuatu Mobile Force, and with NZAID funding, a team of New Zealand Army engineers assisted in the conversion of the Police Barracks in Luganville into a temporary prison over April and May 2006. The project was part of a wider NZAID supported Corrections programme in Vanuatu.

### *Cook Islands and Samoa*

Appropriate training support is provided to both the Cook Islands and Samoan Police forces, with an emphasis on developing the skills required for the effective operation of their Police patrol boats, and strengthening the information technology capacity of the Samoan Police.

### *Southeast Asia*

Southeast Asia remains a key area for New Zealand's security interests. Terrorism continues to be the major security concern in the region. New Zealand engages in high-level relationships with defence partners in the region and defence officials contribute to the regional security dialogue. This includes the annual Shangri-La Dialogue in Singapore, which now occupies an important place in the regional security architecture. The Minister of Defence was one of seventeen Defence Ministers from, or with close security interests in, the Asia-Pacific region who attended this year's meeting.

## Five Power Defence Arrangements

The Five Power Defence Arrangements (FPDA) continues to make an important contribution to regional security. The Arrangements bring the defence forces of Australia, Malaysia, New Zealand, Singapore, and the United Kingdom together to exercise, and provide a valuable forum for Defence Ministers and officials to exchange views on defence issues of relevance to all members. The FPDA continues to evolve to meet today's security challenges.

New Zealand participates in the full range of FPDA activities. These have recently been expanded to include scenarios based around combating non-conventional threats, such as maritime terrorism, piracy and people smuggling. In June 2006, the Minister of Defence met with his FPDA counterparts in Singapore and Malaysia to discuss these developments. A commitment was also made to explore options for enhanced cooperation in humanitarian assistance and disaster relief.

### *ASEAN Regional Forum*

The ASEAN Regional Forum (ARF), which brings together twenty-four countries and the European Union, is the only Asia-Pacific pan-regional forum devoted to discussing security issues. New Zealand values the ARF and actively supports greater defence participation under its auspices.

New Zealand defence officials attended the Ministerial Meeting in Laos in July 2005; the Intersessional Group Meetings in Honolulu in October 2005 and the Philippines in March 2006; and the Senior Officials' Meeting and Security Policy Conference in Malaysia in May 2006. New Zealand also participated in a range of ARF confidence-building measures.

### *Singapore*

New Zealand's extensive and long-standing defence links with Singapore are an integral part of the wider relationship between the two countries. The defence relationship is sustained through exercises, training and exchanges, and an annual schedule of meetings, including at senior levels. The Minister of Defence held talks with his Singaporean counterpart, Rear Admiral Teo Chee Hean, at the Shangri-La Dialogue in Singapore in June 2006. The introduction of formal army-to-army talks in September 2005 and the deepening of defence industry links underline the value in continuing to grow the relationship with Singapore.

### *Malaysia*

New Zealand has a long history of defence association with Malaysia based on an annual programme of exercises, bilateral meetings, multilateral cooperation within the FPDA, and training provided to the Malaysian Armed Forces through the Mutual Assistance Programme. Malaysia also offers training to the New Zealand Defence Force at its United Nations Peacekeeping School. The Minister of Defence met the Malaysian Deputy Prime Minister and Minister of Defence, Dato' Tan Sri Mohammed Najib, during the FPDA Ministers' Meeting in June 2006.

### *Timor-Leste*

New Zealand responded swiftly to the recent crisis in Timor-Leste through the deployment of 200 Defence Force personnel as part of the Australian-led regional task force to restore civil order. Prior to the unrest, New Zealand had been providing modest assistance to the Timor-Leste defence force in an advisory capacity with logistic and human resource support, and small arms training. Over the reporting period, New Zealand also provided one military liaison officer to the United Nations Special Political Mission to Timor-Leste (UNOTIL).

## Other Southeast Asian Nations

New Zealand's defence relationships with Brunei, the Philippines and Thailand centre primarily on the Mutual Assistance Programme. Joint military exercises were held with the Royal Bruneian Armed Forces in Brunei in July/August 2005 and in Central Otago in January/February 2006. The Minister of Defence held bilateral meetings with both the Deputy Minister of Defence of Brunei and the Secretary of National Defence of the Philippines at the Shangri-La Dialogue in Singapore. Defence links with Vietnam are developing and there has been considerable interaction with other Southeast Asian countries through the ARF defence dialogue process.

### *North Asia*

North Asia is strategically important for New Zealand. Our strong economic links with the region make its ongoing stability critical to this country's prosperity. Relations between the countries of North Asia have a significant impact on the security of the wider Asia-Pacific region. New Zealand's defence engagement with China, the Republic of Korea and Japan has developed in line with growth in the overall bilateral relationships.

### *China*

New Zealand's defence relationship with China continues to centre on visits and exchanges. Prominent events in the past year included the visit to New Zealand by Vice Admiral Wu Shengli, People's Liberation Army Deputy Chief of General Staff, in September 2005. A People's Liberation Army officer continues to attend the New Zealand Defence Force Command and Staff Course. New Zealand reciprocates by sending an officer to Beijing for six-weeks to attend the International Symposium on Regional Security Issues at China's National Defence University.

### *Republic of Korea*

New Zealand's defence links with the Republic of Korea (ROK) extend back to New Zealand's participation in the Korean War. Bilateral defence engagement over the past year has included high-level visits, annual talks and academic exchanges. In November 2005, the Minister of Defence visited the ROK and met with his counterpart, Mr Yoon Kwang Woong. New Zealand defence officials held defence talks with their ROK counterparts in Seoul in October 2005. In May 2006, a Defence Force officer began a twelve-week attachment at the Korea National Defence University as a visiting professor. The ROK Joint Staff College visited New Zealand in June 2006 and a Korean student is attending the New Zealand Defence Force Command and Staff Course.

New Zealand's contribution to the multinational United Nations Command underpins New Zealand's commitment to security on the Korean Peninsula and inter-Korean reconciliation. The Minister of Defence met with the then Commander United Nations Command, General Leon J. LaPorte, during his visit to the ROK in November 2005. Three Defence Force officers serve with the United Nations Command Military Armistice Commission.

### *Japan*

New Zealand's defence relationship with Japan took a significant step forward with the formalisation in 2005 of annual bilateral defence talks. Previously this dialogue had taken place as security consultations on an ad-hoc basis. New Zealand defence officials visited Tokyo in December 2005 for the first talks in the new format. We reciprocated in May 2006 by hosting a visit by Japanese officials in Wellington. There will be opportunities for further bilateral engagement in the future as Japan continues its efforts to increase its participation in international peace support operations.

### *United Kingdom*

Our defence relationship with the United Kingdom is long-standing, close and very important. Cooperation across all three Services continues to play a key role in maintaining our professional standards and interoperability with key defence partners. New Zealand continues to contribute to British peace support operations in Bosnia through our commitment to the European Union-led stabilisation force.

The Minister of Defence met with then United Kingdom Secretary of State for Defence, John Reid in February this year; and met with the current Secretary of State for Defence, Des Browne, in London, in early June 2006. He also met with the Secretary of State for the Armed Forces, Adam Ingram, in June in Singapore and Malaysia.

## North America

### *United States*

The relationship with the United States remains an important one for New Zealand. We continue to work alongside United States Forces in a number of international operations in pursuit of shared interests. A key component of New Zealand's bilateral defence relationship with the United States is the international campaign against terrorism. New Zealand is one of a growing number of countries contributing military forces to the stabilisation effort in Afghanistan; and we also actively contribute to, and participate in, the United States-led Proliferation Security Initiative. Such commitments are recognised and appreciated by Washington, including at very senior levels.

The Minister of Defence met his United States counterpart, Donald Rumsfeld, in Washington D.C. in April this year. The commanders of the United States' Pacific (Admiral William Fallon) and Central (General John Abizaid) Commands also visited New Zealand in January and February 2006, respectively.

### *Canada*

New Zealand and Canada enjoy a close and cordial defence relationship. An important development in the relationship this year was the inaugural New Zealand-Canada political-military talks in Ottawa in May 2006. The talks reflect a strengthening of the bilateral relationship in recent years through shared experience in peace support operations, expanded training activities, and defence procurement.

## Peace Support Operations

New Zealand has been a consistent contributor to peacekeeping missions for half a century. The Asia-Pacific region remains New Zealand's first priority for peacekeeping contributions, but our commitment to collective security and the rule of law requires ongoing contributions well beyond our region. Our current commitments are global in reach, with personnel carrying out peacekeeping activities in the Pacific, Middle East, Asia, Europe and Africa. As at 30 June 2006, approximately 411 New Zealand Defence Force personnel were deployed on overseas missions, the bulk of them in Timor-Leste, Solomon Islands, Afghanistan and the Middle East.

### *Afghanistan*

New Zealand supports international efforts to stabilise Afghanistan and build indigenous capabilities. The focal point of this activity is the provision of a Provincial Reconstruction Team of over 120 personnel, a commitment that has been extended to September 2007. Working in Bamyan Province, this team aims to assist the Afghan authorities extend their influence beyond Kabul. Its emphasis is on improving the security environment, as well as facilitating the provision of humanitarian support and development assistance to the Afghan people. New Zealand Defence Force personnel are also training the Afghan National Army and a Military Liaison Officer is working with the United Nations Assistance Mission in Afghanistan.

## Proliferation Security Initiative

The Proliferation Security Initiative (PSI) is a multilateral United States-initiated effort to counter the growing challenge to international security posed by the global proliferation of weapons of mass destruction (WMD), their delivery systems, and related materials-in a manner that is consistent with relevant domestic legal requirements and international law. The PSI objectives, which were launched in 2003, are encompassed in its Statement of Interdiction Principles. New Zealand expressed its support for the PSI Interdiction Principles in April 2004, and has been a member of the governing Operational Expert Group since November of that year. Since joining the PSI, New Zealand defence officials have attended several plenary and Operational Expert Group meetings; and the New Zealand Defence Force have contributed to the ongoing series of workshops and training exercises.

The contribution of a Royal New Zealand Air Force Boeing 757 aircraft, aircrew, and support personnel to the Australian-led PSI exercise, Exercise Pacific Protector, in April 2006 was significant.

This enhanced our credentials as an active PSI contributor, particularly in our region.

### *Acquisition of Defence Equipment*

The Ministry, through the Acquisitions Division, is responsible for procuring all major items of capital equipment for the New Zealand Defence Force. The procurement process is often lengthy. It commences with the Government giving approval in principle to the acquisition process on the basis of concepts of operations and functional performance specifications. These are determined by the New Zealand Defence Force and, at times, in consultation with external agencies. The Acquisition Division develops the necessary documentation for tender purposes, invites tenders, evaluates tender responses, undertakes risk assessments, and identifies preferred bidders. Once government approval is given, the Division negotiates and manages the contract arrangements through to the delivery of the equipment to the Defence Force.

Major projects over the last year have covered all three services, with the majority in the delivery phase. The light armoured vehicles and tactical communications projects are generally complete, following the delivery and introduction into service of the equipment, but some accessories remain to be delivered. Both projects are expected to be delivered within the Government approved budget.

## Upgrading the Army

### *Light armoured vehicles*

105 light armoured vehicles were purchased from General Dynamics Land Systems, Canada. All but one of these vehicles is now in service with the New Zealand Army. One vehicle will remain with the manufacturer to provide a systems validation and a test platform for Army operational purposes. Spare parts, special tools, and test equipment have been delivered and the project is in the final stages of completion.

### *Light operational vehicles*

This project involves the acquisition of 321 light operational vehicles, in six variants, to meet the Army's motorisation requirements. Deliveries commenced in October 2004, and 131 non-armoured vehicles were in service with the Army by 30 June 2005. During the past 12 months all but one of the remaining non-armoured vehicles have been delivered to New Zealand, leaving five armoured variants outstanding at 30 June 2006.

At the request of the New Zealand Defence Force, five light operational vehicles were purchased for the Royal New Zealand Air Force. While the additional vehicles were funded separately from the Defence Force's capital programme minors, the Ministry assisted in their acquisition through the existing contract with the manufacturer.

### *Tactical Communications*

This project covers tactical communications for the Army and supporting Royal New Zealand Air Force units. Final deliveries were received in the fourth quarter of 2005, and the project is now in the closure phase.

### *Very Low Level Air Defence*

This project will provide alerting, cueing and identification of friend or foe systems for the Mistral very low-level air defence system, which is already in service. The systems will be delivered in the fourth quarter of 2006.

### *Medium Range Anti-Armour Weapon*

This project will provide a medium-range anti-armour weapon, the Javelin missile, manufactured by Raytheon/Lockheed Martin Joint Venture. Proceeding under the United States' foreign military sales programme, the training equipment was delivered in June 2006. The missiles will be delivered in the fourth quarter of 2006.

### *Upgrading the Navy*

Following the Government's endorsement of the Maritime Forces Review, Project Protector was initiated to purchase new vessels for the Royal New Zealand Navy. In July 2004, a contract was signed with Tenix Defence Systems for one Multi-Role Vessel, two Offshore Patrol Vessels and four Inshore Patrol Vessels. The Multi-Role Vessel was launched in Rotterdam in February 2006, undertaking contractor sea trials in late June 2006. The Offshore and Inshore Patrol Vessels are being built in Melbourne and Whângarei respectively. All seven ships will be delivered during 2007.

## Upgrading the Air Force

### *C-130 Life Extension*

A contract was signed with L-3 Spar Aerospace in December 2004 to upgrade and extend the life of the Royal New Zealand Air Force's C-130 Hercules fleet. In October 2005, the first aircraft was inducted into the life-extension programme at L-3 Spar Aerospace in Edmonton, Canada.

### *P-3 Orion Communications and Navigation Systems Upgrade*

A contract was signed with L-3 Communications Integrated Systems in October 2004 to upgrade the communications and navigation systems of the Air Force's P-3 Orion fleet. The early Electro Optics installation was completed in New Zealand. Work commenced on the fit out of the new systems in the first aircraft following its arrival at the L-3 communications facility in Greenville, Texas, in September 2005.

### *Boeing 757 Purchase and Modifications*

A contract to re-configure the Air Force's two Boeing 757 aircraft for cargo, as well as passengers, was signed with Mobile Aerospace Engineering in October 2005. Modification of the first aircraft will begin in the second quarter of 2007.

### *Helicopter Replacement*

Work is proceeding on replacing the Air Force's Iroquois helicopters. The Government approved NATO Helicopters Industries (NHI), supplier of the NH90 medium utility helicopter, as preferred tender in March 2005. The Ministry has been engaged with NHI to obtain full costings for the NH90. Government approval was granted on 10 July 2006 to commence contract negotiations for the acquisition of eight NH90 helicopters. Work is also proceeding on identifying a suitable Training/Light Utility Helicopter to replace the Air Force's Sioux helicopters. The evaluation of the Registration of Interest has been completed and Requests for Tenders will be sought in the fourth quarter of 2006.

## A Joint Approach

The acquisition of a joint command and control system (JCCS) will provide Defence Force commanders, at strategic, operational, and tactical levels, with the means to execute, command and control their forces individually, jointly, within a combined force, and within a coalition environment. It will also provide a sustainable framework that is interoperable with our partners, including relevant non-defence partners.

## New Zealand Industry Involvement

### *New Zealand Defence Industry Association*

The Ministry has continued to support local companies seeking to obtain defence work from major acquisition projects and through exports. The main conduit for this assistance has been the New Zealand Defence Industry Association. During the year, the Ministry provided regular briefings at New Zealand Defence Industry Association meetings. Assistance was also provided to the Association for the annual two-day Defence Industry Seminar held at Te Papa Museum in Wellington in late October 2005.

### *Defence Industry Committee of New Zealand*

The Ministry provided support for the Defence Industry Committee of New Zealand. This Ministerial appointed committee provides industry feedback to Defence and briefs the Minister on industry issues.

The Defence Industry Committee of New Zealand sponsors the Defence Industry Committee Awards of Excellence. These are awarded annually to companies that have provided Defence with excellence in products or services. The awards were part of the Defence Industry Seminar 2005.

### *Evaluation*

Under section 24(2)(e) of the Defence Act 1990, the statutory role of the Evaluation Division is to carry out assessments and audits of any function, duty or project of the New Zealand Defence

Force. The Division also conducts audits of the Ministry's activities relating to the procurement of major military equipment.

These assessments and audits are undertaken when required by the Minister of Defence, or to a programme approved under authority delegated by the Minister to the Secretary of Defence and the Chief of Defence Force. Reports of completed audits are submitted to the responsible chief executive and the Minister.

The Secretary of Defence and the Chief of Defence Force, together with an external member, met twice during the year as the Defence Evaluation Board, to approve the programme of work for the Evaluation Division, receive reports on audits completed, and to monitor follow-up action on past audits. The Evaluation Division also undertakes internal audits of the Ministry for the Secretary of Defence. In addition to undertaking audits to meet the Secretary's responsibilities under the Defence Act, the Evaluation Division undertakes audits under section 3(6) of the Hazardous Substances and New Organisms Act 1996.

### *Corporate*

The Corporate Division provides support services and policy advice in the areas of human resources, information management and technology, and legal. The Corporate Division is responsible for all aspects of Ministerial services and support including the handling of Ministerial correspondence, requests under the Official Information Act 1982, and miscellaneous enquiries.

A major emphasis over the last year has been on progressing the new Defence building that will accommodate the two Defence organisations. This is scheduled for completion in February 2007.

The last year proved to be another challenging and rewarding one for the Ministry. As well as the continued focus on re-equipping the New Zealand Defence Force and operational deployments, substantial efforts were devoted to implementing the changes initiated under the DSI. While significant advances have been made, the next phase in the development of the Ministry and the New Zealand Defence Force will bring new challenges. Ensuring that sound policy continues to drive advice on defence capabilities and operations will remain the core function of the Ministry. The Ministry is very conscious of the high international standing in which our Defence Force personnel are held and that New Zealanders take pride in the good work they do. The greater certainty provided by the DSI for defence planning and the investment in new capabilities mentioned above will ensure that these high standards are maintained well into the future.-

## Canada-Australia Defence Relations

Canadians and Australians enjoy very close defence relations having fought side-by-side in the two World Wars and the Korean War. More recently, Canada contributed forces to the International Force East Timor operation. The two countries cooperated closely during combat against terrorism operations in Afghanistan and both have participated in numerous Arabian Gulf deployments enforcing UN Security Council sanctions and embargoes.

Against the background of the historically close linkage brought on by the long standing support and interaction with Australians, the Canadian Defence Advisor (CDA) at the High Commission in Canberra works to maximise the opportunities for the two countries to operate together and further progress the increased interoperability that results from such occasions. Her Majesty's Canadian Ship CALGARY's recent successful ship visits to Fremantle/Perth and Sydney is a manifest example of the activities that epitomise the close relationship fostered by the two nations.

The office of the CDA is responsible for furthering defence and defence intelligence issues between Canada and Australia. The CDA also acts to assist, where possible, in defence-related trade matters. In addition, although Ottawa staff handle the main administration load for the personnel, the Canberra office covers those Canadians on exchange with Australian Defence units and formation, who number some 20 individuals at the time of writing.

## International Relations and Defence

### *Australian Foreign Policy Principles*

"I am one of those old-fashioned Australian politicians who think that our nation's foreign policy should not be aimed at noisy demonstration or assertion. A little man waving a big stick is not only faintly absurd, but liable to lose his balance. Situated as we are in the world, washed on our western and northern shores by potentially hostile seas, and numerically incapable - despite intense defence preparations - of defending ourselves for long against all-out attack by a great power without massive aid from our friends, it seems to me to be clear (and my Government acted on that belief) that our foreign policy should be to cultivate friendly relations with our neighbours; to do what we could to help their development and stability; to encourage every means of peaceful economic and financial co-operation; to avoid avoidable war; to play our part in helping to prevent tensions among our neighbours; to be loyal members of the United Nations while having no illusions about its present protective effectiveness.

## Nationalism and the United Nations

"When the United Nations Organisation was being established, there was a widespread belief that we were making a notable experiment in a direction which favoured an inter-nationalism which would reduce the occasions of conflict in the world. After the war it was though that nations would, seeing the advantages of international action, become less nationalistic; less self-contained; more conscious of the existence and interest of other countries. I confess that I have seen no symptoms that this result has been achieved. On the contrary, I would think that the tendency all around the world and particularly in the newer countries is to intensify nationalism. We are frequently told that strange and revolutionary events in many of the new countries are merely evidence of a struggle for nationalism. Yet there are some paradoxes. These new nations get their national existence acknowledged by membership of the United Nations, but when they attend the General Assembly they fall readily into groups or blocs designed to impose their ideas upon other nations. They are much more concerned, vocally at any rate, to criticise and condemn other nations than to look at themselves and ask how they can make themselves fit into international affairs in a constructive way.

Just as the Commonwealth has begun to fall to pieces because many of the new members, feeling and expressing no obligations to the Commonwealth, devote their energies to telling other members how they ought to run their own affairs, so in the United Nations an exactly similar process goes on. If that process continues, the United Nations will disintegrate for reasons exactly similar to those which we have observed in action in the Commonwealth itself." R.G. Menzies, 'Looking Forward', *Measure of the Years* (1970) 211.

## The United Nations and Domestic Policy

"The United Nations was not created to provide means by which a group of nations can without consent interfere, if necessary by arms, with the domestic affairs of another country; quite the contrary. But should this deplorable process be encouraged, we may all find ourselves and our autonomy put at risk in the presence of a well-organized 'mob' sentiment." R.G. Menzies, 'A critical examination of the modern Commonwealth', *Afternoon Light* (1967) 225.

## Relations with the United States of America

"The nature and form of our association

I shall begin with a little bit of history. When I made the Jefferson 'oration' at Monticello on 4 July 1963, I took the opportunity to point out that when the famous American Declaration of Independence was made and followed up by a successful War of Independence, the American colonies actually created, without knowing it at the time, two new nations. One was, of course, the United States.

The other was Australia! Up to that time the American colonies had been the recipients of convicts transported from England; many thousands of them; though, as I have sometimes pointed out to England audiences, most of the persons convicted over the period of transportation remained in England! When the American colonies became independent, transportation naturally ended. So another destination had to be found. Thus it came about that the Southern Continent of Australia, especially made known to Great Britain by Captain Cook, received, at Botany Bay and Sydney, the first white settlers, the convicted persons and their military custodians, in the fleet commanded by Captain Phillip in 1788! From this somewhat murky origin has grown a nation of life, character and purpose. This is what I mean when I say that two nations were created by the one act.

Again Australia, sixty-five years ago, became a Federation with a Constitution in some material ways modelled upon that of the U.S.A. We have much experience in common of the problems which are presented in adjusted the relations between a Nation and its constituent States. As a lawyer engaged in Constitutional cases in Australia, I used to read, and occasionally quote, decisions of the United States Supreme Court. I think the traffic was reciprocal; I know in particular that my late friend Mr Justice Felix Frankfurter was an avid and prompt reader of the judgements of the High Court of Australia.

And, most eloquent of all facts, American and Australian troops have fought together in two great wars, and since in Korea and Vietnam, in the common cause. If we recall that these elements in our common history have an enormous background of inheritance of a common history before the late eighteenth century, of language and literature, of the Common Law, of the great principles enshrined in the phrase 'the Rule of Law', of popular self-government, of religious faith, and of a common passion for individual and national freedom, we will at once see that enmity between the United States and Australia would be not only unthinkable, but 'most foul, strange and unnatural'.

"The United States is now the greatest power in the world. In earlier years it was clearly isolationist, and could afford to announce the Monroe Doctrine and its detachment from the problems of the old world in Europe to the new world in the East, because Britain was the greatest naval power; while the long-range aircraft, the inter-continental ballistic missile, and the nuclear and thermonuclear weapons had not been devised.

The First World War snatched her out of her isolationism, but her abstention from membership of the League of Nations turned her thoughts once more to home. Her crucial participation in the Second World War, and her magnificent and generous policy thereafter, changed the picture. Power always connotes responsibility in a civilised country. We had all seen the dreadful Hitlerian tragedy of power without responsibility, and have no desire to see it again. It was the great American sense of responsibility which took her into the Marshall plan, into the Berlin airlift, into NATO, into Korea, into SEATO and Vietnam, into ANZUS.

It was inevitable that questioning voices should be raised in the United States, for the burdens lie heavy on the American people, 'Why should we be the world's gendarme?' But, as I took the liberty of pointing out in a recent lecture at the University of Texas, there is a vital middle course between being a defender everywhere abroad, and a defender nowhere except at home. I have always believed and said no more than this, that great powers have great responsibilities, and that the greatest has the greatest. We in Australia are by no means a great power; but we are sufficiently rich and strong to have responsibilities to our neighbours and discharge them, as we do in relation to Papua and New Guinea, the Colombo Plan, SEATO and its consequences, and in various other ways.

The truth is that a great power cannot make itself available at call anywhere, as if it were a fire-brigade. It must select tasks commensurate with its resources and the willingness of its people. As a world power, it will know the sources of world danger to the freedom of which it is an exemplar and defender. America's policy and actions in relation to Western Europe are a splendid example; but they are reasonably predicated upon Western European powers, including Britain, taken their fair share of the burden. It is not called upon to intervene in every local conflict, or, for that matter, in every limited war. But it intervened Vietnam because, more clearly than any of the European powers, it saw the defence of South Vietnam as a defence against the aggression of Communist china, an aggression which is backed by a vast population and a developing technology, including nuclear capacity, and which, if unrestrained, could threaten the peace and security of the whole world.

Looking to the future, I cannot see the United States going isolationist; withdrawing its overseas support, and leaving the rest of the world to look after itself. From a moral point of view, such a policy would be repellent to respectable and respected American opinion. From a hard-bitten, practical point of view, it would, in the long run, gravely damage the United States."

"But a great and civilized power must accept world responsibilities, must set out to discharge them, not priggishly, but with a real vision of what the world needs for the prosperity and happiness of its people. In the performance of its duties, it will need patience and tolerance. It will encounter selfish objections in various quarters. It should never seek to make excuses, but if objections arise, it must have no fear of them. A true consciousness of destiny is not to be brushed aside as 'imperialism'.

For a great nation without a sense of purpose will not remain great very long. What it gives to the world will be the true measure of its greatness." R.G. Menzies, 'Our Relations with The United States of America', *Afternoon Light* (1967) 261. "America has not become our friend and defender simply for love of the countries we inhabit. On the contrary, she knows that, in the most real sense, we are the same kind of people, with the same ideas, with the same ideals, with the same high faith, with the same basic belief that governments exist for the people, that they are the servants and not the masters."

## ANZUS

"Now, apart from our ancient and largely unwritten ties with Great Britain and the Commonwealth, the most significant features of Australia's modern foreign policy was this mutually defensive treaty with the U.S.A. and New Zealand, ratified in accordance with constitutional requirements in all three countries. Its continued validity and effectiveness have been affirmed by successive American Presidents and Secretaries of State. It amply deserves some brief explanation in the context of this chapter.

At a period when it has become almost fashionable to make critical remarks about America and American policy, such remarks being made both at home and abroad, it is good for Australians to recall the provisions and circumstances of the ANZUS Treaty. Nothing can better demonstrate the role which the United States has accepted since the Second World war, and its willingness to match great responsibilities with great power, than this brief but significant treaty.

The United States has seventeen or eighteen times the population of Australia and almost sixty times the population of New Zealand. Clearly what Australia and New Zealand could do to assist the United States would be a very small fraction of what the United States would be a very small fraction of what the United States could do for Australia and New Zealand. But the Americans made the treaty and ratified it."

## Britain's Contribution to the World

"I invite you to remember with pride that it was in the free world that the two great institutions of liberty, parliamentary self-government and the rule of honestly administered law, were fashioned. They have made a mark on this century compared to which a Sputnik is unimportant. It is too frequently forgotten, and sometimes by countries which should remember it, that, if Great Britain has not as yet fired a satellite into space, she has, by a creative modern policy, converted colonies into independent nations, founded upon parliamentary sovereignty and enriched by the rule of law, while the Soviet Union has been busy converting independent nations into colonies under the rule not of law, but of the tank and the bomb."

### *South East Asia*

"My final observation is that, given a satisfactory conclusion to the Vietnam war, Australia will be more and more occupied with the great tasks of establishing our relations with [South East Asian] countries on a basis of friendship and co-operation; with an increasing supply of technical assistance and financial and economic aid being provided by Australia. For we should see these nations, protected against aggression, not only as a *codron sanitiare* between us and the potential enemy, but as a source of economic strength, making an important contribution to the world and providing a good neighbourhood for them and for ourselves."

### *Papua New Guinea*

"The ultimate granting of political independence was always our objective. Whether the time is ripe should be a matter for their own decision, and not a matter for Canberra along. We should not prematurely wash our hands of responsibility for the government of the territories, and run the risk of another Congo. On the other hand, we should not delay action too long, so that when self-government comes it arrives in an atmosphere or resentment and hostility. In other words, 'much too soon' would provoke disaster; 'a little too soon' would be preferable to 'a little too late'. That these territories will achieve independence, I have no doubt. That they will, after political independence, need large economic and financial aid from Australia is inevitable. That they will get it is certain. They will not become a State in the Australian Federation; the difficulties so created would, in my opinion, be politically insuperable.

## *Colombo Plan*

"For we saw quite clearly that one of the greatest underlying problems, which, until it is solved, will produce tensions which threaten the peace, is that of the gap between the living standards of the great industrialised nations with enormous physical and technological resources and therefore rapid growth, and those of the emergent nations with more primitive industry, limited industrial assets, and slower growth. Clearly, if this gap is to continue to widen, there will be much ill-will and frustration. New countries, having increased their export surpluses with technical and financial aid, must be provided with markets for their products at prices which will enable them to develop their capital resources and living standards.

This was the first major initiative of my new Government. It was a positive approach looking well into the future. It involved Australia closely with the countries and peoples of Asia. This association has persisted ever since and has been a major element not only in the policies and dealings of the Australian Government but also in helping to shape the background and attitude of individual Australians. Australian ministers and officials, private firms, and universities are in frequent contact with their counterparts in Asian countries. Many thousands of Asian students had studied in Australia by the time I retired, and the process continues. The daily association of Australians with students and scholars from Asian countries has greatly widened the experience and understanding of our own people, and is a major achievement for which our Government can claim credit.

The Colombo Plan was also important in another respect. We wanted the industrialised countries of North America and Western Europe to give more attention to the economic needs of Asia. After the Second World War great economic aid had gone to Europe, primarily from the United States. The Marshall Plan which followed was a major and most generous programme by the United States to set Western Europe on its feet again economically. The justification for concentrating on Western Europe at that time was that it already had the skills and the basic economic capacity to enable it to become again a major element in the world economy and therefore to contribute to the economic well-being of all. At the same time, in the United Nations valuable work was being done in helping to promote and give practical effect to the idea of international responsibilities for economic development."." R.G. Menzies, 'Pacific Policy', *Measure of the Years* (1970) 51-52. Nuclear weapons "It is hard for me to understand those who would seek to abolish nuclear and thermonuclear weapons as the first step to disarmament and peace. In common with most democratic leaders, I am convinced that, uneasy though the peace may be which the existence of these weapons protects, their disappearance tomorrow would dreadfully increase the dangers of war."

## Weaponry and Freedom

"Let us constantly remember that scientific defence provision is, for us, solely a means of preserving democratic freedom and civilized individual rights. It would be the ultimate tragedy to abandon the purpose of defence in order to prepare as the potential enemy prepares. In actual war, we put many particular freedoms in pawn so as to preserve the great freedom. But such a process should not long survive when war has been won. A *fortiori,* it should not become an established feature of what may well be a prolonged period of uneasy peace. If provision for military scientific research and development comes to be regarded not as a free national effort but as something requiring the abandonment of freedom and the acceptance of authoritarian control, we shall have abandoned the case against Communism in the very course of making ourselves ready to maintain it."

# 2

# Defence Relation : India and Other Countries

## Introduction

India takes an active role in assisting reconstruction efforts in Afghanistan, having committed some $1.2 billion to this cause, as well as contributing some 4,000 workers and opening numerous consulates there (much to the dismay of Pakistan, which fears strategic encirclement and takes note of India's past support for Afghan Tajik and Uzbek militias). Among Indian assistance to Afghanistan are funding for a new $111 million power station, an $84 million roadbuilding project, a $77 million dam project, and construction of Kabul's new $67 Parliament building, to be completed in 2010. There are reported to be several hundred Indian commandos stationed in Afghanistan to provide protection for Indian reconstruction workers. The United States has welcomed India's role in Afghanistan. A July 2008 suicide bombing at India's Kabul Embassy was taken as a stark message to Indian leaders that Taliban militants and their allies want New Delhi to withdraw from Afghanistan. Prime Minster Singh instead responded by vowing $450 million in new Indian aid for Afghan reconstruction.

Looking to the north, New Delhi supports consolidation of Nepal's democratic and conflict resolution processes, in particular through continued political assimilation of the Maoists. India remains concerned by political instability in Kathmandu and by the cross-border infiltration of Maoist militants into India. In April 2008, Nepali Maoists won a surprise electoral victory in taking more than onethird of Kathmandu's Constituent Assembly seats to oversee a new coalition government. The new Kathmandu government has since threatened to abrogate the 1950 Indo-Nepal Peace and Friendship Treaty, which allows for unrestricted travel and residency across the shared border. While Indian officials are fairly sanguine about the development and vow openness to working with the new Nepali government, they are likely to have concerns about the potential for instability in Nepal to exacerbate India's own internal insecurities.

To the east, and despite India's key role in the 1971 creation of neighboring Bangladesh, New Delhi's relations with Dhaka have been fraught with tensions related mainly to the cross-border infiltration of Islamic and separatist militants, and tens of millions of illegal migrants into India. New Delhi is undertaking a $1.2 billion project to fence India's entire 2,000-mile shared border with Bangladesh. The two countries' border forces engage in periodic gunbattles. Still, New Delhi and Dhaka have cooperated on counterterrorism efforts and talks on energy cooperation continue. The Bangladeshi faction of the Harakat ul-Jihad-I-Islami – an Islamist militant outfit that was designated as a Foreign Terrorist Organization under U.S. law in March 2008 and that has links to Pakistan-based terrorist groups – has been implicated in several terrorist attacks inside India, including May 2008 terrorist bombings that killed at least 63 people in Jaipur, Rajasthan. Bangladesh's militarybacked interim government, which took power in 2007, may benefit India by reducing anti-India rhetoric and by addressing the apparently growing influence of Islamist forces that are seen as a threat to Indian interests.

In the island nation of Sri Lanka off India's southeastern coast, a Tamil Hindu minority has been fighting a separatist war against the Sinhalese Buddhist majority since 1983. A Norwegian-brokered cease-fire unraveled in 2006 and, after a series of military successes in 2007, the Colombo government abrogated the cease-fire in January 2008. More than 60 million Indian Tamils live in southern India and tens of thousands of Sri Lankan Tamil refugees have fled to India in recent months and years. India's armed 1987 intervention to assist in enforcing a peace accord resulted in the deaths of more than 1,200 Indian troops and led to the 1991 assassination of former Indian Prime Minister Rajiv Gandhi by Tamil militants. Since that time, New Delhi has maintained friendly relations with Colombo while refraining from any deep engagement in third-party peace efforts. New Delhi resists Colombo's push for more direct Indian involvement and insists there can be "no military solution" to the island's ethnic troubles. The Indian Navy played a key role in providing disaster relief to Sri Lanka following the catastrophic December 2004 Indian Ocean tsunami. Moscow was New Delhi's main foreign benefactor for the first four decades of Indian independence. Russia continues to be "indispensable to India's foreign policy interests," according to Prime Minister Singh, who calls energy cooperation the core of the two countries' "strategic partnership." India's single largest foreign investment is a $1 billion stake in a joint oil and gas venture on Russia's Sakhalin Island. Moreover, and despite some post-Cold War diversification of its defence suppliers, India continues to obtain the bulk of its imported military hardware from Russian firms. In 2007, Russian President Vladimir Putin paid a visit to New Delhi, where he met with top Indian officials; signed several bilateral agreements on energy, science, and space cooperation; and offered to sell four new 1,000-megawatt nuclear reactors to India. In November, Prime Minister Singh visited Moscow, where he and Putin discussed economic, energy, and defence ties. Agreement for the construction of four new nuclear reactors was deferred due to "technical hitches." Some commentators believe the U.S. government pressured New Delhi to avoid the deal. Russia's status as a main supplier of Indian defence equipment currently is threatened by several disputes, including over the refitting of an aircraft carrier (which has seen major delays and cost overruns), a spat over Russia's allegedly substandard upgradation of an Indian attack submarine, and other irritants.

India's relations with Japan only began to blossom in the current decade after being significantly undermined by India's 1998 nuclear weapons tests. Today, leaders from both countries acknowledge numerous common values and interests. They are engaging a "strategic dialogue" formally launched with a 2007 visit to Tokyo by Foreign Minister Mukherjee, who spoke of Japan as a "natural partner in the quest to create an arc of advantage and prosperity" in Asia. Mukherjee emphasized India's desire for economic integration in Asia and cooperative efforts to secure vital sea lanes, especially in the Indian Ocean. Japan's support for the latter initiative has included plans for unprecedented joint naval exercises. New Delhi and Tokyo also share an interest in seeing membership of the U.N. Security Council expanded; both governments aspire to permanent seats. India seeks Japan's endorsement for proposed U.S.-India civil nuclear cooperation, which has not been forthcoming to date. A mid-2007 visit to New Delhi by Japanese Prime Minister Shinzo Abe, who was effusive in his praise of India as a "partner and friend," was seen by many as part of a long-term Japanese effort to hedge against China's growing regional influence. Abe and Prime Minister Singh issued a "Roadmap for New Dimensions to the Strategic and Global Partnership" outlining plans for security cooperation and comprehensive economic engagement. Singh met with the new Japanese Prime Minister, Yasuo Fukada, in Singapore in November and reiterated a commitment to the India-Japan "strategic and global partnership."

The U.S. and Japanese governments have sought India's participation in a prospective quadrilateral "axis of democracy" that would include Australia and could conceivably have a security alliance dimension (Australian officials reportedly are skeptical of such a pact for fear of alienating China). In 2007, U.S., Indian, and Japanese naval vessels conducted unprecedented combined exercises off Japan's east coast. In September of that year, India hosted unprecedented five-country naval exercises in the Bay of Bengal (with Australian and Singaporean vessels also participating). Officials stressed that the exercises – which involved a total of 27 ships and submarines, among them two U.S. aircraft carriers – were not prompted by China's growing military strength. New Delhi favours greater trilateral India-U.S.-Japan cooperation, especially in the areas of trade and energy security, but shies from anything that could be construed as a multilateral security alliance.

## Political Setting

India is the world's most populous democracy and remains firmly committed to representative government and rule of law. As a nation-state, India presents a vast mosaic of hundreds of different ethnic groups, religious sects, and social castes. U.S. policymakers commonly identify in the Indian political system shared core values, and this has facilitated increasingly friendly relations between the U.S. and Indian governments. In 2008, the often-cited Freedom House again rated India as "free" in the areas of political rights and civil liberties.

### *National Elections*

With a robust and working democratic system, India is a federal republic where the bulk of executive power rests with the prime minister and his or her cabinet (the Indian president is a ceremonial chief of state with limited executive powers). Most of India's prime ministers have come from the country's Hindi-speaking northern regions and all but two have been upper-caste Hindus. The 543-seat Lok Sabha (People's House) is the locus of national power, with directly elected representatives from each of the country's 28 states and 7 union territories. A smaller upper house, the Rajya Sabha (Council of States), may review, but not veto, most legislation, and has no power over the prime minister or the cabinet. National and state legislators are elected to five-year terms. The most recent parliamentary elections were held in the spring of 2004.

National elections in October 1999 had secured ruling power for a Bharatiya Janata Party (BJP)-led coalition government headed by Prime Minister Vajpayee. That outcome decisively ended the historic dominance of the Nehru-Gandhi-led Congress Party, which was relegated to sitting in opposition at the national level (its members continued to lead many state governments). However, a surprise Congress resurgence under Sonia Gandhi in the 2004 elections brought to power a new leftleaning coalition government led by former finance minister and Oxford-educated economist Manmohan Singh, a Sikh and India's first-ever non-Hindu prime minister. Many analysts attributed Congress's 2004 resurgence to the resentment of rural and poverty-stricken urban voters who felt left out of the "India shining" campaign of a BJP more associated with urban, middle-class interests. Others saw in the results a rejection of the Hindu nationalism associated with the BJP.

The current Congress-led United Progressive Alliance (UPA) ruling coalition has marked nearly four years in power, exceeding the expectations of some observers. Opinion surveys suggest that both Prime Minister Singh and party chief Gandhi have remained fairly popular national figures. However, February 2007 state elections in Punjab and Uttaranchal saw Congress candidates decisively defeated by the BJP and its allies, causing some pundits to suggest that national economic policies and rising inflation may have damaged the ruling coalition's standing. Such arguments were forwarded when the Bahujan Samaj Party (BSP) won an outright majority in May 2007 state assembly elections in Uttar Pradesh, India's most populous state. During its four years overseeing a national ruling coalition, the Congress Party has lost 12 assembly elections and was dislodged by the main opposition BJP in four states, including Karnataka and Punjab.

Meanwhile, under the party presidency of Rajnath Singh, the BJP has enjoyed seven consecutive election victories. Congress's surprise May 2008 loss in Karnataka set the party on its heels in the run-up to national polls expected in early 2009, with many analysts concluding that national political momentum has shifted away from the party. Some observers saw in the Karnataka election dynamics signs that urban voters are exercising new-found muscle in ways that could weaken the country's traditionally pro-rural politicians.

Prime Minister Singh, though widely admired as an honest and intelligent figure, has been unable to succeed in pushing through most of the UPA agenda, and his party's state-level electoral setbacks have most analysts predicting no bold policy initiatives before the next national election expected in 2009. This is especially so in the wake of the New Delhi government's inability to consummate a civil nuclear cooperation deal with the United States, an issue upon which the UPA leadership has staked considerable political capital. By most accounts, 2007 was a particularly unsuccessful year for the incumbent national government.

### *The Congress Party*

Congress's electoral strength reached a nadir in 1999, when the party won only 110 Lok Sabha seats. Observers attributed the poor showing to a number of factors, including the failure of Congress to make strong preelection alliances (as had the BJP) and perceptions that party leader Sonia Gandhi lacked the experience to lead the country. Support for the Congress, which dominated Indian politics for decades, had been in fairly steady decline following the 1984 assassination of Prime Minister Indira Gandhi and the 1991 assassination of her son, Prime Minister Rajiv Gandhi.

Sonia Gandhi, Rajiv's Italian-born, Catholic widow, refrained from active politics until the 1998 elections. She later made efforts to revitalize the party by phasing out older leaders and attracting more women and lower castes – efforts that appear to have paid off in 2004. Today, Congress again occupies more parliamentary seats (145) than any other party and, through unprecedented alliances with powerful regional parties, it again leads India's government under the UPA coalition. As party chief and UPA chair, Gandhi is seen to wield considerable influence over the coalition's policy making process. Her foreign origins have presented an obstacle and likely were a major factor in her May 2004 decision to decline the prime ministership. As key Congress party figures express support for the future leadership of her son and new parliamentarian, Rahul Gandhi, Manmohan Singh's political authority is correspondingly undermined.

### *The Bharatiya Janata Party (BJP)*

With the rise of Hindu nationalism, the BJP rapidly increased its parliamentary strength during the 1980s. In 1993, the party's image was tarnished among some, burnished for others, by its alleged complicity in serious communal violence in Bombay and elsewhere. Some hold elements of the BJP, as the political arm of extremist Hindu groups, responsible for the incidents (the party has advocated "Hindutva," or an India based on Hindu culture, and views this as key to nation-building).

While leading a national coalition from 1998-2004, the BJP worked – with only limited success – to change its image from right-wing Hindu fundamentalist to conservative and secular, although 2002 communal rioting in Gujarat again damaged the party's credentials as a moderate organization. The BJP-led National Democratic Alliance (NDA) was overseen by party notable Prime Minister Atal Vajpayee, whose widespread personal popularity helped to keep the BJP in power. After 2004, the BJP was weakened by leadership disputes, criticism from Hindu nationalists, and controversy involving party president Lal Advani (in 2005, Advani ceded his leadership post and Vajpayee announced his retirement from politics). The party did, however, take control of the Karnataka state government in November 2007, the first time the BJP has held power in southern India. In preparing for a new round of national elections, the party may adhere to its core Hindutva philosophy; it has nominated hardliner Advani to be its next prime ministerial candidate and may continue efforts to demonize India's Muslim minority as part of a long-standing electoral strategy. Some observers, however, believe the party is looking beyond its traditional vote bank to appeal to urban, middle-class concerns such as governance and commerce, especially in the wake of party notable Narendra Modi's reelection as Chief Minister of the western Gujarat state in December 2007.

### *Regional Parties*

The influence of regional and caste-based parties has become an increasingly important variable in Indian politics; the 2004 national elections saw such parties receiving nearly half of all votes cast. Never before 2004 had the Congress Party entered into pre-poll alliances at the national level, and numerous analysts attributed Congress's success to precisely this new tack, especially thorough arrangements with the Bihar-based Rashtriya Janata Dal and Tamil Nadu's Dravida Munnetra Kazhagam. The newfound power of both large and smaller regional parties, alike, is seen to be reflected in the UPA's ministerial appointments, and in the Congress-led coalition's professed attention to rural issues and to relations between state governments and New Delhi.

Two significant regional parties currently independent of both the ruling coalition and the BJP-led opposition are the Samajwadi Party, a largely Muslim-and lower caste-based organization highly influential in Uttar Pradesh, and the Bahujan Samaj Party (BSP) of Bihar, which also represents mainly lower-caste constituents. State assembly elections in Uttar Pradesh – home to more than 170 million Indians and one of only four states where the Congress Party is not in power – concluded in May 2007 and saw a major victory for the BSP and its lower-caste, female leader Mayawati, who reached out to upper-caste and other groups to secure an outright majority, the first time in 14 years that a single party secured such status. Mayawati is believed to have national political aspirations and her party's success with castebased politics may erode support for the Congress party in expected 2009 national elections. The outcome may have been an important indicator of national political trends, especially in gauging satisfaction with the current centre coalition. In June 2007, eight regional parties formally launched a new "Third Front" that might emerge as a national alternative to the UPA and NDA. Well-known Tamil Nadu politician Jayalalithaa is a notable leader.

### *The Left Front*

Although the Communist Party of India (Marxist) seated the third largest number of parliamentarians in 2004, its vote bank is almost wholly limited to West Bengal and Kerala (the Left Front coalition holds about 11% of all Lok Sabha seats). Communist parties have in the past been bitter rivals of the Congress in these states, but a mutual commitment to secularism appears to have motivated their cooperation against the BJP in 2004.122 Early alarm was sounded that the new influence of communists in New Delhi might derail India's economic reform efforts; Indian industrial leaders sought to assure foreign investors that Left Front members are not "Cuba-style communists," but could be expected to support the UPA reform agenda. The communist Chief Minister of West Bengal, Buddhadeb Bhattacharya, has himself actively sought corporate investment in his state. However, since coming to power, the Congress-led coalition has slowed most aspects of its economic reform program, including suspending major government disinvestment and special economic zone initiatives. These moves are widely viewed

## Bilateral Issues

### *"Next Steps in Strategic Partnership" and Beyond*

The now-concluded Next Steps in Strategic Partnership (NSSP) initiative encompassed several major issues in U.S.-India relations. New Delhi has long pressed Washington to ease restrictions on the export to India of dual-use hightechnology goods (those with military applications), as well as to increase civilian nuclear and civilian space cooperation. These three key issues came to be known as the "trinity," and top Indian officials insisted that progress in these areas was necessary to provide tangible evidence of a changed U.S.-India relationship. There were later references to a "quartet" when the issue of missile defence was included. In January 2004, President Bush and Prime Minister Vajpayee issued a joint statement declaring that the U.S.-India "strategic partnership" included expanding cooperation in the "trinity" areas, as well as expanding dialogue on missile defence. This initiative was dubbed as the NSSP and involved a series of reciprocal steps.

In July 2005, the State Department announced successful completion of the NSSP, allowing for expanded bilateral commercial satellite cooperation, and removal/revision of some U.S. export license requirements for certain dual-use and civil nuclear items. Taken together, the July 2005 U.S.-India Joint Statement and a June 2005 U.S.-India Defence Framework Agreement include provisions for moving forward in all four NSSP issue-areas. Many observers saw in the NSSP evidence of a major and positive shift in the U.S. strategic orientation toward India, a shift later illuminated more starkly with the Bush Administration's intention to initiate full civil nuclear cooperation with India.

### *Civil Nuclear Cooperation*

India's status as a non-signatory to the 1968 Nuclear Nonproliferation Treaty (NPT) has kept it from accessing most nuclearrelated materials and fuels on the international market for more than three decades. New Delhi's 1974 "peaceful nuclear explosion" spurred the U.S.-led creation of the Nuclear Suppliers Group (NSG) — an international export control regime for nuclear-related trade — and Washington further tightened its own export laws with the Nuclear Nonproliferation Act of 1978 (P.L. 95-242). New Delhi has long railed at a "nuclear apartheid" created by an apparent double standard inherent in the NPT, which, they maintain, allows certain states to legitimately employ nuclear deterrents while other states cannot. Senior Indian officials reiterate the widely-held Indian perspective that reaching a civil nuclear deal with the United States remains crucial to the process of removing constraints placed on India by "an increasingly selective, rigorous, and continually expanding regime of technology denial," claiming that only by "turning the nuclear key" will India be able to open the door to global trade in dual use and other sophisticated technologies.

Under U.S. and international law, civil nuclear cooperation with India cannot commence until Washington and New Delhi finalize a peaceful nuclear cooperation agreement (and Congress endorses such an agreement), until New Delhi concludes its own safeguards agreement with the International Atomic Energy Agency, and until the NSG allows for such cooperation. At present, nuclear power accounts for less than 3% of India's total electricity generation, and an Indian government official has estimated that, even under optimistic scenarios, this percentage would likely no more than double over the next 25 years.

### *The Bush Administration Policy Shift*

Differences over nuclear policy bedeviled U.S.-India ties for decades and – given New Delhi's lingering resentments – have presented a serious psychological obstacle to more expansive bilateral relations. In a major policy shift, the July 2005 U.S.-India Joint Statement notably asserted that "as a responsible state with advanced nuclear technology, India should acquire the same benefits and advantages as other such states," and President Bush vowed to work on achieving "full civilian nuclear energy cooperation with India." As a reversal of three decades of U.S. nonproliferation policy, such proposed cooperation stirred controversy and required changes in both U.S. law and in NSG guidelines. India reciprocally agreed to take its own steps, including identifying and separating its civilian and military nuclear facilities in a phased manner and placing the former under international safeguards. Some in Congress express concern that civil nuclear cooperation with India might allow that country to advance its military nuclear projects and be harmful to broader U.S. nonproliferation efforts. While the Bush Administration previously had insisted that such cooperation would take place only within the limits set by multilateral nonproliferation regimes, it later actively sought adjustments to U.S. laws and policies, and has approached the NSG in an effort to adjust that regime's guidelines, which are set by member consensus. In March 2006, President Bush and Prime Minister Singh issued a Joint Statement that included an announcement of "successful completion of India's [nuclear facility] separation plan." After months of complex and difficult negotiations, the Indian government had presented a plan to separate its civilian and military nuclear facilities as per the July 2005 Joint Statement. The separation plan would require India to move 14 of its 22 reactors into permanent international oversight by the year 2014 and place all future civilian reactors under permanent safeguards. Shortly thereafter, legislation to waive the application of certain requirements under the Atomic Energy Act of 1954 with respect to India was, at the President's request, introduced in the U.S. Congress.

### *Potential Benefits and Costs*

Secretary of State Rice appeared before key Senate and House committees in April 2006 to press the Bush Administration's case for civil nuclear cooperation with India. The Administration offered five main justifications for making changes in U.S. law to allow for such cooperation, contending that doing so would

- benefit U.S. security by bringing India "into the nonproliferation mainstream;"
- benefit U.S. consumers by reducing pressures on global energy markets, especially carbon-based fuels;
- benefit the environment by reducing carbon emissions/ greenhouse gases;
- benefit U.S. business interests through sales to India of nuclear reactors, fuel, and support services; and
- benefit progress of the broader U.S.-India "global partnership."

Many leading American experts on South Asian affairs joined the Administration in urging Congress to support the new policy, placing particular emphasis on the "necessary" role it would play in promoting a U.S.-India global partnership. The U.S. Chamber of Commerce – which, along with the U.S.-India Business Council, lobbied vigorously in favour of President Bush's initiative – speculated that civil nuclear cooperation with India could generate contracts for American businesses worth up to $100 billion, as well as generate up to 27,000 new American jobs each year for a decade. A more modest estimate foresees the deal generating as much as $40 billion in new foreign investment into India. However, foreign companies such as Russia's Atomstroyexport and France's Areva may be better poised to take advantage of the Indian market. Moreover, U.S. nuclear suppliers will likely balk at entering the

Indian market in the absence of nuclear liability protection, which New Delhi does not offer at present.

Further hearings in the Senate and House during mid-2006 saw a total of fifteen independent analysts weigh in on the potential benefits and/or problems that might accrue from such cooperation. Numerous nonproliferation experts, scientists, and former U.S. government officials warned that the Bush Administration's initiative was ill-considered, arguing that it would facilitate an increase in the size of India's nuclear arsenal, potentially leading to a nuclear arms race in Asia, and would undermine the global nonproliferation regime and cause significant damage to key U.S. security interests. Some experts opined that the Administration's optimism, perhaps especially as related to the potential effects on global energy markets and carbon emissions, could not be supported through realistic projections.

### *Geopolitical Motives*

In the realm of geopolitics, much of the Administration's argument for moving forward with the U.S.-India nuclear initiative appears rooted in an anticipation/expectation that New Delhi will in coming years and decades make policy choices that are more congruent with U.S. regional and global interests (a desire for such congruence is, in fact, written into the enabling legislation, P.L. 109-401). Proponents suggest that this U.S. "gesture" will have significant and lasting psychological and symbolic effects in addition to the material ones, and that Indian leaders require such a gesture in order to feel confident in the United States as a reliable partner on the world stage. Skeptics aver that the potential strategic benefits of the nuclear initiative are being over-sold. Indeed, centuries of Indian anti-colonial sentiments and oftentimes prickly, independent foreign policy choices are unlikely to be set aside in the short run, meaning that the anticipated geopolitical benefits of civil nuclear cooperation with India remain speculative and at least somewhat dependent upon unknowable global political developments.

### *Congressional Action*

After months of consideration, key House and Senate committees took action on relevant legislation in June 2006, passing modified versions of the Administration's proposals by wide margins. The new bills (H.R. 5682 and S. 3709) made significant procedural changes to the Administration's original proposal, changes that sought to retain congressional oversight of the negotiation process, in part by requiring the Administration to gain future congressional approval of a completed peaceful nuclear cooperation agreement with India (this is often referred to as a "123 Agreement," as it is negotiated under the conditions set forth in Section 123 of the Atomic Energy Act). During the final months of its tenure, the 109th Congress passed enabling legislation with broad bipartisan support. So-called "killer amendments" were rejected by both chambers (Indian government and Bush Administration officials had warned that certain proposed new provisions, such as those requiring that India halt its fissile material production or end its military relations with Iran, would trigger New Delhi's withdrawal from the entire negotiation).

In a December 2006 "lame duck" session, congressional conferees reconciled the House and Senate versions of the legislation and provided an explanatory statement (H.Rept. 109-721). President Bush then signed the Henry J. Hyde United States-India Peaceful Atomic Energy Cooperation Act of 2006 (P.L. 109-401 or the "Hyde Act") into law, calling it a "historic agreement" that would help the United

States and India meet the energy and security challenges of the 21st century. The President also issued a signing statement asserting that his approval of the act "does not constitute [his] adoption of the statements of policy as U.S. foreign policy" and that he will construe such policy statements as "advisory." Some in Congress expressed concern that President Bush would seek to disregard Congress's will. In mid-2007, as negotiations on a 123 Agreement were underway, experts, scholars, and former U.S. government officials signed a letter urging Senators to hold the Bush Administration to the "set of core conditions and limitations" of the Hyde Act, including termination of assistance upon an Indian nuclear test, permanent and unconditional safeguards on civilian Indian facilities, and prohibitions on reprocessing and enrichment technologies. A July letter to President Bush signed by 23 Members of the House stressed the need for any civil nuclear cooperation agreement with India to conform to "the legal boundaries set by Congress." The letter noted that the U.S. Constitution provides Congress with the sole authority to regulate foreign commerce, and it expressed ongoing concerns about "India's deepening military-to-military relationship with Iran... [which] places congressional approval of the Agreement for Nuclear Cooperation in jeopardy."

### *Indian Concerns*

Almost immediately upon the release of the July 2005 Joint Statement, key Indian political figures and members of the country's insular nuclear scientific community issued strong criticisms of the bilateral civil nuclear initiative; some such criticisms continue to this day. Former Prime Minister Vajpayee, along with many leading figures in his opposition BJP party, insisted that the deal as envisioned would place unreasonable and unduly expensive demands on India, particularly with regard to the separation of nuclear facilities. In reaction to the U.S. Congress's passage of enabling legislation in late 2006, the BJP listed numerous continuing objections, and went so far as to call the deal "unacceptable" and aimed at "capping, rolling back, and eventually eliminating India's nuclear weapons capability." Many analysts view the BJP's opposition as political rather than substantive, especially in light of the fact that the 2004 NSSP initiative was launched during the BJP's tenure.

Some Indian analysts, wary of U.S. intentions in pursuing bilateral civil nuclear cooperation, believe the initiative may be cover for a broader effort to cement India's cooperation in a number of non-energy-related areas, such as defence trade and New Delhi's relations with Iran. From this perspective, the U.S. government repeatedly "shifted the goalposts" to forward its own (veiled) nonproliferation goals. India's influential communist parties, whose Left Front provides crucial support to the Congress-led ruling coalition in New Delhi, have focused their ire on geopolitical aspects of the civil nuclear initiative. In late 2006, the leader of India's main communist party declared the U.S.-India civil nuclear deal "not acceptable" as it would "seriously undermine India's independent foreign policy." Previously, the Left Front had called India's two IAEA votes on Iran a "capitulation" to U.S. pressure. Indian leftists thus have been at the forefront of political resistance to India's becoming a "junior partner" of the United States. Equally stinging and perhaps more substantive criticism came from several key Indian scientists, whose perspectives on the technical details of the civil nuclear initiative are considered highly credible. India's nuclear scientific community, mostly barred from collaboration with international civil nuclear enterprises as well as direct access to key technologies, has worked for decades in relative isolation, making its members both proud of their singular accomplishments and sensitive to any signs of foreign "interference." Many viewed the enabling legislation passed by the U.S. Congress as being more about nonproliferation and less about energy cooperation. They considered it both intrusive on and preclusive of their activities. The major criticisms of existing plans for U.S.-India civil nuclear cooperation made by Indian commentators (and at times by the Indian government) are summarized as follows:

- India's unilateral moratorium on nuclear tests was being codified into a bilateral obligation through a clause that would allow the United States to reclaim any supplied nuclear equipment if India were to test a nuclear device;
- India was being denied nuclear reprocessing technologies warranted under "full cooperation;"
- India was not being given prior authorization to reprocess spent fuel;
- India was not being given assurances that it will receive uninterrupted fuel supplies in perpetuity; and
- language on securing India's assistance with U.S. efforts to prevent Iran from obtaining weapons of mass destruction would limit New Delhi's foreign policy independence.

Prime Minister Singh stood firm against such wide-ranging and high-profile criticisms, repeatedly assuring his Parliament that relevant negotiations with the United States have not altered basic Indian policies or affected New Delhi's independence on matters of national interest. Within this context, however, Singh expressed concern about some of the points listed above. Regardless of the legally binding or non-binding nature of certain controversial sections of the U.S. legislation, New Delhi found many of them to be either "prescriptive" in ways incompatible with the provisions of the July 2005 and March 2006 Joint Statements, or "extraneous" and "inappropriate to engagements among friends."

## Bilateral Negotiations Completed

In July 2007, the United States and India announced having concluded negotiations on a peaceful nuclear cooperation ("123") agreement, calling it a "historic milestone" in the bilateral strategic partnership. The announcement came one week after a fifth round of formal bilateral negotiations had ended in Washington, where a high-level Indian delegation led by National Security Advisor M.K. Narayanan had met with numerous top U.S. officials, including Vice President Cheney and Secretary of State Rice. Under Secretary of State Burns, the lead U.S. negotiator, called the deal "perhaps the single most important initiative that India and the United States have agreed to in the 60 years of our relationship" and "the symbolic centerpiece of a growing global partnership between our two countries." U.S. officials urged New Delhi to move rapidly toward completing remaining steps to consummation of the pact. Among the text's more salient provisions are the following:

- India is granted authorization to reprocess spent fuel at a national reprocessing facility that New Delhi plans to establish under International Atomic Energy Agency safeguards.
- In the event of a future nuclear test by India, the two countries would launch immediate bilateral consultations to "consider carefully the circumstances" and take into account whether the circumstances resulted from "serious concern about a changed security environment or as a response to similar actions by other states which could impact national security." While the U.S. President would have a right to demand the return of all U.S.-supplied nuclear equipment and material in such a circumstance, the text recognizes that "exercising the right of return would have profound implications" for bilateral relations and calls for both parties to "take into account the potential negative consequences" of any termination of ongoing cooperation.
- India is given assurances that supplies of fuel for its civilian reactors will not be interrupted – even if the United States terminates the 123 Agreement – through U.S. commitments to "work with friends and allies... to create

the necessary conditions for India to obtain full access to the international fuel market," and to "support an Indian effort to develop a strategic reserve of nuclear fuel."

Press reports had indicated that U.S. granting of unambiguous reprocessing rights, along with an Indian insistence on U.S. guarantees of an uninterrupted fuel supply for all imported reactors, had become a central obstacle in the lead-up to the talks, and that Indian negotiators had taken uncompromising positions in both areas. Subsequent reports suggested that U.S. negotiators made considerable concessions to Indian demands and that the agreement could face resistance in Congress if its legal stipulations are seen to deviate from those found in the Hyde Act. In early 2008, External Affairs Minister Mukherjee reassured the Indian Parliament of his government's view that the Hyde Act is relevant only to interaction between the legislative and executive branches of the U.S. government, and that only the provisions of the 123 Agreement will be binding upon New Delhi. This distinction was echoed by Assistant Secretary of State Boucher during his contemporaneous visit to New Delhi.

### *Civil Space Cooperation*

India has long sought access to American space technology; such access has since the 1980s been limited by U.S. and international "red lines" meant to prevent assistance that could benefit India's military missile programs. India's space-launch vehicle technology was obtained largely from foreign sources, including the United States, and forms the basis of its intermediate-range Agni ballistic missile booster, as well as its suspected Surya intercontinental ballistic

The NSSP called for enhanced U.S.-India cooperation on the peaceful uses of space technology, and the July 2005 Joint Statement anticipated closer ties in space exploration, satellite navigation and launch, and in the commercial space arena. Major conferences on India-U.S. space science and commerce were held in Bangalore (headquarters of the Indian Space Research Organization) in both 2004 and 2005. During President Bush's 2006 visit to India, the two countries committed to move forward with agreements that will permit the launch of U.S. satellites and satellites containing U.S. components by Indian space launch vehicles and they later agreed to include two U.S. scientific instruments on India's planned Chandrayaan lunar mission. In 2007, a meeting of the U.S.-India Joint Working Group on Civil Space Cooperation was held in Washington, where officials expressed satisfaction with growing bilateral ties in the aerospace field.

## *High-Technology Trade*

U.S. Commerce Department officials have sought to dispel "trade-deterring myths" about limits on dual-use trade by noting that less than 0.5% of total U.S. trade value with India is now subject to licensing requirements and that the great majority of dual-use licensing applications for India are approved (about 95% in 2007). July 2003 saw the inaugural session of the U.S.-India High-Technology Cooperation Group (HTCG), where officials discussed a wide range of issues relevant to creating the conditions for more robust bilateral high technology commerce; the sixth HTCG meeting was held in New Delhi in February 2008 (at the 2007 session, U.S. Commerce Secretary Carlos Gutierrez had unveiled a new "Trusted Customer" program designed to facilitate greater high-tech trade with India). In 2005, the inaugural session of the U.S.-India High-Technology Defence Working Group was held under HTCG auspices. Commerce's Bureau of Industry and Security formally designated India as an eligible country under its "Validated End-User" program in October 2007.

This designation will allow certain trusted Indian buyers to purchase high-technology goods without an individual license. Since 1998, a number of Indian entities have been subjected to case-by-case licensing requirements and appear on the U.S. export control "Entity List" of foreign end users involved in weapons proliferation activities.

In 2004, as part of NSSP implementation, the United States modified some export licensing policies and removed the Indian Space Research Organization (ISRO) headquarters from the Entity List. Further adjustments came in 2005 when six more subordinate entities were removed. Indian entities remaining on the Entity List are four subordinates of the ISRO, four subordinates of the Defence Research and Development Organization, three Department of Atomic Energy entities, and Bharat Dynamics Limited, a missile production agency.

## Security Issues

### *The Indian Military*

With more than 1.3 million active personnel, India's is the world's third-largest military (after China and the United States). The country's defence budget grew by 11% to about $28 billion in 2007 and is up more than 30% since 2000 (adjusted for inflation). The army — more than one million strong and accounting for nearly half of the budget — has traditionally dominated, but the navy and air force are becoming more important as India seeks to project its power and protect an Exclusive Economic Zone of more than two million square kilometers. For 2007, the air force procurement budget of $3.75 billion was nearly 44% of the service-specific total, with the navy receiving another $2.56 billion. The Indian army possesses more than 4,000 main battle tanks and some 4,500 towed artillery tubes. The navy has grown rapidly in recent years, currently operating 48 principal surface combatants (including one aircraft carrier) and 16 submarines. There also is a significant amphibious capacity: 17 landing ships (including one recently acquired from the United States) can carry nearly 5,000 troops or 100 tanks. The navy is developing an indigenous nuclear-powered attack submarine to be armed with nuclear-tipped cruise missiles and also plans to lease a Russian Akula-class submarine as part of its "sea-based strategic deterrence." The air force flies 565 combat-capable aircraft, the majority of them Russian-built MiGs, along with some late-model Sukhoi-30, as well as French-built Mirage and Anglo-French Jaguar aircraft. It also possesses modest airborne early warning and in-flight refueling capabilities provided by Russian-made platforms. A Strategic Forces Command oversees as many as 170 intermediate-and short-range ballistic missiles capable of delivering nuclear warheads, and has plans to field a new Agni-IV missile with a range that would give it inter-continental capabilities.

New Delhi increasingly seeks to shift advanced military imports from finished platforms to co-production with foreign suppliers. A 2005 deal with France provides for technology transfers and Indian construction of six Scorpene submarines to be delivered in 2012-2017. In seeking to replace its aging arsenal of MiG-21 fighters, India may purchase up to 186 new jets (126 for the air force and 60 for the navy) and has signalled a desire for technology sharing and co-production in this effort: only 18 of the new air force jets are to be manufactured abroad. In addition to the Scorpene submarines, other notable recent purchases for the Indian military include hundreds of the latest Russian T-90 tanks and upgrades on 600 existing T-72s; 3 new Russianbuilt missile frigates; 24 new MiG-29K naval jets for deployment on the *INS Vitramaditya* (formerly the Russian *Gorshkov*); 40 upgraded Su-30 MKI ground attack aircraft, major upgrades on existing MiG and Jaguar combat aircraft; and 66 jet trainers from Britain.

Russia continues to provide the bulk of India's imported defence wares. In recent years, however, Israel has roughly equaled Russia in the value of defence exports to India, with each country providing about $1.5 billion worth of defence supplies in 2006. Moreover, India and Israel are engaging in new joint development projects involving missile technology. India was the leading developing world arms purchaser from 1999-2006, making arms transfer *agreements* totaling $22.4 billion during that period. As India seeks to expand its power projection capabilities, it has come under fire from some for continuing to prepare for a conventional interstate war that may be unlikely to occur. According to one report, of the country's nearly two million persons in uniform, only about 5,000 have meaningful counterterrorism training.

## *U.S.-India Security Cooperation*

Defence cooperation between the United States and India is in the early stages of development (unlike U.S.-Pakistan military ties, which date back to the 1950s). Since September 2001, and despite a concurrent U.S. rapprochement with Pakistan, U.S.-India security cooperation has flourished; U.S. diplomats rate military cooperation among the most important aspects of transformed bilateral relations. The India-U.S. Defence Policy Group (DPG) – moribund since India's 1998 nuclear tests and ensuing U.S. sanctions – was revived in late 2001 and meets annually.

In June 2005, the United States and India signed a ten-year defence pact outlining planned collaboration in multilateral operations, expanded two-way defence trade, increasing opportunities for technology transfers and co-production, expanded collaboration related to missile defence, and establishment of a bilateral Defence Procurement and Production Group. The agreement may be the most ambitious such security pact ever engaged by New Delhi. A Maritime Security Cooperation Agreement, inked in 2006, commits both countries to "comprehensive cooperation" in protecting the free flow of commerce and addressing a wide array of threats to maritime security, including piracy and the illicit trafficking of weapons of mass destruction and related materials. In April 2007, the Commander of the U.S. Pacific Command, Adm. Tim Keating, told a Senate panel that the Pentagon intends to "aggressively" pursue expanding military-to-military relations with India. During his August 2007 visit to New Delhi, Adm. Keating lauded U.S.-India defence relations as "solid, good, and improving steadily." The sentiment was echoed by Secretary of Defence Gates during his February 2008 visit to the Indian capital. The United States views defence cooperation with India in the context of "common principles and shared national interests" such as defeating terrorism, preventing weapons proliferation, and maintaining regional stability. Many analysts view increased U.S.-India security ties as providing an alleged "hedge" against or "counterbalance" to growing Chinese influence in Asia, though both Washington and New Delhi repeatedly downplay such probable motives. Still, while a congruence of U.S. and Indian national security objectives is unlikely in the foreseeable future, convergences are being identified in areas such as shared values, the emergence of a new balance-of-power arrangement in the region, and on distinct challenges such as WMD proliferation, Islamist extremism, and energy security. There also remain indications that the perceptions and expectations of top U.S. and Indian strategic planners are divergent on several key issues, including the role of Pakistan, approaches to conflict resolution in Iraq and in Palestine, and Indian's relations with Iran, as well as with repressive governments in places such as Burma and Sudan.

### *Combined Military Exercises*

Since early 2002, the United States and India have held a series of unprecedented and increasingly substantive combined exercises involving all military services. "Cope India" air exercises have provided the U.S. military with its first look at advanced Russian-built Su-30MKIs; in 2004, mock air combat saw Indian pilots in late-model Russian-built fighters hold off American pilots flying older F-15Cs, and Indian successes were repeated versus U.S. F-16s in 2005. Indian pilots joined military aviators from South Korea and France to participate in August 2008 U.S. Air Force training exercises over Nevada. U.S. and Indian special forces soldiers have held at least five "Vajra Prahar" joint exercises, and at least 133 U.S. Special Forces soldiers have attended India's Counter-Insurgency Jungle Warfare School. Moreover, major annual "Malabar" joint naval exercises are held off the Indian coast. The seventh and most recent of these came in September 2007, when India hosted a total of 27 warships from five countries – including the United States, Japan, Australia, and Singapore – for maneuvers in the Bay of Bengal. It was the first time such exercises were conducted off India's east coast. U.S. and Indian officials tout ongoing joint maneuvers as improving interoperability and as evidence of an overall deepening of the bilateral defence relationship.

### *Arms Sales*

Along with increasing military-to-military ties, the issue of U.S. arms sales to India has taken a higher profile, with some analysts anticipating that New Delhi will spend as much as $40 billion on weapons procurement over the next five years. The first-ever major U.S. arms sale to India came in 2002, when the Pentagon negotiated delivery of 12 counter-battery radar sets (or "Firefinder" radars) worth a total of $190 million. India also purchased $29 million worth of counterterrorism equipment for its special forces and has received sophisticated U.S.-made electronic ground sensors to help stem the tide of militant infiltration in the Kashmir region. In 2004, Congress was notified of a sale to India involving up to $40 million worth of aircraft self-protection systems for mounting on the Boeing 737s that carry India's head of government. Moreover, the State Department has authorized Israel to sell to India the jointly developed U.S.-Israeli Phalcon airborne early warning system, an expensive asset that some analysts believe may tilt the regional strategic balance even further in India's favour.

In 2006, Congress authorized and New Delhi approved the $44 million purchase of the *USS Trenton*, a decommissioned American amphibious transport dock. The ship, which became the second largest in the Indian navy when it was commissioned as the *INS Jalashwa* in June 2007, set sail for India carrying six surplus Sikorsky UH-3H Sea King helicopters purchased for another $39 million. In May 2007, the Pentagon notified Congress of a possible sale to India of six C-130J Hercules military transport aircraft (along with related equipment, training, and services) in a deal that could be worth more than $1 billion to the manufacturer, Maryland-based Lockheed Martin. In January 2008, Washington and New Delhi signed an agreement to finalize the deal, which represents the largest-ever U.S. defence sale to India.

The Indian government reportedly possesses an extensive list of desired U.S.-made weapons, including PAC-3 anti-missile systems, electronic warfare systems, and possibly even combat aircraft. The March 2005 unveiling of the Bush Administration's "new strategy for South Asia" included assertions that the United States welcomed Indian requests for information on the possible purchase of F-16 or F/A-18 fighters, and indicated that Washington is "ready to discuss the sale of transformative systems in areas such as command and control, early warning, and missile defence." India in August 2007 invited foreign tenders for the sale of 126 new multi-role combat aircraft in a deal that could be worth more than $10 billion. Lockheed Martin's F-16 and Illinois-based Boeing's F/A-18 are competing with aircraft built in Russia, France, Sweden, and by a European consortium. Lockheed's pitch reportedly includes offering a "super-cruise" version of the F-16 that saves large amounts of fuel by achieving supersonic speeds without the use of afterburners. Boeing, for its part, has sought to establish multiple joint ventures that could better position the company to become India's preferred aerospace and defence partner. Some top Indian officials express concern that the United States is a "fickle" partner that may not always be relied upon to provide the reciprocity, sensitivity, and high-technology transfers sought by New Delhi. In 2006, the Indian Navy declined an offer to lease two U.S. P-3C maritime reconnaissance aircraft, calling the arrangements too costly. Moreover, India's offset policy states that any defence purchases worth more that $76 million must include offset clauses amounting to at least 30% of the deal's total value. This policy, already described as "narrow" and "fairly restrictive" by the U.S. Ambassador to India, was altered to require that fully half of the value of any multi-role combat aircraft import be attached to offsets. U.S. laws requiring on-site verifications of exported defence equipment may represent a further irritant, as Indian officials reportedly have expressed discomfort with such physical inspections.

Joint U.S.-India military exercises and arms sales negotiations can cause disquiet in Pakistan, where there is concern that induction of advanced weapons systems into the region could disrupt the "strategic balance" there. Islamabad worries that its already disadvantageous conventional military status vis-à-vis New Delhi will be further eroded by India's acquisition of sophisticated "force multipliers." In fact, numerous observers identify a pro-India drift in the U.S. government's strategic orientation in South Asia. Yet Washington regularly lauds Islamabad's role as a key ally in the U.S.-led counterterrorism coalition and assures Pakistan that it will take no actions to disrupt strategic balance on the subcontinent.

## U.S.-India Counterterrorism Cooperation

One facet of the emerging "strategic partnership" between the United States and India is greatly increased counterterrorism cooperation. The U.S. State Department's *Country Reports on Terrorism 2007* identified India as being "among the world's most terror-afflicted countries" and counted more than 2,300 Indian deaths due to terrorism in 2007 alone. State finds numerous problems with New Delhi's capacity to combat terrorism: The Indian government's counterterrorism efforts remained hampered by outdated and overburdened law enforcement and legal systems. The Indian court system was slow, laborious, and prone to corruption; terrorism trials can take years to complete. Many of India's local police forces were poorly staffed, lacked training, and were ill-equipped to combat terrorism effectively. Some Indian analysts complain that the intelligence gathering capabilities of India's security forces remain woefully inadequate and preclude effective law enforcement and preventive action.

In November 2001, President Bush and then-Indian Prime Minster Vajpayee agreed that "terrorism threatens not only the security of the United States and India, but also our efforts to build freedom, democracy and international security and stability around the world." In 2002, India and the United States launched the

Indo-U.S. Cyber Security Forum to safeguard critical infrastructures from cyber attack. The June 2005 "New Framework for the U.S.-India Defence Relationship" lists "defeating terrorism and violent religious extremism" as one of four key shared security interests, and it calls for a bolstering of mutual defence capabilities required for such a goal. An April 2006 session of the U.S.-India Joint Working Group on Counterterrorism — the seventh such meeting since the group's founding in January 2000 — ended with a statement of determination from both countries to further advance bilateral cooperation and information sharing on such areas of common concern as bioterrorism, aviation security, advances in biometrics, cyber-security and terrorism, WMD terrorism, and terrorist financing. Expanding military-to-military links have included company-level joint counterinsurgency training of army units. In October 2005, the United States and India concluded a treaty on criminal matters that would institutionalize law enforcement cooperation and create a regularized channel for mutual assistance. Among the hoped-for benefits has been more effective counterterrorism efforts. It was reported in May 2006 that the United States had offered demining assistance, counterinsurgency training for police forces, and humanitarian relief for persons internally displaced by conflict related to the Maoist rebellion. Moreover, three months after the July 2006 Bombay terrorist bombings, senior CIA officials reportedly travelled to New Delhi to discuss improving counterterrorism cooperation with Indian leaders, and an FBI official later called for closer law enforcement and intelligence coordination with India in light of terrorist attacks in that country's interior. There have been signs that U.S. government agencies have taken greater notice of links apparent between Pakistanbased terrorist groups and wanted Indian criminal boss Dawood Ibrahim, who is suspected of residing in Karachi, Pakistan. In 2003, the U.S. Department of the Treasury formally designated Ibrahim as a terrorist supporter and accused him of collaborating with Al Qaeda in South Asia.

## Nuclear Weapons and Missile Proliferation

Many policy analysts consider the apparent arms race between India and Pakistan as posing perhaps the most likely prospect for the future use of nuclear weapons by states. In May 1998, India conducted five underground nuclear tests, breaking a self-imposed, 24-year moratorium on such testing. Despite international efforts to dissuade it, Pakistan quickly followed. The tests created a global storm of criticism and represented a serious setback for two decades of U.S. nuclear nonproliferation efforts in South Asia. Following the tests, President Clinton imposed full restrictions on nonhumanitarian aid to both India and Pakistan as mandated under Section 102 of the Arms Export Control Act. India currently is believed to have enough fissile material, mainly plutonium, for 55-115 nuclear weapons; Pakistan, with a program focused on enriched uranium, may be capable of building a similar number. Both countries have aircraft capable of delivering nuclear bombs. India's military has inducted short-and intermediate-range ballistic missiles, while Pakistan itself possesses short-and medium-range missiles (allegedly acquired from China and North Korea). All are assumed to be capable of delivering nuclear warheads over significant distances.

Proliferation in South Asia is part of a chain of rivalries – India seeking to achieve deterrence against China, and Pakistan seeking to gain an "equalizer" against a conventionally stronger India. In 1999, a quasi-governmental Indian body released a Draft Nuclear Doctrine for India calling for a "minimum credible deterrent" (MCD) based upon a triad of delivery systems and pledging that India will not be the first to use nuclear weapons in a conflict. In 2003, New Delhi announced creation of a Nuclear Command Authority. After the body's first session in September of that year, participants vowed to "consolidate India's nuclear deterrent." India thus appears to be taking the next steps toward operationalizing its nuclear weapons capability. According to the director of the U.S. Defence Intelligence Agency in a 2007 statement to a Senate panel, India is building its stockpile of fission weapons and is likely to continue work on advanced warhead and delivery systems.

### *U.S. Nonproliferation Efforts and Congressional Action*

Soon after the May 1998 nuclear tests in South Asia, Congress acted to ease aid sanctions through a series of legislative measures. In September 2001, President Bush waived remaining sanctions on India pursuant to P.L. 106-79. During the 1990s, the U.S. security focus in South Asia sought to minimize damage to the nonproliferation regime, prevent escalation of an arms race, and promote Indo-Pakistani bilateral dialogue. In light of these goals, the Clinton Administration set out "benchmarks" for India and Pakistan based on the contents of U.N. Security Council Resolution 1172, which condemned the two countries' nuclear tests.

These included signing and ratifying the Comprehensive Nuclear Test Ban Treaty (CTBT); halting all further production of fissile material and participating in Fissile Material Cutoff Treaty negotiations; limiting development and deployment of WMD delivery vehicles; and implementing strict export controls on sensitive WMD materials and technologies.

Progress in each of these areas has been limited, at best, and the Bush Administration quickly set aside the benchmark framework. Along with security concerns, the governments of both India and Pakistan face the prestige factor attached to their nuclear programs and domestic resistance to relinquishing what are perceived to be potent symbols of national power.

Neither has signed the CTBT, and both appear to be producing weapons-grade fissile materials. (India has consistently rejected the CTBT, as well as the Nuclear Nonproliferation Treaty, as discriminatory, calling instead for a global nuclear disarmament regime. Although both India and Pakistan currently observe self-imposed moratoria on nuclear testing, they continue to resist signing the CTBT — a position made more tenable by U.S. Senate's rejection of the treaty in 1999.)

The status of weaponization and deployment is unclear, though there are indications that this is occurring at a slow but steady pace. Section 1601 of P.L. 107-228 outlined U.S. nonproliferation objectives for South Asia. Some in Congress identify "contradictions" in U.S. nonproliferation policy toward South Asia, particularly as related to the Senate's rejection of the CTBT and U.S. plans to build new nuclear weapons. In May 2006, the United States presented in Geneva a draft global treaty to ban future production of fissile material (a Fissile Material Cutoff Treaty) that it hopes will be supported by India. Some analysts speculated that the move was meant to bolster U.S. congressional support for proposed U.S.-India civil nuclear cooperation.

## India's Economy and U.S. Interests

India is in the midst of a major and rapid economic expansion, with an economy projected to soon be the world's third largest. Although there is widespread and serious poverty in the country, observers believe long-term economic potential is tremendous, and recent strides in the technology sector have brought international attention to such new global high-tech centers as Bangalore and Hyderabad. However, many analysts and business leaders, along with U.S. government officials, point to excessive regulatory and bureaucratic structures as a hindrance to the realization of India's full economic potential.

The high cost of capital (rooted in large government budget deficits) and an "abysmal" infrastructure also draw negative appraisals as obstacles to growth. Constant comparisons with the progress of the Chinese economy show India lagging in rates of growth and foreign investment, and in the removal of trade barriers. Just prior to his March 2006 visit to New Delhi, President Bush noted India's "dramatic progress" in economic reform while insisting "there's more work to be done," especially in lifting caps on foreign investment, making regulations more transparent, and continuing to lower tariffs.

According to the Economist Intelligence Unit, India's per capita GDP was only about $824 in 2007. The highly-touted information technology and business processing industries employ only about one-third of one percent of India's work force and, while optimists vaunt an Indian "middle class" of some 300 million people, a larger number of Indians subsists on less than $1 per day. Yet, even with the existence of ongoing problems, the current growth rate of India's increasingly service-driven economy is among the highest in the world and has brought the benefits of development to many millions of citizens. The U.N. Development Program ranked India 128th out of 177 countries on its 2007/2008 human development index (between Morocco and Laos), down from 126th in 2006.184 After enjoying an average growth rate above 6% for the 1990s, India's economy cooled with the global economic downturn after 2000. Yet sluggish, Cold War-era "Hindu rates of growth" had become a thing of the past. For the fiscal year ending March 2006, real change in GDP was 8.5%, the second-fastest rate of growth among the world's 20 largest economies. During FY2006/

2007, India's economy expanded by a blistering 9.2% and nearly matched this rate again in FY2007/2008 with a 9% expansion. Robust growth in the services, manufacturing, and industry sectors continues, but is moderated by a weak agricultural sector (low productivity levels in this sector, which accounts for nearly one-fifth of the country's GDP, are a drag on overall growth). Short-term estimates are encouraging, predicting expansion well India's central bank warned in early 2007 that rising inflation and surging stock and property markets were "signs of overheating" in the country's economy. Some analysts criticize the bank for being too timid in reining in domestic demand. Consumer price inflation rose somewhat in mid-2007, then appeared to level off at a lower rate toward year's end (with a year-on-year rate of 5.5% in January), but may rise again in 2008. The soaring Bombay Stock Exchange tripled in value from 2001-2006, then apparently overheated with the worst-ever daily decline of its benchmark Sensex index on May 22, 2006, when almost 11% of its total value was lost (related also to political developments). The market subsequently stabilized and then recovered mightily, reaching new highs in the closing months of 2006. More new record highs became even more frequent in the latter half of 2007 and the Sensex was up nearly 40% for the year. India now boasts more billionaires than any other Asian country and has the fourth most in the world, trailing only the United States, Germany, and Russia. The bounty of India's newly-super-wealthy is traced largely to phenomenal gains in the country's stock market, but, in a further indicator of serious income disparity, only about 2% of the country's working-age population hold any stock at all.

A major U.S. concern with regard to India is the scope and pace of reforms in what has been that country's quasi-socialist economy. Reforms begun in 1991, under the Congress-led government of Prime Minister Rao and his finance minister, current Prime Minister Singh, boosted growth and led to major new inbound foreign investment in the mid-1990s. Reform efforts stagnated, however, under weak coalition governments later in the decade, and combined with the 1997 Asian financial crisis and international sanctions on India (as a result of its 1998 nuclear tests) to further dampen the economic outlook. Following the 1999 parliamentary elections, the BJP-led government launched second-generation economic reforms, including major deregulation, privatization, and tariff-reducing measures. Once seen as favouring domestic business and diffident about foreign involvement, New Delhi appears to gradually be embracing globalization and has sought to reassure foreign investors with promises of transparent and nondiscriminatory policies. A January 2007 report from global investment banking and securities firm Goldman Sachs called India's recent high growth rates a result of structural rather than cyclical increases and projected a sustainable growth rate of about 8% through 2020. It identified political developments – including a rise in protectionism; supply-side restraints, including business climate, education, and labour market reforms; and environmental degradation – as representing major risks to future growth. An October 2007 country survey from the Paris-based Organization for Economic Cooperation and Development (OECD) traced India's economic successes to reforms that reduced the role of the state in economic affairs and claimed that New Delhi's pursuit of further "ambitious and wide-ranging reforms" could push India's growth rate to a sustainable 10% annually. Other analyses identify water shortages, urban woes, and pollution as further potential threats to Indian prosperity.

### *Trade and Investment*

As India's largest trade and investment partner, the United States strongly supports New Delhi's continuing economic reform policies. A U.S.-India Trade Policy Forum was created in November 2005 to expand bilateral economic engagement and provide a venue for discussing multilateral trade issues. The United States currently accounts for about one-sixth of all Indian exports. India was the 16th largest export market for U.S. goods in 2007 (up from 21st the previous year). Levels of U.S.-India trade, while relatively low, are blossoming; the total value of bilateral trade has doubled since 2001 and the two governments intend to see it doubled again by 2009. U.S. imports from India in 2007 were valued at $24 billion (up 10% over 2006). Leading imports included cotton apparel; textiles; and pearls, gemstones, and jewellery. Exports to India in 2007 totalled $17.6 billion (up 75% over 2006), with civilian aircraft; telecommunications equipment; finished pearls, gemstones, and jewellery; and chemical fertilizers as leading categories. Bilateral trade in private commercial services was worth more than $13 billion more, split evenly between imports and exports.

Annual inward direct investment to India from all countries rose from a mere $74 million in 1991 to $5.5 billion in 2001 and $17.5 billion in 2006.192 Net portfolio investment added another $7.1 billion in FY2006/2007. According to Indian officials, about one-seventh of foreign direct investment in India since 1991 has come from U.S. firms; in recent years, the major U.S.-based companies Microsoft, Dell, Oracle, and IBM have made multi-billion-dollar investments in India (U.S. firms invested about $2 billion in India in 2006; Indian companies invested roughly the same amount in the United States). The stock of U.S. foreign direct investment in India was just below $9 billion for 2006. India's foreign exchange reserves were at a record $300 billion in August 2008. India has moved to raise limits on foreign investment in several key sectors, although U.S. officials prod New Delhi to make more rapid and more substantial changes to foreign investment ceilings, especially in the retail, financial services, and banking sectors. In March 2006, the U.S.-India CEO Forum – composed of ten chief executives from each country representing a cross-section of key industrial sectors – issued a report identifying India's poor infrastructure and dense bureaucracy as key impediments to increased bilateral trade and investment relations.

In a May 2007 speech on U.S.-India relations, Under Secretary of State Burns captured all the major U.S. concerns (and advice) with regard to bilateral economic issues with India, saying New Delhi must insure that new regulations or old red tape don't impeded growth, and that foreign companies have a clear path to settling commercial disputes when they arise. The Indian government should also continue economic reforms and liberalizations that have been the basis of India's economic boom so far.... In order to achieve higher growth rates as well as broad rural development, India requires world-class airports, irrigation, and communications networks. It needs modern power grids, ports, and highways, and many other infrastructural improvements that could be vastly accelerated by greater investment, both public and private.... Our focus is on facilitating and promoting foreign direct investment, enhancing bilateral consultations on reducing tariff and non-tariff barriers to trade in industrial goods, services, and agriculture, preventing the illicit use of the financial system, and strengthening India's regime for intellectual property rights.

In September 2007, U.S. Ambassador Mulford opined that, "Continued reform and liberalization will help further boost... and spread the benefits of rapid economic growth to more recipients across India." During his October 2007 visit to India, U.S. Treasury Secretary Paulson told a Mumbai audience, In the long term, India can take a number of steps to become even more competitive, such as reducing requirements that financial institutions hold large amounts of government debt, reducing requirements for banks to provide credit to certain priority sectors, and removing various restrictions and caps on foreign investment. Limits on debt and equity financing, and asset allocation restrictions on financial institutions, are impediments to putting resources to their most productive use.

### *Barriers to Trade and Investment*

Despite significant tariff reductions and other measures taken by India to improve market access, according to the 2008 report of the United States Trade Representative (USTR), a number of foreign trade barriers remain, including high tariffs, especially in the agricultural sector. The USTR asserts that "continued reduction of the bilateral trade deficit will depend on significant additional Indian liberalization of the trade and investment regime." The Commerce Department likewise encourages New Delhi to continue lowering tariffs as a means of fostering trade and development. Indian Finance Minister Chidambaram agrees that high rates of investment must be maintained to sustain the country's economic growth. In 2007, India regained full investment-grade status after a 15-year hiatus when Standard & Poor's upgraded India's sovereign rating, but the country's public finances remain much weaker than comparable states: India has a public debt-to-GDP ratio (85%) more than three times higher than China's, and interest consumes nearly one-third of total revenue.

India's extensive trade and investment barriers have been criticized by U.S. government officials and business leaders as an impediment to its own economic development, as well as to stronger U.S.-India ties. For example, in 2004, then-U.S. Under Secretary of State Alan Larson opined that "trade and investment flows between the U.S. and India are far below where they should and can be," adding that "the picture for U.S. investment is also lackluster." He identified the primary reason for the suboptimal situation as "the slow pace of economic reform in India." In 2007, Under Secretary of the Treasury Tim Adams urged India to further reduce trade and investment barriers, liberalize its financial sector, and improve its business climate as key means to "compete effectively in the global economy."

Inadequate intellectual property rights protection is another long-standing issue between the United States and India. The USTR places India on its Special 301 Priority Watch List for "inadequate laws and ineffective enforcement" in this area. The International Intellectual Property Alliance (IIPA), a coalition of U.S. copyrightbased industries, estimated U.S. losses of $913 million due to copyright piracy in India in 2007, with some 95% of this in the categories of business and entertainment software (estimated loss amounts do not include motion picture piracy, which in 2004 was estimated to have cost some $80 million). The IIPA expresses frustration that "little significant progress" is being made in more effectively enforcing copyright protection in India. In December 2006, Under Secretary of Commerce and Director of the U.S. Patent and Trademark Office Jon Dudas told a New Delhi audience that "further modifications are necessary" in India's intellectual property rights protection regime and that India's copyright laws are "insufficient in many aspects." He also warned that "piracy and counterfeiting rates will continue to rise without effective enforcement."

While the past two decades have seen a major transformation of the Indian economy, it remains relatively closed in many aspects. The Heritage Foundation's SEZ-related troubles continued in late 2007 with an upsurge in political violence in West Bengal and reports that state officials may have been complicit in attacks on farmers. *2008 Index of Economic Freedom* — which some say may overemphasize the value of absolute growth and downplay broader quality-of-life measurements — rated India's economy as being "54% free" and ranked it 115th out of 162 countries. The index highlights restrictive trade policies, heavy government involvement in the banking and finance sectors, rigorous investment caps, demanding regulatory structures, and a high incidence of corruption. Berlin-based Transparency International placed India 72nd out of 179 countries in its 2007 "corruption perceptions index." The group's 2006 "bribery index" found India to be the worst offender among the world's top 30 exporting countries. The Vancouver-based Fraser Institute provides a more positive assessment of economic freedom in India, while also faulting excessive restrictions on capital markets.

### *Special Economic Zones (SEZs)*

In 2005, New Delhi announced plans to allow Indian states to establish Chinese-style special economic zones that would encourage foreign investment and boost employment by bypassing the country's strict labour and tax laws. Parliament soon approved implementation and, in early 2006, the SEZ Act went into effect. With well over 200 such zones approved and hundreds more planned, SEZs became a matter of significant controversy. Proponents view them as sensible means of growing the economy through greatly increased investment, as well as improving infrastructure. Yet the policy has elicited energetic opposition from interest groups representing the political left and right, alike. Some critics say building SEZs on fertile agricultural land will impoverish farmers without adequate compensation. Even Congress Party chief Sonia Gandhi openly opposed exposing farmers to "unscrupulous developers." Other detractors, including India's finance minister, warn that the government will be denied billions of dollars in tax revenues lost due to special concessions offered to participating firms. In early 2007, after Left Front parties demanded extensive curbs on the initiative, New Delhi suspended approval of 304 more SEZs pending decisions on issues including compensation for displaced farmers. In March of that year, police in Nandigram, West Bengal, opened fire on a group of protesters who were demonstrating against state land appropriations for a planned SEZ. At least 14 people were killed and the incident led to days of violent protests against the state government's action. Soon after, the West Bengal government dropped its plans and the federal government vowed to "refine" its SEZ policy to make it more equitable.

## Multilateral Trade Negotiations

In 2006, the World Trade Organization's "Doha Round" of multilateral trade negotiations were suspended due to disagreement among the WTO's six core group members – which include the United States and India – over methods to reduce trade-distorting domestic subsidies, eliminate export subsidies, and increase market access for agricultural products. The United States and other developed countries seek substantial tariff reductions in the developing world. India, like other members of the "G-20" group of developing states, has sought more market access for its goods and services in the developed countries, while claiming that developing countries should be given additional time to liberalize their own markets. In particular, India is resistant to opening its markets to subsidized agricultural products from developed countries, claiming this would be detrimental to tens of millions of Indian farmers and result in further depopulation of the countryside. According to Indian officials, the WTO's narrow focus on economic issues excludes political and social variables which are equally sensitive for New Delhi and which constrain the options available to the Indian government. They seek greater U.S. understanding of this dynamic. The Indian economy could benefit significantly from lowered farm subsidies in developed countries and expanded trade in services, but indigenous industries could also be harmed if New Delhi were to reduce tariffs that currently protect India's exporting sectors, especially in textiles and garments.

Indian Commerce Minister Nath has blamed U.S. intransigence for the Doha Round's collapse. In mid-2007, Indian officials rejoined the negotiations, then claimed the talks had again "collapsed" due to lack of convergence among the major actors. U.S. Trade Representative Schwab later expressed surprise at how "rigid and inflexible" India (and Brazil) were during the negotiations, and she suggested that "some countries... really don't want a Doha round outcome." In September, however, Nath again expressed optimism in identifying a new and "greater comprehension of India's sensitivities" on the effects of U.S. farm subsidies. Indian leaders were reported to be especially dissatisfied with draft documents they believe are too restrictive of their domestic policies meant to protect Indian farmers from a flood of foreign imports. The U.S. government, for its part, continues to insist that it can only cut its own domestic farm subsidies if advanced developing states such as India (and China and Brazil) do more to open their own markets to foreign goods. In June 2008, a Commerce Department official called India a "roadblock to success" in the negotiations by treating them as a "donor's conference" and resisting all reasonable liberalization proposals, even those being offered by other developing countries. When dialogue was rejoined in July, Commerce Minister Nath assumed the mantle of unofficial spokesman for the world's developing economies, frustrating many Western negotiators by creating what seemed an intractable obstacle to progress. The potentially final collapse of talks came when U.S. negotiators could not agree with their Indian and Chinese counterparts on levels for a "safeguard clause" meant to protect developing states from unrestricted imports, which the Americans believed were being set too low. Some commentators said the Doha Round's failure marked a conclusive end to an era in which free trade was organized around rules set in the West.

## *The Energy Sector and Climate Change*

India's continued economic growth and security are intimately linked to the supply of energy resources. Indeed, Indian leaders insist that energy security is an essential component of the country's development agenda, calling for an integrated national energy policy, diversification of energy supplies, greater energy efficiency, and rationalization of pricing mechanisms. The country's relatively poor natural energy resource endowment and poorly functioning energy market are widely viewed as major constraints on continued economic growth. Estimates indicate that maintaining recent rates of growth will require that India increase its commercial energy supplies by 4%-6% annually in coming years. The U.S. government has committed to assist India in promoting the development of stable and efficient energy markets there; a U.S.-India Energy Dialogue was launched in July 2005 to provide a forum for bolstering bilateral energy cooperation, meeting most recently in New Delhi in April 2008.213

## *Increasing Energy Consumption*

India is the world's fifth largest energy consumer and may become third by the middle of this century. Overall power generation in the country more than doubled from 1991 to 2005.214 Coal is the country's leading commercial energy source, accounting for more than half of national demand. India is the world's third most productive coal producer, and domestic supplies satisfy most demand (however, most of India's coal is an inefficient low-grade, high-ash variety). Oil consumption accounts for some onethird of India's total energy consumption; about 70% of this oil is imported (at a rate of 1.7 million barrels per day in 2006), mostly from the West Asia/Middle East region. India's domestic natural gas supply is not likely to keep pace with demand, and the country will have to import much of its natural gas, either via pipeline or as liquefied natural gas. Hydropower, especially abundant in the country's northeast and near the border with Nepal, supplies about 5% of energy needs. Nuclear power, which Indian government officials and some experts say is a sector in dire need of expansion, currently accounts for only 1% of the country's energy supplies and less than 3% of total electricity generation. Even optimistic projections suggest that nuclear power will provide less than 10% of India's generation capacity in 25 years and there are doubts about New Delhi's projected goal of generating 20 gigawatts of nuclear power by 2020.

Roughly one-fifth of the India's power is consumed by farmers' irrigation systems, making the farm lobby a powerful obstacle to curtailing subsidies provided by State Electricity Boards, which collectively lose billions of dollars annually. Moreover, from one-quarter to one-half of India's electricity is said to disappear though "transmission losses," i.e., theft. In the summer of 2007, worsening shortfalls were causing electrical outages of up to nine hours per day in the industrial and agricultural belts of Punjab, Gujarat, and Maharashtra; the capital of Delhi often has power for only 14 hours each day. A burgeoning electricity crisis may be severely hampering India's continued economic security and growth.

During a March 2007 visit to New Delhi, U.S. Energy Secretary Sam Bodman held wide-ranging talks with numerous Indian officials and business leaders to discuss India's energy needs and strategies for relevant bilateral cooperation. Secretary Bodman stressed "the absolute necessity of substantial and sustained investment in innovation on a global scale" and listed five major global goals for all countries, including the United States and India: 1) diversifying the available supply of conventional fuels and expanding their production; 2) diversifying energy portfolios through expanded use of alternative and renewable sources, including nuclear energy; 3) promoting increased energy efficiency and conservation; 4) reducing pollution and energy intensity in the global economy; and 5) protecting critical energy infrastructure.

### *Climate Change Policies*

With emissions of more than 500 million tons of carbon dioxide per year, India is the world's fourth-largest producer of greenhouse gases (GHGs) (after the United States, China, and Russia). Per capita emissions are, however, only about one-sixteenth those of the United States. The negative impact of climate change likely will be seen across India's broad range of ecosystems, with agriculture, infrastructure, and water resources most affected. Indian officials, who note that India accounts for 17% of the earth's population but only 4% of its GHG emissions, thus far reject any policies or international agreements that would set limits on their own national emissions while calling it "imperative" that developed countries commit themselves to reducing their own emissions. New Delhi criticizes Washington for failing to take "historical responsibility for cumulative emissions" and for bringing "extraneous considerations of industrial competitiveness and employment" to bear on the debate. India asserts that its own continued economic development and poverty reduction efforts preclude capping its GHG emissions and claim there has been a "persistent attempt" by some developed countries to "avoid their legal obligations" under international treaties. In June 2008, the New Delhi government unveiled India's first-ever "national action plan" to address climate change, with Prime Minister Singh acknowledging that the country faced a "dangerous problem" and vowing to devote greater attention to renewable energy, water conservation, and preserving natural resources. The plan sets forth eight "national missions" for sustainable development: (1) solar energy; (2) enhanced energy efficiency; (3) sustainable habitat; (4) conserving water; (5) sustaining the Himalayan ecosystem; (6) a "Green India;" (7) sustainable agriculture; and (8) a Strategic Knowledge Platform for Climate Change."

### *Collaborative Efforts*

India is a party to both the U.N. Framework Convention on Climate Change and the Kyoto protocol. According to the principles in both these treaties of "common but differentiated responsibility,"

India is a developing country not required to set legally binding emissions limits under these agreements. In July 2005, the United States joined with India, China, Japan, Australia, and South Korea in the Asia-Pacific Partnership (APP) on Clean Development and Climate, a U.S.-led effort to accelerate the development and deployment of clean energy technologies through a voluntary public-private partnership among six major Asia-Pacific nations. Sydney, Australia, hosted the inaugural meeting in January 2006 and the body's second ministerial meeting was held in October 2007 in New Delhi, where the United States announced providing grant funds for 23 clean technology projects in India under the Partnership's aegis. However, funding shortfalls have hampered the APP initiative since its inception. India also participates in the Major Economies Meeting (MEM) on Energy Security and Climate Change, initiated by President Bush in 2007. The process involves 16 nations (plus the EU) that are major greenhouse gas emitters. Its third session was held in Paris in April 2008.

224 Most estimates list from 41,000 to 66,000 related deaths. The Pakistan-based Kashmir Media Service claims that more than 92,000 Kashmiris have been "martyred" in the fighting. Some in Congress have sought to increase international cooperation on energyrelated matters, including with India. The Energy Diplomacy and Security Act of 2007 (S. 193) was reported out of the Senate Foreign Relations Committee in April 2007. The bill includes provisions for establishing energy crisis response mechanisms in cooperation with the governments of India and China. In February, H.R. 1186, to promote global energy security through increased U.S.-India cooperation, was introduced in the House. The International Climate Cooperation Re-engagement Act of 2007 (H.R. 2420) was reported out of the House Foreign Affairs Committee in June. The bill contains provisions for expanding efforts to promote U.S. exports in clean and efficient energy technologies to India and China. The Clean Energy Partnership With India Act of 2008 (H.R. 5705), referred to House committee in April 2008, would establish a commission for improving and promoting bilateral renewable energy cooperation with India.

### *The Kashmir Issue*

Although India suffers from several militant regional separatist movements, the Kashmir issue has proven the most lethal and intractable. Gunbattles and bomb blasts in India's Jammu and Kashmir state reportedly killed an average of 5 or 6 people every day over the period 1989-2006. Conflict over Kashmiri sovereignty also has brought global attention to a potential "flashpoint" for interstate war between nuclear-armed powers. The problem is rooted in competing claims to the former princely state, divided since 1948 by a military Line of Control (LOC) separating India's Muslim-majority Jammu and Kashmir state and Pakistan-controlled Azad [Free] Kashmir. The dispute relates to the national identities of both countries: India has long sought to maintain its secular, multi-religious credentials, in part by successfully incorporating a Muslim-majority region, while Pakistan has since independence been conceived as a homeland for the subcontinent's Muslims. India and Pakistan fought full-scale wars over Kashmir in 1947-1948 and 1965. Some Kashmiris seek independence from both countries. Spurred by a perception of rigged state elections in 1989, an ongoing separatist war between Islamic militants (and their supporters) and Indian security forces in Indian-held Kashmir is ongoing and has claimed tens of thousands of lives.

India blames Pakistan for supporting "cross-border terrorism" and for fueling a separatist rebellion in the Muslim-majority Kashmir Valley with arms, training, and militants. Islamabad, for its part, claims to provide only diplomatic and moral support to what it calls "freedom fighters" who resist Indian rule and suffer alleged human rights abuses in the region. New Delhi insists that the dispute should not be "internationalized" through involvement by third-party mediators and India is widely believed to be content with the territorial status quo. In 1999, a bloody, six-weeklong battle in the mountains near the LOC at Kargil cost more than one thousand lives and included Pakistani army troops crossing into Indian-controlled territory. Islamabad has sought to bring external major power persuasion to bear on India, especially from the United States. The longstanding U.S. position on Kashmir is that the issue must be resolved through negotiations between India and Pakistan while taking into account the wishes of the Kashmiri people.

During the early years of the Kashmir insurgency, hundreds of thousands of indigenous Hindu "Pandits" were driven from the region in what amounted to a form of "ethnic cleansing." Up to half a million Kashmiri Pandits, accounting for the vast majority of Hindus then living in the area around Srinagar, fled their homes after coming under threat from Muslim militants. For many Indians, the Kashmir dispute cannot be resolved without arrangements for the return of these refugees, more than 100,000 of whom continue to live in camps with government support. Resolutions in the 110th Congress (H.Con.Res. 55 and S.Con.Res. 38) call for the safeguarding of the physical, political, and economic security of the Kashmiri pandits.

Some separatist groups, such as the Jammu and Kashmir Liberation Front (JKLF), continue to seek an independent or autonomous Kashmir. Others, including the militant Hizbul Mujahideen (HuM), seek union with Pakistan. In 1993, the All Parties Hurriyat [Freedom] Conference was formed as an umbrella organization for groups opposed to Indian rule in Kashmir. The Hurriyat membership of more than 20 political and religious groups has included the JKLF (originally a leading militant force, now a political group) and Jamaat-e-Islami (the political wing of the HuM). The Hurriyat Conference, which states that it is committed to seeking dialogue with the Indian government on a broad range of issues, calls for a tripartite conference on Kashmir, including Pakistan, India, and representatives of the Kashmiri people. Hurriyat leaders demand Kashmiri representation at any talks between India and Pakistan on Kashmir. The Hurriyat formally split in 2003 after a dispute between hardliners allied with Islamabad and moderates favouring negotiation with New Delhi. Subsequent efforts to reunify the group failed. In 2005, the Congress Party-led government renewed high-level contact with moderate Hurriyat leaders begun by the previous BJP-led coalition. Two years later, however, Hurriyat leader and noted Kashmiri cleric Mirwaiz Umar Farooq said talks between the Indian government and moderate Kashmiri separatists had suffered a "complete breakdown of communication," and he accused New Delhi of lacking the will needed to find a political solution to the problem.

In December 2006, Pakistani President Musharraf issued a newly-modified version of his "out-of-the-box" thinking on resolution to the Kashmir problem, saying Pakistan is "against independence" for Kashmir, and offering instead a fourpoint proposal that would lead to "self-governance," defined as "falling between autonomy and independence." Many analysts saw the proposal as being roughly in line with New Delhi's Kashmir position. Some Kashmiri separatist groups rejected the proposal as an abandonment of Islamabad's long-held policy, but Indian leaders welcomed Musharraf's statements; in February 2007, Prime Minister Singh said the Pakistani government was "saying the right thing" in rejecting armed militancy as a solution to the Kashmir problem. Still, a lack of consensus among Kashmiri leaders and political parties has hampered progress. Even Kashmiri political figures who accept the principle of a solution within the framework of the Indian Constitution cannot agree on what such a solution may look like, and the Hurriyat Conference – which may have contributed to its own marginalization by boycotting the state's 2002 elections – remains rife with its own divisions. Some analysts urge greater U.S. efforts to prod the New Delhi and Islamabad governments along in the ongoing search for a final resolution.

At least 8,000 Kashmiris have "disappeared" during the conflict; some of these may occupy the nearly 1,000 unmarked graves discovered near the LOC in early 2008.228 When measured in terms of human deaths, levels of violence in Kashmir were high and steady through the mid-and late 1990s, peaked in 2001, and have been in decline since. Despite waning rates of infiltration and separatist-related violence, the issue continues to rankle leaders in New Delhi and remains a serious impediment to progress in the current India-Pakistan peace initiative. Even as the normalization of India-Pakistan relations moves forward – and to some extent in reaction to their apparent marginalization in the face of this development – separatist militants continue their attacks on both civilians and Indian security forces, and many observers in both India and the United States believe that active support for Kashmiri militants remains Pakistani policy. The militants, seeing their relevance and goals threatened by movement toward peaceful resolution, regularly lash out with bloody attacks meant to derail the process.

Despite some ongoing violence, many indicators point to positive long-term trends. The steadily reduced rates of infiltration may be attributed to the endurance of India-Pakistan dialogue and, with a flurry of diplomatic exchanges in late 2006, many analysts saw prospects for a meeting of minds between New Delhi and Islamabad as being better than ever before (determining and incorporating the desires of the Kashmiri people remain highly problematic). In 2006, India's army chief credited much of a 20% drop in levels of violence in the region to the surrender of more and more "disillusioned" militants. At the same time, the state's political leadership has lauded a major decline in reported human rights abuses by security forces, attributing the improvement to policies of restraint launched by the Peoples Democratic Party-Congress Party coalition which took power in 2002.231 New Delhi has more recently vowed to pull troops out of Kashmir if militant infiltrations and violence there cease, but to date only nominal troop withdrawals have come in response to a somewhat improved security situation in the region. In late 2007, India's Home Ministry stated that the "overall stable security situation in the [Jammu and Kashmir] State is indicative of transition to normalcy." There appears to be widespread public support among Kashmir Valley citizens for demilitarization of the region and a major reduction in the number of India troops stationed there.

While those responsible for Kashmir's security remain vigilant and convinced that the Islamabad government still "controls the tap" of cross-LOC infiltration, the people of the Muslim-majority Kashmir Valley have been widely approving of the "flexibility" exhibited by Pakistan's president and hopeful that such flexibility will be mirrored in New Delhi so as to create a resolution that works for all stakeholders.

## Other Regional Dissidence

The United States maintains an ongoing interest in India's domestic stability and the respect for internationally recognized human rights there. The U.S. Congress has held hearings in which such issues are discussed. As a vast mosaic of ethnicities, languages, cultures, and religions, India can be difficult to govern. Internal instability resulting from diversity is further complicated by colonial legacies such as international borders that separate members of the same ethnic groups, creating flashpoints for regional dissidence and separatism. Beyond the Kashmir problem, separatist insurgents in remote and underdeveloped northeast regions confound New Delhi and create international tensions by operating out of neighboring Bangladesh, Burma, Bhutan, and Nepal. New Delhi has at times blamed the governments of those countries for "sheltering" separatist groups beyond the reach of Indian security forces, and New Delhi has launched joint counter-insurgency operations with some of these neighbours. At the same time, Maoist rebels continue to operate in numerous states and represent a growing threat to internal sovereignty. India also has suffered outbreaks of serious communal violence between Hindus and Muslims, especially in the western Gujarat state.

### *The Northeast*

Since the time of India's foundation, numerous militant groups have fought for greater ethnic autonomy, tribal rights, or independence in the country's northeast region. Some of the tribal struggles in the small states known as the Seven Sisters are centuries old. It is estimated that more than 50,000 people have been killed in such fighting since 1948, including about 20,000 killed in a 28-yearold Naga insurgency and another 10,000 deaths in 15 years of fighting in the Assam state. In the small state of Manipur alone there are said to be more than 20 separatists groups fighting the Indian army at a cost of more than 8,000 lives over two decades, and the writ of the central government there is tenuous, at best. As militant groups are seen to benefit from highly profitable criminal activities such as informal taxation, kidnaping, and smuggling, many observers conclude that only more effective economic development and integration of India's northeast will allow for the resolution of myriad ethnic conflicts there.

According to India's Home Ministry, the states of Chhattisgarh and Jharkhand account for two-thirds of the country's Naxalite incidents and three-quarters of related casualties. The United Liberation Front of Assam (ULFA), the National Liberation Front of Tripura, the National Democratic Front of Bodoland (NDFB), and the United National Liberation Front (seeking an independent Manipur) are among the approximately 40 militant groups at war with the central government. These groups reportedly field a total of no more than 20,000 trained cadres. ULFA, like other groups, accuses New Delhi of exploiting their state's resources while doing little to forward development and allowing thousands of non-indigenous people (often Hindispeakers from Bihar) to flood the local job markets. In 2005, the U.S. State Department's Counterterrorism Office listed ULFA among its "other groups of concern," the first time an Indian separatist group outside Kashmir was so named. In June 2008, six ULFA field commanders abjured violence and vowed to seek peaceful resolution through negotiation.

### *Maoist Insurgency*

Also operating in India are "Naxalites" — Maoist insurgents ostensibly engaged in violent struggle on behalf of landless laborers and tribals. These groups, most active in inland areas of east-central India, claim to be battling oppression and exploitation in order to create a classless society. Their opponents call them terrorists and extortionists. The groups get their name from Naxalbari, a West Bengal village and site of a militant peasant uprising in 1967. In 2006, Prime Minister Singh identified a worsening Maoist insurgency as "the single biggest internal security challenge" ever faced by India, saying it threatened India's democracy and "way of life." Some of these groups may be growing poppy and extorting farmers and opium traders to fund their activities. Further reports indicate the rebels are placing new emphasis on recruiting child soldiers. Some analysts warn that, by blocking access to raw materials vital to India's manufacturing sector, the Naxalite movement could deter investors and so thwart India's long-term economic success. Naxalites now operate in about half of India's 28 states; related violence has killed more than 6,000 people over the past two decades, including some 650 deaths in 2007. Indian government officials seek to downplay the threat by pointing out that only 2% of the country's 650,000 villages are affected and only 2% of the country's 14,000 police stations report Naxalite activity.

The most notable of India's Maoist militant outfits are the People's War Group (PWG), mainly active in the southern Andhra Pradesh state, and the Maoist Communist Centre of West Bengal and Bihar. In 2004, the two groups merged to form the Communist Party of India (Maoist). Both appear on the U.S. State Department Counterterrorism Office's list of "groups of concern" and both are designated as terrorist groups by New Delhi, which claims there are nearly 10,000 Maoist militants active in the country. Other estimates see some 20,000 such fighters in India, including up to 5,000 in the central Chhattisgarh state alone. Such militants possess sophisticated weapons and communications equipment. PWG cadres were behind a 2003 landmine attack that nearly killed the chief minster of Andhra Pradesh. In 2004, that state's government lifted an 11-year-old ban on the PWG, but the Maoists soon withdrew from ensuing peace talks, accusing the state government of breaking a cease-fire agreement. Violent attacks on government forces then escalated in 2005 and have continued with even greater frequency since.

The Chhattisgarh state government has since 2005 sponsored a grassroots anti-Maoist effort. This "Salwa Judum" ("Campaign for Peace" or, literally, "collective hunt") militia – comprised of about 5,000 lightly-armed tribal people who are paid about $1 per day – is viewed by some as an effective countervailing people's movement. Others label it a vigilante group that has engaged in its own coercive and violent tactics against innocent tribals, one that only serves to accentuate the conflict as "a cure that is worse than the disease." Following a March 2007 raid on a Chhattisgarh police camp by up to 600 armed rebels in which 55 people, including 19 policemen, were killed, Maoist leaders threatened further attacks if the Salwa Jundum was not dismantled. A May 2008 report for India's Planning Commission recommended that the Salwa Jundum campaign represented "an abdication of the state itself" and should immediately be ended. New York-based Human Rights Watch later called on the New Delhi and Chhattisgarh governments to end all official support for the campaign, including provision of weapons, and to launch"serious and independent investigations" of related human rights abuses.

Analysts warn that Naxalite activity – including swarming attacks on government facilities and coordinated, multi-state economic blockades – is spreading and becoming more audacious in the face of incoherent and insufficient Indian government policies to halt it. A shortage of police personnel appears to be a key problem. In late 2007, Prime Minister Singh asked India's states to establish specialized, dedicated forces to address Maoist militancy. In mid-2008, the federal government announced plans to create a new 10,000-strong force trained specifically to fight the rebels. However, these efforts do not address the "intellectual appeal" of the Maoists, which India's national security advisor says remains a key problem.

### *Hindu-Muslim Tensions*

Some elements of India's Hindu majority have at times engaged in violent communal conflict with the country's Muslim minority. In 1992, a huge mob of Hindu activists in the western city of Ayodhya demolished a 16th century mosque said to have been built at the birth site of the Hindu god Rama. Ensuing communal riots in cities across India left many hundreds dead.

Bombay was especially hard hit and was the site of coordinated 1993 terrorist bombings believed to have been a retaliatory strike by Muslims. In 2002, another group of Hindu activists returning by train to the western state of Gujarat after a visit to the Ayodhya site of the now razed Babri Mosque (and a proposed Hindu temple) were attacked by a Muslim mob in the town of Godhra; 58 were killed. Up to 2,000 people died in the fearsome communal rioting that followed, most of them Muslims. The BJP-led state and national governments came under fire for inaction; some observers saw evidence of state government complicity in anti-Muslim attacks.

The U.S. State Department and human rights groups have been critical of New Delhi's largely ineffectual efforts to bring those responsible to justice; some of these criticisms were echoed by the Indian Supreme Court in 2003. In 2005, the State Department made a controversial decision to deny a U.S. visa to Gujarat Chief Minster Narendra Modi under a U.S. law barring entry for foreign government officials found to be complicit in severe violations of religious freedom.

The decision was strongly criticized in India. More than five years after the Gujarat riots, international human rights groups express serious concerns about obstacles faced by victims seeking justice, the continuing internal displacement of thousands of families who lack basic necessities, and large numbers of uninvestigated related criminal cases (despite the Indian Supreme Court's 2004 order to reopen nearly 1,600 such cases). A 2006 central government report found deep communal divisions continuing to haunt Gujarat, concretely expressed through ghettoization and religious segregation. In 2008, a U.N. envoy said such divisions combine with a culture of impunity to raise the risk of future violence. Sporadic communal violence continues to affect several Indian states.

### *Human Rights Issues*

Many of India's more than one billion citizens suffer from numerous and oftentimes serious human rights abuses. Some analysts are concerned that, as Washington pursues a new "strategic partnership" with New Delhi, U.S. government attention to such abuses has waned. According to the U.S. State Department's *Country Report on Human Rights Practices, 2007*, the Indian government "generally respected the human rights of its citizens; however, numerous serious problems remained." These included extensive societal violence against women; extrajudicial killings, including faked encounter killings; excessive use of force by security forces, arbitrary arrests, and incommunicado detentions in Kashmir and several northeastern states; torture and rape by agents of the government; "harsh, life-threatening" prison conditions and lengthy pretrial detentions without charge; "pervasive" police corruption; forced prostitution; child prostitution and female infanticide; forced child labour; human trafficking; and "ubiquitous" caste-based discrimination and violence, among others. Terrorist attacks and kidnapings also remained grievous problems, especially in Kashmir and the northeastern states. Indian law provides for extensive human rights protections, but enforcement is "lax" and convictions rare.

The 2007 annual report from New York-based Human Rights Watch noted that India has a vibrant press and civil society, but also suffers from a number of chronic human rights problems. It called impunity a "critical issue" involving officials and members of the security services abusing their power and who are "rarely if ever brought to justice for torture, arbitrary detentions and extrajudicial killings...." Listed among other human rights concerns in India is the alleged "failure to implement policies that protect the rights of children, religious minorities, those living with HIV/AIDS or those belonging to vulnerable communities such as tribal groups, Dalits and other 'backward' castes." London-based Amnesty International's 2007 annual report also claims that perpetrators of human rights violations in India, in particular those related to 2002 communal rioting in Gujarat, continued to enjoy impunity, and it asserts that concerns over protection of economic, social, and cultural rights of already marginalized communities grew in 2006.248 The State Department itself recognizes impunity as a major human rights problem in India, asserting in an April 2007 report that "A widespread culture of impunity among police and security forces and pervasive corruption continued to be the principal obstacles to improving human rights" there.

The State Department's Bureau of Democracy, Human Rights, and Labour has claimed that India's human right abuses "are generated by a traditionally hierarchical social structure, deeply rooted tensions among the country's many ethnic and religious communities, violent secessionist movements and the authorities' attempts to repress them, and deficient police methods and training." India's 1958 Armed Forces Special Powers Act, which gives security forces wide leeway to act with impunity in conflict zones, has been called a facilitator of "grave human rights abuses" in several Indian states (in December 2006, Prime Minister Singh said he would seek to amend the controversial Act). In 2007, the problem of "staged encounters" in which police officers kill suspects in faked shootouts came to the fore. India generally denies international human rights groups official access to Kashmir and other sensitive areas.

### *Human Trafficking*

The State Department's latest annual report on trafficking in persons (issued June 2008) said, "India is a source, destination, and transit country for men, women, and children trafficked for the purposes of forced labour and commercial sexual exploitation." It placed India on the "Tier 2 Watch List" for the fifth consecutive year for "failure to provide evidence of increasing efforts to combat trafficking in persons" and for "making no progress" in efforts to address the problem of bonded labour, which affects an estimated 20-65 million Indians.

Moreover, State criticized the India's federal and state governments for largely ignoring "the pervasive problem of government complicity in trafficking." Upon the report's release, the head of State's trafficking office, Ambassador Mark Lagan, said "India still doesn't recognize the degree to which bonded labour is a substantial human trafficking problem in its country. It has weak anti-corruption efforts and prosecutions are too few."

### *Religious Freedom*

An officially secular nation, India has a long tradition of religious tolerance (with periodic lapses), which is protected under its constitution. The population includes a Hindu majority of 82% as well as a large Muslim minority of some 150 million (14%). Christians, Sikhs, Buddhists, Jains, and others total less than 4%. Although freedom of religion is protected by the Indian government, human rights groups have noted that India's religious tolerance is susceptible to attack by religious extremists. In its annual report on international religious freedom released in September 2007, the State Department found "no change in the status of respect for religious freedom" by India's national government:

[G]overnment policy continued to contribute to the generally free practice of religion; however, problems remained in some areas. Some state governments enacted and amended "anti-conversion" laws and police and enforcement agencies often did not act swiftly enough to effectively counter societal attacks, including attacks against religious minorities. Despite Government efforts to foster communal harmony, some extremists continued to view ineffective investigation and prosecution of attacks on religious minorities, particularly at the state and local level, as a signal that they could commit such violence with impunity, although numerous cases were in the courts at the end of the reporting period. The National Government, led by the United Progressive Alliance (UPA), continued to implement an inclusive and secular platform that included respect for the right to religious freedom.

The report added that a "Hindutva" — or Hindu nationalist— ideology continued to influence some government policies and actions at the state and local levels over the previous year.

A May 2008 report of the U.S. Commission on International Religious Freedom noted continued improvements since the 2004 election of the Congress-led coalition, but warned that concerns about religious freedom in India remain. These include ongoing attacks against religious minorities, perpetrated mainly by Hindu activists and most often in states with BJP-led governments. The Commission also continued to criticize allegedly insufficient state efforts to pursue justice in cases related to 2002 communal rioting in Gujarat. More than five years after those riots, the victims are said to still face serious challenges and obstacles in securing justice, and a large number of related criminal cases remain uninvestigated and unresolved.

## *Caste-Based Discrimination*

The millennia-old Hindu caste system reflects Indian occupational and socially-defined hierarchies. Sanskrit sources refer to four social categories: priests (Brahmin), warriors (Kshatriya), traders (Vayisha) and farmers (Shudra). Tribals and lower castes were long known as "untouchables" – a term now officially banned but still widely used – or Dalits. Although these categories are understood throughout India, they describe reality only in the most general terms. National-level legislation exists to protect India's lower castes, yet, according to the U.S. State Department, "The Scheduled Castes and Scheduled Tribes (Prevention of Atrocities) Act lists offenses against disadvantaged persons and prescribes stiff penalties for offenders; however, this act had only a modest effect in curbing abuse and there were very few convictions." In July 2007, H.Con.Res. 139, expressing the sense of Congress that the United States should address the ongoing problem of untouchability in India, was passed by the full House.

## *Female Infanticide and Feticide*

Given traditional societal discrimination against females, uneven female-to-male ratios are a matter of concern for India. The incidence of female infanticide and gender-selective abortions is identified as a growing human rights problem in India. The diffusion of enabling medical technology and the existence of unethical doctors have made sex-selective abortions more common there. Prime Minister Singh has called female feticide in India a "national shame" and said the government has a responsibility to curtail the widespread practice. The country's most recent census (in 2001) found only 927 girls aged 0-6 for every 1,000 boys nationwide. Wealthier states, such as Delhi, Punjab, and Gujarat, have the lowest ratios (Punjab's was the lowest at 798).257 A 2006 study in the British medical journal *Lancet* estimated that up to

10 million Indian females are "missing" due to sex-selective abortions and infanticide over the past two decades, and that some 500,000 girls are being "lost" annually. According to a June 2008 nongovernmental report, the incidence of female feticide is only increasing. The most recent U.S. State Department *Country Report on Human Rights* for India (released March 2008), claims that, in many Indian states,

Baby girls were either aborted or, after birth, left in the cold to contract pneumonia and perish. NGOs alleged that medical practitioners and government workers often were complicit in pushing or persuading women to abort their girl children. Sex determination tests are illegal under the 1994 Pre-Natal Diagnostic Techniques Act. However, NGOs reported that some family planning centers continued to reveal the sex of fetuses. According to the NGO IFES, feticide is a $116 million industry.

In 2007, the New Delhi announced the establishment of a series of orphanages to raise unwanted baby girls in an effort to reduce the incidence of female infanticide.

### *HIV/AIDS*

The United Nations has estimated that 5.7 million Indians are infected with HIV / AIDS, giving India the largest such population worldwide (India overtook South Africa in this category in 2006). However, a July 2007 U.N.-backed study found that India's infected population was about 2.5 million and the U.S. government estimate rises only to 3.1 million. Due to the country's large population, prevalence rates among adults remain below 1%. India's AIDS epidemic has become generalized in four states in the country's south (Andhra Pradesh, Tamil Nadu, Karnataka, and Maharashtra) and two in the northeast (Manipur and Nagaland). According to USAID, these six states account for 80% of the country's reported AIDS cases. India first launched its AIDS control program in 1992; New Delhi boosted related funding to about $120 million in the most recent fiscal year and in July 2007 launched a new $2.8-billion National AIDS Control Program that will expand free treatment for HIV-positive persons, as well as boost the number of awareness and prevention campaigns. Stigma, gender inequalities, and discrimination present major obstacles to controlling India's HIV / AIDS epidemic. In the country's traditional society, open discussion of sexuality and risk of infection is rare, making education difficult: one Indian government survey found that nearly half of Indian women had not even heard of the disease. Analysts opine that substantially greater resources are needed to address HIV/AIDS in India than are currently available.

As part of its foreign assistance program in India, the U.S. government supports integrated HIV/AIDS prevention, treatment, and support services in high prevalence states. India received nearly $30 million in direct U.S. assistance for such programs in FY2007 under the President's Plan for AIDS Relief (PEPFAR), for a projected total of some $136 million for FY2004-FY2008. In January 2007, H.R. 175, to provide assistance to combat HIV/AIDS in India, and for other purposes, was introduced in the House, but has not moved out of committee to date.

### *U.S. Assistance*

A total of more than $15 billion in direct U.S. aid went to India from 1947 through 2007, nearly all of it in the form of economic grants and loans, more than half as food aid. In February 2007, in response to several years of rapid Indian economic expansion and New Delhi's new status as a donor government, the State Department announced a 35% reduction in assistance programs for India.

The bulk of the cuts are to come from development assistance and food aid programs. Another smaller decrease came in 2008 "in recognition of the continuing growth of the Indian economy and the ability of the government to fund more"development programs.

Economic. According to the U.S. Agency for International Development (USAID), India has more people living in abject poverty (some 385 million) than do Latin America and Africa combined. USAID programs in India, budgeted at about $69 million in FY2008, concentrate on six areas: (1) *health* (improved overall health with a greater integration of food assistance, reproductive services, and the prevention of HIV/AIDS and other infectious diseases); (2) *environment* (improved access to clean energy and water); (3) *education* (improved literacy and teacher capacity); (4) *economic opportunity* (agricultural reform and improved financial markets); (5) *disaster response*; and (6) *tsunami recovery*.

Security. The United States has provided about $169 million in military assistance to India since 1947, more than 90% of this distributed from 1962-1966. In recent years, modest security-related assistance has emphasized export control enhancements, counterterrorism and counternarcotics programs, and military training. Early Bush Administration requests for Foreign Military Financing were later withdrawn, with the two countries agreeing to pursue commercial sales programs. The Pentagon reports military sales agreements with India worth $429 million in FY2002-FY2007.

## India's Foreign Policies on Pakistan Reach a Dead-end

India's foreign policies on Pakistan have been brought to a dead-end with the dawn of the year 2009. Painfully, it needed the Mumbai 9/11 murderous massacres on November 26, 2008 by Pakistani Special Forces trained Islamic Jihadi commando terrorists to bring home the realization to India's political leaders and the policy establishment that India's policies and formulations on Pakistan have been an utter failure.

India's foreign policies on Pakistan, and more specifically in the first decade of the 21st Century, stand failed because Pakistan as a state in fractional asymmetry to India, strategically and politically, existing on borrowed and reflected strengths of the United States and China has forced India to run out of decisive options in the post-Mumbai 9/11 phase. India's foreign policies on Pakistan have failed in the lost 63 years because India submitting itself to external pressures and shirking from the use of her preponderant strengths over Pakistan, fostered a perception in the Pakistani military establishment that India could be trifled with impunity and without punitive reprisals.

Pakistan as a "garrison state" run by a military adventurist Pakistan Army required an Indian foreign policy based on Indian national security determinants only, without conceding strategic space to the national interests of the intrusive external powers in South Asia. Strangely, in the last fifteen years, India's political leaders and its foreign policy establishment failed to translate India's growing global economic clout into political and strategic muscle to attain its foreign policy objectives of neutralizing Pakistan and its state-sponsored terrorism against India in the name of

Islamic Jihad. The measure of India's failure in its Pakistan policies has been brought home by the signal change in tunes within a month, of the United States ad Britain from siding with India, to the defence of Pakistan and its instruments of state not being involved in Mumbai 9/11. Where did they get evidence of this? Or is this only a surmise?

India's foreign policies on Pakistan have reached a dead-end not only because of India's own policy flaws and systemic failures but also more significantly because the United States as Pakistan's vital strategic patron has time and again forgiven Pakistan's strategically destablizing policies against India. In this process Pakistan stood further emboldened, conscious that Pakistan would not be disciplined by the United States. India's foreign policies on Pakistan have reached a dead-end and a policy audit is required in addition to looking into the immediate future, as to where should India now go from here.

This is covered under the following heads in brief outline:

- India's Political Leadership: Faulty Political and Strategic Perceptions on Pakistan
- India's Foreign Policy Establishment: Rudderless Policy Formulations on Pakistan
- United States Needs to be De-hyphenated from India's Pakistan Policies
- The Way Ahead: Immediate Indian Imperatives of Hard-Line Declaratory Policies towards Pakistan

## India's Political Leadership: Faulty Political and Strategic Perceptions on Pakistan

The Indian political leadership, irrespective of political affiliations, has successively failed in providing a realistic political template of assessments on Pakistan, on which the Indian foreign policy establishment and the Indian military establishment could base their operational strategies on.

The Indian political leadership's failure, strictly in the political sense, arises from:

- Perceptional failings in their readings of Pakistan's political dynamics, Pakistani political leaders, and the propensities of the Pakistan Army. Historical patterns are neither studied nor paid attention to in their assessments, if any.

- Indian political leaders failing to perceive that, 60 years of India's peaceful and conciliatory policies towards Pakistan, restraint against grave provocations and Track II diplomacy has not yielded any success to India in the evolution of a peaceful India-Pakistan relationship.
- Political leadership not indulging in independent analysis of Pakistani events but totally dependant on estimates of party think-tanks comprising retired senior diplomats, intelligence officials and military officers, most of whom try to 'situate' their assessments to be in line with their political patrons' views or being out of touch with contemporary realities

Indian political leaders have failed to strike personal links with political leaders of major countries which could facilitate informal and non-institutional exchange of political perceptions and also as an alternative to pressurize Pakistan. Indian political leaders have denied themselves vital inputs by:

- Remaining strategically ill-equipped by not spending time on frequent briefings and brain-storming with India's uniformed fraternity but relying on bureaucratic inputs.
- Not facilitating the growth of an independent Indian strategic culture.
- Not giving primacy to India's national security determinants over political expediency in Pakistan policy formulations.
- Strategic fears in the Indian political leadership and their policy advisors that should India undertake military strikes against Pakistan, there would be forceful retaliation by Pakistan. Of course there would be Pakistani retaliation and expectedly so. Should that deter India as an emerging power to stop using the prerogatives of its power and buckle down against Pakistani "War of Terror" against India.

Cumulatively arising from the above, in relation to Pakistan, India's political leadership was led to the following strategic blunders:

- Nehru agreeing to a cease-fire in Kashmir on 1948-49 when the Indian Army was virtually on the doorsteps of Muzaffrabad and the whole of Kashmir would have been of India.
- Shastri agreeing to return the Haji Pir Bulge & Kargil Heights after India's victory over Pakistan in 1965 war.
- Indira Gandhi agreeing to return 90,000 Pakistan prisoners of war captured by Indian Army in 1971 without written guarantees from Bhutto on Kashmir and relying on his verbal assurances.
- Rajiv Gandhi very nearly agreed to a compromise on Siachen with Benazir Bhutto.
- Vajpayee policy blunders of convening Agra Summit and not pushing PRAKARM to its logical conclusion.

Dr. Manmohan Singh, the present Indian Prime Minister, has more strategic blunders to account for in relation to Pakistan, namely:

- Implicitly trusting Musharraf under US nudging
- Siachen was virtually sold out.
- India's Pakistan policy was totally subordinated to United States policies, perceptions and strategic interests in Pakistan.
- Signing the infamous Havana Declaration with Musharraf and setting up a Joint Terror Mechanism - a virtual "Dance with the Wolves".
- Following it, major terrorist strikes against India from Pakistan kept taking place without any reprisals from India.
- Policy paralysis in not exercising the hard option against Pakistan post-Mumbai 9/11.

## India's Foreign Policy Establishment: Rudderless Policy Formulations on Pakistan

As a spin-off of the above and without institutional assertiveness by India's diplomatic establishment, India's foreign policy on Pakistan growingly stood encroached by the Prime Minister's Office. The resultant outcome has been as what can be described as rudderless policy formulations on Pakistan, divorced from institutional strategic vision, deliberation and analysis. This stood further compounded by the following factors:

- India's High Commissioners in Pakistan, with few exceptions, focused more on being "cultural ambassadors" rather than the diplomatic representatives of South Asia's only regional power and consequently indulging in hard-headed diplomacy.
- Reliance on "Special Envoys" system of the Prime Minister which distorted policy formulations. Nor did any substantial diplomatic gains accrued from the system of "Special Envoys".
- Unjustified confidence in Track II diplomacy with Pakistan. It has not produced any results.
- Indian Foreign Office's propensity lately to take cues from Washington on Indian foreign policy formulations on Pakistan and reliance on US assessments of Pakistan's political and military establishment.
- India's diplomatic establishments inability in the last 63 years to come up with policies which could provide "Indian leverages on Pakistan". India today has no independent political, military, economic or multi-lateral leverages over Pakistan.

The lowest ebb in India's foreign policy establishment role lately was in the following:

- Incessant helpless refrain that India will do business with whosoever was in power in Pakistan. Did that presage dealing with the Taliban also?
- The Prime Minister not being dissuaded from signing the Havana Agreement with Musharraf and thereby devaluating and neutralizing India's stands and credibility on Pakistan's proxy war and state-sponsored terrorism. Mumbai 9/11 can be in a sense said to have been the out come of this mis-step.
- Not prevailing on the political leadership to go in for the hard-option post-Mumbai 9/11.

India's foreign office and its diplomatic establishment must realize that they are as much "custodians of India's national security" as are the armed forces, and in this custodial responsibility they should not allow the politicians (who come and go and are influenced by domestic political considerations) to play around with India's security due to perceptive failures or ignorance of strategic realities.

## United States Needs to be De-hyphenated from India's Pakistan Policies Formulations

United States involvement in the shaping of India's Pakistan-policies formulations would have been a welcome step had the United States played the rule of an "honest broker" in South Asia. The record has been otherwise, even with President Bush who has been the best US President that India could have so far.

United States actions and role in post-Mumbai 9/11 fall into the above category. It does not inspire confidence in India. After supporting India's demands initially on Pakistan in relation to a Mumbai 9/11 they have down-slided to support Pakistan's adamancy

As far back as December 2002, the observations made by this Author in his Paper: " India's Foreign Policy Predicaments" (SAAG Paper 570 dated 24.12.2002) need to be highlighted once again in the present context:

- "US policies and actions post-9/11 belies the earlier stated and mutual high expectations of a "natural allies" relationship."
- If it were truly so, then the combination of 9/11 and 13/12 would have spurred the United States to recognize, respect and integrate the Islamic Jehadi threats against India with the overall American operations against global terrorism (read Islamic Jehadi terrorism)"
- "More inexplicable has been the US shielding of Pakistan from Indian military wrath post 13/12. It virtually amounted to a Papal condonation of Pakistan's mortal sins".
- "India therefore needs to develop a more conditional foreign policy relationship with USA."
- "India's foreign policy responses to the United States must depend on the American respect for India in the context of its South Asian policies. India is in a position to lay

down bench-marks, this strength should emanate from her strategic potential in South Asia and the Indian Ocean Region."

History seems to be repeating itself once again. Instead of Pakistan being subjected to punitive approaches by the United States for its role in Mumbai 9/11, the United States is pressurizing India to exercise restraint. On the contrary moves are afoot once again to use the Kashmir issue as a leverage against India and in favour of Pakistan and further US military supplies to Pakistan continue.

Just as the United States claims it has de-hyphenated its India-Pakistan relationships, India must realize that in terms of her national security interests, India has to "de-hyphenate" the United States-Pakistan relationship" in its foreign policies on Pakistan.

## Line Declaratory Policies Towards Pakistan

The following recommendations were made by the Author in the above quoted Paper in December 2002 in terms of India's declaratory policy assertions.

- "Kashmir is non-negotiable and all external powers need to lay-off this issue."
- "India's dominance model may be an anathema for Pakistan but that country has to adjust and adapt to this strategic reality. India's foreign policy initiatives must emphasize to external powers to respect this reality and prevail over their protégé Pakistan, to recognize it."
- "India must declare that any threats to its external or internal security will be met with disproportionate force if necessary."
- "No external pressures will be accepted by India to deflect it from its pursuance of just war or preemptive strikes to deter aggression against India."

These assertions would eater to the neutralization of Pakistan's main strategies against India in terms of Kashmir, proxy war and terrorism. They as declaratory policies would lay down 'red lines' for Pakistan. Six years down the line, Indian political leadership nor its policy establishment has made any such assertions due to obliviousness to national security imperatives or having no time from political chicanery pre-occupations or lacking the sheer will to make forceful declarations.

Post-Mumbai 9/11, India has already fore-closed its military strike options in reprisals against Pakistan, and all that it has left now is to indulge in the non-military options to pressurize Pakistan. The following non-military options, if implemented immediately could be perceived as hard-line options to foreclose any further state-sponsored terrorism from Pakistan in the wake of Mumbai 9/11.

- Break diplomatic relations with Pakistan.
- Abrogate the Havana Agreement
- Declare Pakistan as a "terrorist state" and the ISI as a "terrorist organization."
- Snap all CBM's implemented on Kashmir from cross-border travel to trade etc.
- Review Indus Waters Treaty and stop flow of river waters to Pakistan
- Snap all Pak transit overflights
- Stop train and air services to Pakistan.
- Peace Process and Composite Dialogue to be called off.
- Black-list all countries selling defence equipment to Pakistan and not invite them to tender for Indian military purchases.
- Resume 'covert operations' against Pakistan with focus on Pakistan's military establishment and terrorist organization.
- India should give political, moral and material support to the "freedom fighters" in Baluchistan, Northern Areas and Pakistan-occupied Kashmir.
- Isolate Pakistan in South Asia by disbanding SAARC and focus on alternative regional organizations excluding Pakistan.
- Psychological warfare, visibly exposing Pakistan Army's and ISI disruptive activities in neighbouring countries. "Radio Free Pakistan" and TV channels be established. The emphasis in this campaign should be that India and Indians are not against the Pakistani people and that India is definitely against the Pakistan Army establishment, the

ISI and their affiliated terrorist organisations indulging in unrestrained "War of Terror" against India, Afghanistan and in Pakistan's frontier areas.

- Establish a maritime 'cordon sanitairre' in the North Arabian Sea excluding all trade by dhows and fishing trawlers traffic.
- No tourists from Pakistan or foreigners transiting through Pakistan be given entry to India.
- India should not pursue the Iran-Pakistan-India gas pipeline project both in the present context and otherwise too.

In the execution of the above measures, India should not become amendable to any external pressures. Should Pakistan consequently ratchet on the above, the military confrontation along the LOC or the other borders, India should prepare itself for war. USSR's first Foreign Minister, Leon Trotsky was recently quoted by noted Indian journalist M J Abbar, in another context as: "*You may not be interested in war, but war is interested in you.*" India's political leaders should be mindful of this maxim as war is a recurrent reality in global affairs and cannot be wished away.

## Concluding Observations

India's peaceful and conciliatory approaches to Pakistan and traditional exercise of restraint despite grave provocations by Pakistan in the last 63 years have been misread by Pakistan as responses from a timid state devoid of political will for hard responses. It seems to be convinced that Indian political leaders lack the courage to come up with firm responses. The dead-end reached by India in its foreign policies towards Pakistan is a by-product of the above. India can only by-pass this dead-end by hard-line policies if not hard strike reprisals for Mumbai 9/11.

India's political leaders can no longer ignore the overwhelming Indian public opinion that the time has come for India to deal with Pakistan firmly. Pakistan cannot be saved from its 'dysfunctional state' downslide by India's permissiveness of tolerating endless Pakistan-originated terrorists strikes. Nor can Pakistan be saved from military rule by Indian restraint. Pakistan can only be saved by the people of Pakistan rising against their military establishment as did the Iranians. who overthrew the powerfully backed Shah of Iran and his Imperial Ground Forces in 1979 as a result of groundswell of public unrest. As written elsewhere by this Author, India needs to assert itself against Pakistan boldly and fearlessly, if it believes that it has a 'Manifest Destiny" to emerge as "the regional power" and an aspirant for global power status.

India s should not be cowed down or its leaders deterred by fears of Pakistan's military retaliation. Of course, there would be human and material losses. But then India's political leaders need to recognize the strategic reality that: "Power Status does not come cheaply and nor does it come without the guts to bear losses in the pursuit of power. Power accrues only to those who are bold and audacious."

## India, Bangladesh to Discuss Defence Relations

A high-level Bangladesh Air Force delegation led by the country's air chief, Air Marshal S.M. Zia-ur-Rehman, is in New Delhi to discuss defence ties between the neighboring countries, a senior Indian Defence Ministry official said. India is ready to export to Bangladesh defence equipment, including the Advanced Light Helicopter, and to assist the country in building warships, the ministry official said. New Delhi is concerned about the increasing levels of defence supplies being sent from China to Bangladesh, Defence Ministry sources here said. There are reports the Chinese Navy has access to Bangladesh's Chittagong port, the sources said. China already has a military base on the Coco islands, leased from Myanmar, near India's Andaman islands, which is considered a listening post over the eastern part of India, including India's ballistic missile centre in the eastern state of Orissa. China is also helping Pakistan build the Gwadar deep-sea port.

China has sold artillery systems, combat aircraft and small arms to Bangladesh in the last two years. The Bangladesh air chief will hold talks with Indian Defence Minister A.K. Antony, Indian Navy Chief Adm. Sureesh Mehta and Army Chief Gen. Deepak Kapoor. India helped Bangladesh, formerly East Pakistan, during its 1971 independence war against Pakistan. Fire has been exchanged along the border between the countries in cases relating to forced migration and smuggling.

3

# Religious Nationalism and Foreign Policy: India and Israel Compared

The emergence of India and Israel as independent states in 1947-48 highlighted the power of religious identity to shape political outcomes. While India was partitioned as a result of the demand for a separate Pakistan for the subcontinent's Muslims, Israel came into being as the fulfilment of the Zionist vision of Palestine as a homeland for Jews throughout the world. Yet the post-independence leadership of both countries sought to create states informed by secular rather than religious political principles. This paper examines the role of religion in foreign policy in India and Israel with particular reference to the recent salience of Hindu nationalism and religious Zionism. It explores the influence of religion in shaping the foreign policy environment and the perceptions of Indian and Israeli policymakers, focusing in particular on the relationship between secular state interest and nationalism predicated on religious identity. The argument is that for both countries it is imperative to transcend religious nationalism if they are to secure their international position.

Few observers concerned themselves with the significance of 'Hindu' nationalism for Indian foreign policy until the rise of the Bharatiya Janata Party (BJP) to leading the national government, followed almost immediately by the nuclear tests of May 1998. Now it is widely accepted as a significant factor in considering India's foreign policy (e.g. Haynes 2007: 367,374), being seen as reinforcing longstanding hostility towards Pakistan and inspiring a more aggressive Indian attitude (Jones 2004: 27,29). In the case of Israel too, despite the central role of religious identity in bringing the Jewish state into being in 1948, religion was rarely mentioned in discussing the foreign policy of that state. However, by the early 1990s the success of Jewish fundamentalism in shaping the public discourse in Israel was admitted (Silberstein 1993: 21-2). In fact, some even saw religion as having replaced secular right-and left-wing expressions of Zionism as 'the source of political legitimation for the state' (Ehrlich 2003: 93).

The similarities in the political trajectory followed by India and Israel have not escaped attention. Ilan Pappe has commented on how 'Both parties [the neo-Zionists and the BJP] wish to demolish a past of a few hundred years old in the name of a distant past a few thousand years old' (Pappe 2003: 55). (When the right-wing Likud Prime Minister Ariel Sharon became the first Israeli premier to visit India in September 2003, as a guest of the BJP-led government, critics denounced the apparent emerging convergence in Indian and Israeli foreign policy, one describing it as an entente 'between Hindutva and Sharonism in the shadow of US imperialism' (Prashad 2003: 10).)

The paper begins by looking at the connection between religion, nationalism and the creation of the modern state in India and Israel before discussing the role, if any, that religion played in shaping the foreign policy of both states under their first prime ministers, Jawaharlal Nehru and David Ben-Gurion. It then turns to the growth of religious nationalism as a political force in both countries from the late 1960s on and its influence on government in the last twenty or thirty years. The paper considers how far the development of a certain strategic convergence in the foreign and defence policies of India and Israel can be ascribed to the role of religious nationalism before ending by emphasising the dangers and limitations of the ideologies encapsulated by the terms Hindutva (Hindu-ness) and Eretz Israel (Land of Israel) in informing foreign policy in the 21 st century.

## *Religion, Nationalism and Statehood*

While Israel, like Pakistan, is ineffably marked by its creation on the basis of religious identity, few nation states can disclaim the influence of religion on their nationhood (Neuberger 1999: 77). For nationalism requires a human community and signifiers of identity and religion were often invaluable in providing both

(Dieckhoff 2003: 128). In the case of Israel, Akiva Orr makes the telling point that 'There is no secular definition of Jewishness.' (Orr 1994: 50). Even the socialist Zionist collectivism of the early 20th century European Jewish settlers in Palestine may be seen as merely a secular variation of the kehilla, the Jewish congregation that served as the bedrock of traditional Jewish society (Dieckhoff 2003: 10). Abraham Isaac Kook, the first Ashkenazi Chief Rabbi of Palestine, rationalised the relationship between secular Zionism and religion thus, The spirit of Israel is so closely linked to the spirit of God that a Jewish nationalist, no matter how secularist his intention may be, is, despite himself, imbued with the divine spirit even against his own will.

In India the modern idea of Hinduism as a distinct religion developed in parallel with that of nationalism through the nineteenth and twentieth centuries. The Hindu social reform movements that arose in British India from the early 19 th century helped form the intellectual climate in which a nascent western-educated predominantly upper caste and urban middle class began to inculcate notions of national political identity and self-government. (Derek Penslar has drawn a parallel between this and how the late 18 th and 19 th century European Jewish enlightenment (Haskalah) contributed to the emergence of secular ideologies such as Zionism.

With the rise of Mahatma Gandhi to the leadership of Congress in the years immediately after the First World War, the connection between religion and Indian nationalism found its most striking embodiment. The transformation of Congress into much more of a mass movement over the next decades was marked by his use of the language and symbolism of religion to imbue it with a popular character. While this was not exclusively Hindu, it came to be widely perceived as predominantly so, especially by Muslims. Yet for many Congressmen, most notably Jawaharlal Nehru, it was an article of faith that India should not be defined by religious identity, that a distinction had to be maintained between the broad civilisational legacy that they laid claim to and any narrowly defined Hindu religious identity (Nehru 1961: 74-6) – "if India was anything at all, it was not a 'Hindu Pakistan'" (Guha 2007: 751). Yet the dilemma after the partition of the subcontinent in 1947 was that as long as Pakistan existed it would sustain Hindu 'fundamentalists' in India. In the event the constitution that India endowed itself when it became a republic in 1950, while seeking to uphold the idea of a common, secular citizenship, created devices that affirmed religious and caste identities. It included provisions reserving seats in legislatures and shares in public jobs and educational institutions for low caste people, empowering the state to open all Hindu religious institutions to all classes of Hindus, protecting the right of minorities to establish and administer their own educational institutions, and even a non-justiciable directive principle urging the prohibition of the slaughter of cows, anathema to Brahminical Hindus. The ambiguity of Indian secularism reflected the contradictions besetting post-independence India: between the secular form of the modern state and a religious society, the demands of a putative nation state and the realities of a diverse federal polity.

Despite the distinct identity of the Jewish people being the raison d'etre for the state of Israel, what the nature of that state should be proved an irresoluble problem. Was it to be a Jewish State or a State of-or for – the Jews (Klein 2005: 242)? If the former, religious Jews expected the state to be one governed by religious law, the Torah and the Talmud. If the latter, what mattered was Jewishness as an ethnic badge rather than a religious identity. The Constituent Assembly elected in 1949 was unable to agree on drafting a constitution, resolving instead that the parliament (Knesset) should pass a series of Basic Laws that would substitute, eleven being passed between 1958 and 1994.

This represented the outcome of a historic compromise between the secular socialist Zionist leadership of the fledgling state and the ultra-orthodox anti-Zionist or non-Zionist Haredi Jews, the majority of whom refused to recognise the credentials of the Zionist state. The compromise was based on a June 1947 letter addressed by David Ben-Gurion to the leadership of Agudat Israel, an umbrella organisation of the ultra-Orthodox. The kernel of this included recognition of the Jewish Sabbath, maintaining kashrut (Jewish dietary laws) in public institutions, state funding of religious public schools, and the acceptance of Orthodox rabbinical authority over marriage and divorce (Dowty 1998: 166). It reflected the fact that Judaism was both a religion of law (halakhah) and a national religion (Ravitzky 2005: 137). The consequence has been a state marked by Jewish symbols (e.g. the Shield of David carried on the national flag and the menorah that is the national emblem), institutions (the unique statutory authority of the Sephardic and Ashkenazi Chief Rabbinate), language (Hebrew), holidays (Jewish Holy Days) and, of course, the 1950 Law of Return granting all Jews the right to Israeli citizenship (Dowty 1998: 187). As one writer pithily put it, there may be freedom of religion in Israel but no freedom from religion (Neuberger 1999: 78).

Jawaharlal Nehru reportedly told Andre Malraux that one of the greatest difficulties he faced was 'creating a secular state in a religious country' (Malraux 1968: 145) and the formula devised in post-independence India, carrying on the anti-colonial Indian National Congress aspiration to be a kind of 'political Noah's Ark' of all species of Indians (Guha 2007: 751), was one of enshrining the notion of 'unity in diversity'. While there was no denying the religiosity of the mass of India's population at independence, Israeli political leaders were also, as already noted, aware of the potential for a deeply divisive Kultukampf (the word was actually used by one former prime minister, Yitzhak Shamir) over the relationship between state and religion (Shamir 1994: 160). Even though surveys in the 1990s found a fifth or quarter of Israeli Jews secular and non-observant, between a fifth and a third were found to be religiously observant, and the largest group-around half-were classed as somewhat observant or 'traditional'.

## Pragmatic Idealism and Muscular Realism

As new states in an international environment defined by the Cold War there were certain obvious, if crude, parallels between India and Israel. Both were erstwhile British territories that had to cope with the traumatic legacy of a bloody partition based on religious identity, a legacy that included unsettled borders with hostile Muslim neighbours. Both were led for the greater portion of the first two decades of their existence by professedly socialist Western-oriented prime ministers (Nehru and Ben-Gurion) at the head of political parties (Congress and Mapai/Labour) that dominated government for thirty years after independence. In addition, in both secularly inclined elites faced the task of managing the disruptive potential of the politics of religious identity. However, foreign policy choices made were shaped, in large part, by the great differences between India and Israel - of geography, size, religion and colonial and pre-colonial history. India under Nehru opted for a foreign policy often expressed in idealist terms but leavened by a measure of pragmatism while Israel under Ben-Gurion embodied a muscular realism, albeit rationalised in idealistic language.

Taking office in 1995 in the wake of the assassination of his predecessor, Yitzhak Rabin, by a Jewish religious extremist, Prime Minister Shimon Peres recalled how he had 'learned from my teacher and mentor David Ben-Gurion that to be "a light unto the nations" is a Jewish vision, and must be an Israeli strategy' (Peres 1995). However, this often repeated Zionist reference to the words of the prophet Isaiah was in practise tempered by 'the harsh reality of the Middle East and of world politics [compelling Israel's founding fathers] to learn the rules of Realpolitik' (Navon 2004: 1). Such realism, in Ben-Gurion's case found expression in what became known as mamlachtiyut, or the primacy of state interest, but, at times, also coincided with uncompromising interpretations of Jewish tradition by religious nationalists. The basis for this convergence was provided by a shared belief in the unique nature of the Jewish people. In Ben-Gurion's own words, 'The secret of our survival... is our qualitative superiority, moral and cultural.'.

Such shared ground facilitated the tacit understanding between Ben-Gurion and the religious parties whereby the latter oversaw the secular-religious status quo established upon Israel's creation and acquiesced in the handling of foreign and security policy by the secular Zionist leadership of Mapai/Labour (Maoz 2006: 488).

The religious parties were among the chief material beneficiaries of the segmental autonomy of what has been described by some political scientists (e.g. Hazan 1999) as the consociational features of Israel's politics during its first two decades. State support was crucial for the creation and maintenance of the system of kollel (advanced yeshivah-rabbinical academies) that were central to the ultra-Orthodox being able to pursue their autonomous lifestyle and avoid absorption into secular Israeli society (Reiser 1991: 74). Consequently, up until the rise of militant religious nationalism in the 1970s religious parties typically concentrated on their narrow material interests (state patronage and funding for their own educational institutions and subsidised housing, as well as exemption of Haredi males from compulsory military service) rather than broader issues, including foreign affairs.

Beyond the compact between the socialist and religious Zionists another historic convergence underpinned the evolution of Israeli foreign policy. This was the idea of the 'Iron Wall' associated with the founder of the Revisionist branch of the Zionist movement, Vladimir Jabotinsky, and championed in Israel by the main opponents of Mapai/Labour, the Herut (later expanded to become the Gahal and Likud) group in the Knesset. As early as in 1923 Jabotinsky held that a political agreement between the Zionists and the Palestinian Arabs was impossible and that, therefore, settlement had to 'develop under the protection of a force that is not dependent on the local population, behind an iron wall which they will be powerless to break down' (quoted in Shlaim 2001: 15). Despite being opposed by the Labour Zionists led by Ben-Gurion up until Jabotnsky's death in 1940, they eventually ended up pragmatically adopting the reasoning that lay behind his concept-Ben-Gurion in the period before the Suez War in 1956 successfully countering the attempts of his archrival Moshe Sharett to develop a more accommodative approach in dealing with Israel's Arab foes. Indeed, a recent academic advocate of the 'Iron Wall' credits the 1979 peace treaty with Egypt's to Israel's pursuit of the strategy (Navon 2004: 8).

In the quarter century preceding the establishment of Israel a minority of the Jewish intelligentsia in Palestine advocated an alternative to both the Revisionist 'Iron Wall' strategy and the realist pragmatism of Ben-Gurion. Coming together in the Brit Shalom (Covenant of Peace) and then the Ihud (Unity) movement, men like Judah Magnes, the first Vice-Chancellor of the Hebrew University, and the philosopher Martin Buber, sought a bi-national solution to the conflict between Zionist settlers and the existing Arab inhabitants of Palestine. Dismissed by the Zionist mainstream as dreamers and spurned by the Palestinian Arab leadership, they did not get anywhere but, nevertheless, reflected an idealistic approach to international relations that survived in Israel, albeit on the political fringe.

Buber and Magnes' hope that in the aftermath of World War Two a supra-national future would emerge (Navon 2004: 7) was shared by Nehru in India (Nehru 1961: 536, 540). Nehru, even more than Ben-Gurion, drew the parameters and set the tone for Indian foreign policy. During his seventeen years in power India emerged as a leader of the newly independent states of Asia and Africa, and, spurning alliance with both West and East in the Cold War, of the Non-aligned Movement. Although nonalignment was a strategic as well as a principled choice for the internationally-minded Nehru (Chiriyankandath 2004: 200), it contributed to a moral authority that, together with the legacy of Gandhi's successful non-violent struggle against British colonialism, is still credited with endowing it with 'soft power' in the global arena (Kamdar 2004).

Yet Hindu nationalists regarded this Gandhian legacy as based on illusion. Writing in the 1960s, M.S. Golwalkar, the second Sarsangchalak (supreme philosopher-guide) of the Rashtriya Swayamsevak Sangh (RSS) (National Volunteer Organisation), the parent organisation of the organisational family (sangh parivar) of Hindu chauvinist organisations to which the BJP belongs, stated: the only basis for our free and prosperous national life is invincible national strength – a strength that will strike terror into the hearts of aggressive powers and make other nations seek our friendship.

From this perspective Golwalkar saw India's acquisition of the atom bomb as an imperative (Golwalkar 1980: 429). (In Israel Ben-Gurion had already come to the same conclusion, taking the decision to develop nuclear weapons before leaving office in 1963.

Bharat Karnad, the arch-realist Indian international relations theorist, agrees. He has argued that 'traditional Indian statecraft, built around the concepts of ready use of force, expediency and amorality are, in fact, in sharp contrast to Gandhi's teachings' (Karnad 2002: 3).

Drawing on the ancient Vedas (from the Sanskrit vid, to know) and Puranas (mythologies), as well as the Arthashastra of Kautilya, the Indian treatise on statecraft dating from the fourth century BCE, he holds that traditional Indian doctrines on foreign policy were based on machtpolitik (power politics) rather than Nehru's moralpolitik (Karnad 2002: 18), the latter denoting the conversion of Gandhi's legacy into 'the aggressive use of morality to advance national interest' (Karnad 2002: 3).

## The Rise of Religious Nationalism

The year 1967, two decades following the emergence of India and Israel as independent states, marked a turning point in the politics of both countries. In India three years after Nehru's demise his Congress Party suffered its first severe setback in national elections under his daughter Indira Gandhi with the Hindu chauvinist Bharatiya Jana Sangh, the precursor to the BJP, with nearly a tenth of the popular vote, emerging as its leading opponent in the populous Hindi-speaking states of north India. Three months later the Six-Day War occurred, proving a transformative event for the politics and foreign policy of Israel. Within a decade both Congress and the Labour Alignment were ousted from power by coalitions dominated by right-wing parties including Hindu nationalists in India and militant religious Zionists in Israel.

The Six-Day War gave rise to "religious Zionism" as a significant force in Israeli politics. Israel's lightning triumph over Arab armies that saw the conquest of East Jerusalem and the West Bank of the Jordan was seen by many Orthodox Jews as the providentially redemptive hand of the God of the Jewish people at work and confirmation that they were living in messianic times (Shlaim 2001: 549). Thereafter political discourse in Israel acquired a religious element when it came to discussing foreign policy and security, something that had hitherto been absent (Maoz 2006: 488). However, this shift did not immediately become apparent. It was the 1973 Yom Kippur War, in which Israel initially suffered traumatic reverses, which sharpened disillusion with the post-independence political dispensation.

With the Ashkenazi (European Jewish) Labour leadership resented by Sephardic (Oriental) Jews for their elitism and seeming to have lost the pioneering zeal once symbolised by the kibbutz, the Gush Emunim (Bloc of the Faithful) soon won widespread public acceptance after it was launched in 1974. Its purpose was to secure Israeli ownership of the West Bank (described in Israeli parlance as Judea and Samaria) through the settlement of Jews throughout the occupied territories (Dowty 1998: 228). Gush Emunim's public appeal extended beyond the national religious camp because it seemed to offer a vigorous and decisive Zionist response in the aftermath of the Yom Kippur War.

Historically the religious parties in Israel, unlike the BJP and its precursors in India, have drawn their support almost exclusively from the religious electorate (Hazan 1999: 114). Gush Emunim, though linked to the religious Zionism of the National Religious Party (NRP), did not limit itself to the strictly religious repertoire of the ultra-Orthodox but was more eclectic, drawing upon both religious and Zionist tradition, thus becoming both 'the ideological vanguard of the New [post-Labour or neo-revisionist] Zionism... and ... a bridge between religious and secular nationalists' (Dowty 1998: 118). In this respect its significance for contemporary Israelis has been compared to that of the secular kibbutz movement in an earlier era in providing 'models for Jewish patriotism, Zionist commitment, civic duty, and spiritual guidance' (Lustick 1993: 109).

The electoral rise of the religious parties became marked in the 1990s, peaking at 31 of the 120 Knesset seats in 1999, five being claimed by the religious Zionist National Religious Party and most of the rest by ultra-Orthodox groups including, most notably, Shas, a 1983 Oriental Sephardi Jewish breakaway from the Ashkenazi Orthodox Agudat Israel, which won 17 seats. Shas' spiritual leader, Rabbi Ovadya Yosef, believed that the Oriental Jews historically underprivileged position in Israeli society stemmed from a loss of pride in their cultural/religious heritage and therefore advocated 'a spiritual-religious transformation of an ethnically conscious sector of society' (Weissbrod 2003: 102). Shas has enjoyed striking political success, taking part in all but two of the eleven Israeli governments formed since it entered the Knesset in 1984 (it became the third biggest partner in the governing coalition formed by Prime Minister Ehud Olmert after the 2006 elections).

Although Shas added an ethnic dimension to the politics of religious interest traditionally pursued by Israel's ultra-Orthodox parties, it has not departed fundamentally from their typical approach of focusing on 'narrow interests (funds and patronage) rather than broader issues of principle' (Dowty 1998: 169). It is in this respect that critics of the religious parties such as the late Israel Shahak make a qualitative distinction between the Gush Emunim-NRP form of Jewish 'fundamentalism' from the Haredi form, the potential danger of the former arising from their desire to eventually appropriate the state as the Labour Zionists had succeeded in doing (Shahak 1999: 77).

A rough parallel can be made between the transformative objectives of the national religious camp in Israel and the RSS sangh parivar in India. Started in 1925 by K.B. Hedgewar, a Brahmin doctor, the RSS was led for more than three decades during its formative phase by his successor, M.S. Golwalkar. It concentrated on a wide spread of cultural and social activity aimed at building up a distinct, strong, martial Hindu ethos. Temporarily banned in 1948-49 after a onetime member assassinated Gandhi, the distance it kept from direct involvement in party politics facilitated its steady growth into what by the 1980s was a formidable force in Indian public life. Organised in thousands of shakhas (branches) across India guided in each region by pracharaks (celibate full-time propagandists), its influence was disseminated through the network of linked organisations known collectively as the sangh parivar (organizational family). The latter included the BJP, one of India's two biggest parties from 1991, the second biggest national students and labour federations, as well as a multiplicity of political, religious cultural, intellectual, social service, cooperative, peasants and women's bodies.

Just as the aftermath of the Six-Day and Yom Kippur wars, disillusionment with Labour Zionism and the disaffection of Oriental Jews all played a role in strengthening both the secular and religious right in Israel, several factors made the theme of giving a more distinctly 'Hindu' hue to national identity central to Indian politics in the 1980s and 1990s. First, there was, after Indira Gandhi's return to power in 1980, the increasing exploitation by the Congress Party of the ambiguity of Indian secularism for the political use of religion, especially in the form of populist invocations of a majority Hindu identity. One reason for the movement away from the more secular attitude espoused by Mrs. Gandhi's father, Jawaharlal Nehru, lay in the steady decline of Congress as a mass political institution at a time when its authority was under increasing challenge not only from the Hindu right but also low caste and regional parties. Another was the increasingly strident, even violent, separatist demands on the part of some non-Hindus in peripheral regions, which culminated in the descent into effective civil war of border states like Assam, Punjab and

Kashmir. This was itself to some degree the consequence of short-term Congress stratagems involving the exploitation of communal divisions.

An additional element fostering the growth of Hindu nationalism at this stage in India's development was the liberalisation of the economy, initiated in the 1980s and adopted more wholeheartedly by the minority Congress government of P.V. Narasimha Rao in the wake of a balance of payments crisis in 1991. Some of the repercussions of the economic changes initiated by liberalisation facilitated the growing appeal of a kind of 'syndicated Hinduism' (Thapar 1990: 31). As one commentator put it, the 'overlap between the narratives of communal and consumer identity formation' (Rajagopal 1996: 341), together with the rapid expansion of electronic communication allowed for the emergence of a kind of retail Hindu identity that the Hindu nationalists were able to turn into a valuable political resource. Hindu-Muslim tensions reached a fever pitch in December 1992 when Hindu militants unrestrained by the BJP state government of Uttar Pradesh, and in the presence of party leaders including party president Lal Krishna Advani, destroyed the Babri Masjid in Ayodhya, a disused 16 th century mosque claimed as the birthplace of the Hindu deity Ram (Ram Janmabhoomi). The nationwide communal violence that followed was the worst since partition, claiming at least two thousand lives, and led to the RSS being briefly banned. Although the intensity of the passion whipped up by the Ayodhya confrontation paid rich political dividends for the BJP, in the years that followed the BJP's political strategy, recognising the logic of India's political demography, shifted steadily towards building a network of alliances with regional parties. This aimed at outflanking Congress by gaining strength in areas of the country where Hindu nationalism remained a peripheral force. The strategy proved remarkably successful. Despite continuing to trail Congress in the popular vote, it emerged as the largest single party in parliament in three successive elections (1996, 1998 and 1999). This provided the platform for six years of BJP-led coalition government from 1998 until its unexpected defeat at the hands of a rival Congress-led combination in 2004.

# 4

# India's New Foreign Policy Strategy and Relation

## Introduction

Most nations and large ones at that do not easily alter their international orientation. States tend to be conservative about foreign policy. Fundamental changes in foreign policy take place only when there is a revolutionary change either at home or in the world. Much as the ascent of Deng Xiaoping in the late 1970s produced radical changes in Chinese foreign policy, India's relations with the world have seen a fundamental transformation over the last decade and a half. A number of factors were at work in India. The old political and economic order at home had collapsed and externally the end of the Cold War removed all the old benchmarks that guided India's foreign policy. Many of the core beliefs of the old system had to discarded and consensus generated on new ones. The collapse of the Soviet Union and the new wave of economic globalization left India scrambling to find new anchors for its conduct of external relations. This paper is examines the origin, dynamics and the implications of India's new foreign policy strategy.

Most Indians agree that its first Prime Minister Jawaharlal Nehru had defined a unique foreign policy for India at the very dawn of its independence. Despite many critics of his world view, a broad national consensus had emerged around Nehru's ideas on independent foreign policy, non-alignment, and third world solidarity. Since the 1990s, though, the challenge for the Indian leaders has been to reinterpret Nehru's ideas to suit the new political context that had confronted it. The new Indian leaders could neither denounce Nehru nor formally reject Nehru's ideas, for that would have invited serious political trouble. Yet they had to continually improvise and refashion India's foreign policy to suit the new requirements. This has not been easy. The tension between the imperative of the new and the resistance of the old ideas on how to conduct foreign policy is real and is unlikely to end in the near future. The fear of the new and fondness for the old continue to be reflected in all aspects of Indian diplomacy from engaging the United States to an optimal strategy towards the smallest of the neighbours. The "new" foreign policy of India is indeed work in progress. Yet it is not difficult to see that the direction of Indian diplomacy has changed substantially since the end of the cold war amidst internal and external impulses.

## Structural Changes in India's World View

Underlying India's current foreign policy strategy are a set of important transitions in India's world view. Not all of these were articulated self-consciously or clearly by the Indian political leadership. A few of those changes stand out and are unlikely to be reversed. The first was the transition from the national consensus on building a "socialist society" to building a "modern capitalist" one. The socialist ideal, with its roots in the national movement, had so dominated the Indian political discourse by the early 1970s, that a Constitutional amendment was passed in 1976 to make the nation into a "socialist republic". But 1991 saw the collapse of the Soviet Union, the veritable symbol of socialism, and the edifice of India's state-socialism began to crumble.

Adapting to the new challenges of globalization now became the principal national objective. The change in the national economic strategy in 1991 inevitably produced abundant new options on the foreign policy front. Implicit in this was the second transition, from the past emphasis on politics to a new stress on economics in the making of foreign policy. India began to realize in the 1990s how far behind it had fallen the rest of Asia, including China, in economic development. With the socialist strait jacket gone, and the pressures to compete with other emerging markets, Indian diplomacy now entered uncharted waters. In the past, foreign for aid was so symbolic of Indian diplomacy that sought to meet the government's external financing requirements as well as developmental needs. India was now seeking foreign direct investment, and access to markets in the developed world. The slow but successful economic reforms unleashed the potential of the nation, generated rapid economic growth and provided a basis to transform its relations with great powers, regional rivals Pakistan and China, and the neighbourhood as a whole. A third transition in Indian foreign policy is about the shift from being a leader of the "Third World" to the recognition of the potential that India could emerge as a great power in its own right. While independent India always had a sense of its own greatness, that never seemed realistic until the Indian economy began to grow rapidly in the 1990s. In the early decades of its independent existence, India viewed many of the international and regional security issues through the prism of the third world and "anti-imperialism". The 1990s, however, brought home some painful truths. There was no real third world trade union, that India believed it was leading. After a radical phase in the 1970s, most developing nations had begun to adopt pragmatic economic policies and sought to integrate with the international market. Much of the developing world had made considerable economic advances, leaving the South Asia way behind. While the rhetoric on the third world remained popular, the policy orientation in India's external relations increasingly focused on India's own self interest. There was a growing perception, flowing from the Chinese example, that if India could sustain high growth rates it had a chance to gain a place at the international high table.

The 1990s also saw India begin discarding the "anti-Western" political impulses that were so dominant in the world view that shaped Indian diplomacy right up to 1991. Rejecting the "anti-Western" mode of thinking was the fourth important transition of Indian foreign policy. As the world's largest democracy, India was the most committed to Western political values outside the Euro-Atlantic world. Yet the Cold War saw India emerge as the most articulate opponent of the Western world view. A strong anti-Western bias crept into Indian foreign policy supported by the left as well as the right and underwritten by the security establishment. The disappearance of the Soviet Union and China's rise as a great power demanded that India to break the decades old anti-Western approaches to foreign policy.

Finally, the fifth transition in Indian foreign policy in the 1990s was from idealism to realism. Idealism came naturally to the Indian elite that won independence from the British by arguing against colonialism on the basis of first principles of Enlightenment. The new leaders of India had contempt for "power politics".

They believed it was a negative but lingering legacy from 19th century Europe that had no relevance to the new times of the mid 20th century. India tended to see its role in world politics as the harbinger of a new set of principles of peaceful coexistence and multilateralism which if applied properly would transform the world.

Although Nehru demonstrated realism on many fronts, especially in India's immediate neighbourhood, the public articulation of India's foreign policy had the stamp of idealism all over it. Since the 1990s, India could no longer sustain the presumed idealism of its foreign policy. India had to come to terms with the painful reality that its relative standing in the world had substantially declined during the Cold War. Much like Deng Xiaoping who prescribed pragmatism for China, the Indian leaders began to emphasize practical ways to achieve power and prosperity for India.

## Dynamics of the New Foreign Policy

One area which saw the cumulative impact of all these transitions in a powerful manner was India's nuclear diplomacy. After years of promoting idealistic slogans such as universal disarmament, India by the late 1990s recognized the importance of becoming a declared nuclear weapon power.

Despite the steady nuclearization of its security environment over the decades, India remained ambiguous about its attitudes to its national own nuclear weapons programme. Even as it tested a nuclear device in 1974, India refused to follow through with the nuclear weapons project.

By the late 1990s, though, India found it necessary to make itself an unambiguous nuclear power. The economic growth of the decade gave it the self-confidence that it could ride through the inevitable international reaction to it. India was also right it betting that a country of its size and economic potential could not be sanctioned and isolated for too long. Even more important, India sensed that there might be diplomatic opportunities for getting the great powers acknowledge if not legitimize its nuclear weapons programme and remove the high technology sanctions against it.

Within seven years after its second round of nuclear testing in 1998, India signed the historic nuclear deal with the Bush Administration in July 2005 under which the U.S. agreed to change its domestic non-proliferation law and revise the international guidelines on nuclear cooperation in favour of India.

Another area of transformation was India's relations with the great powers. The end of the Cold War and the collapse of the Soviet Union, allowed India to pursue, without the political inhibitions of the past, simultaneous expansion of relations with all the major powers.

Injecting political and economic substance into the long emaciated relationship with the United States, now the lone super power, became the principal national strategic objective. At the same time, India was unwilling to let its old ties to the Soviet Union, now a weakened Russia wither away. Since the end of the Cold War, Russia has remained an important source of arms and a strategic partner.

Meanwhile India's ties with Europe, China and Japan have all become far more weighty and diversified. The upgradation of the relations with China since the early 1990s has been one of the biggest achievements of India's new foreign policy.

The once wary relationship with China has now blossomed into a strategic partnership for peace and development. China is now all set to emerge as India's single largest trading partner. India and Japan, which drifted apart from the Cold War, have steadily expanded the basis for political cooperation in recent years and have proclaimed a strategic partnership in 2005.

India's new foreign policy was not all about "big power diplomacy". It involved a strong effort to find political reconciliation with two of its large neighbours—Pakistan and China. Since the end of the Cold War, India had sought to cope with Pakistan in the radically changed context that brought nuclear weapons into the bilateral equation and an increased ability of Pakistan to intervene in the disputed state of Jammu and Kashmir through cross-border terrorism. The diplomatic history of Indo-Pak relations in the 1990s is a rich, if frustrating, tapestry that included every possible development—from a limited conventional war to a total military confrontation to many summits that struggled to define a new framework peace between the two neighbours.

A new peace process under way since 2004 has produced the first important steps towards a normalization of Indo-Pak relations, including a serious negotiation on the Kashmir dispute. At the same India is also involved in purposeful negotiations to end the long-standing boundary dispute with China.

For the first time since its independence, India is now addressing its two of most important sources of insecurity—unresolved territorial questions with Pakistan and China. Both involve de-emphasizing territorial nationalism, which in turn carry significant political risks at home. Yet, the Indian political leadership now believes resolving either or both of these problems would fundamentally alter India's security condition.

By the 1990s, India, which always saw itself as the pre-eminent power in South Asia, found its relations with the smaller neighbours had reached a dead end. Recognizing the need to transform its South Asian policy, India embarked on a series of policy innovations that demanded greater generosity and a willingness to walk more than half the distance in resolving its many accumulated problems with smaller neighbours.

As it embarked upon the policy of economic globalization, India also saw the importance of promoting regional economic integration in the Subcontinent, which was a single market until the Partition of the region took place in 1947. While India's weight in the region began to increase it also had to temper the past temptations to unilaterally intervene in the internal conflicts of its neighbours. Unlike in the past, when it sought to keep major powers out of the Subcontinent, India is now working closely with the great powers in resolving the political crises in Nepal and Sri Lanka.

India's unilateralism in the region is increasingly being replaced by a multilateral approach. India has also supported the participation of China, Japan, and the U.S. as observers in the principal mechanism for regionalism, the South Asian Association for Regional Cooperation. Even as India seeks to define a new approach towards smaller neighbours, the regions abutting the Subcontinent beckoned India to reassert its claim for a say in the affairs of the Indian Ocean and its littoral. The 1990s saw India making a determined effort to reconnect with its extended neighbourhood in South East Asia, Afghanistan and Central Asia, and the Middle East. India's renewed engagement with the surrounding regions is within a new framework that emphasized economic relations and energy diplomacy rather than the traditional notion of third world solidarity through the nonaligned movement. The Cold War and India's insular economic policies in the first four decades had undermined India's standing to the East and West of its neighbourhood and prevented New Delhi from ensuring its much vaunted importance in the Indian Ocean littoral. But India's new economic and foreign policies have given India a real opportunity to realize the vision of Lord Curzon, the British viceroy at the turn of the 20th century of Indian leadership in the region stretching from Aden to Malacca. After decades of neglecting economic and political regionalism, India is now an active participant in various regional organizations from the East Asia Summit to the African Union.

During the 1990s Indian diplomacy had to develop a new strategy to deal with the Islamic world. Even as it renewed its engagement with Israel, that was kept at arms length for decades, India also sought to redefine its policies towards key Islamic countries. The reality of a large Islamic population—nearly 150 million today— had always been an important factor in India's foreign policy. In the past it merely meant supporting various Islamic causes. But today, the relationship with the Islamic world is being deepened on the basis of economic and commercial cooperation, energy security and cooperation in combating religious extremism and terrorism. This gave an unprecedented depth and breadth to India's ties to the Islamic world since the end of the Cold War.

## Long Term Implications

The innovations in India's foreign policy strategy since the early 1990s has resulted in the happy situation of simultaneous expansion of relations with all the major powers, growing weight in Asia and the Indian Ocean regions, and the prospect of improved relations with important neighbours. Given its impending relative rise in the international system, India is bound to be confronted by a number of challenges.

First the new focus on the importance of power is not without problems. Despite being marginalized in recent years, the imperatives of idealism and moralism have not completely disappeared from India's foreign policy.

Since 1991, India has moved from its traditional emphasis on the "power of the argument" to a new stress on the "argument of power". Given its noisy democracy, India cannot build domestic political support to foreign policy initiatives purely on the argument of power. It would continue to need a set of values and norms to justify its actions on the world stage. As a consequence the tension between "power and principle" would remain an enduring one in India's foreign policy strategy.

Second, increased power potential will mean that India would have to take positions on major international issues and regional conflicts. In recent years, New Delhi has either avoided or merely substituted them with generalized slogans.

Just as Beijing is being pressed to become a "stake-holder" in the international system, New Delhi too would come under greater pressure to stop being a "free rider". In other words, India would have to often find ways to limit the pursuit of "national interest" in order to contribute to "collective interests" of the international system.

Third, as India emerges as an important element of future balance of power in the world, it would be pressed to make choices in favour of one or the other great powers at least on specific issues. The absence of great power confrontation in the last few years has allowed India the luxury of converting the slogan of "non-alignment" into an "independent" foreign policy. But amidst potential new rivalries among the U.S., China, Europe, Russia, and Japan, New Delhi would be compelled to make often wrenching political choices. While India making potential alliances with one or other major powers cannot be ruled out in the future, as a large country, India would remain loath to limit its freedom of action through formal alliances.

Fourth, the demands on India to contribute to order and stability in its immediate and extended neighbourhood would dramatically increase in the coming decades. This would in turn draw India deeper into great power rivalries in various regions and the internal conflicts of smaller countries. Use of military force, either unilaterally or under multilateral mechanisms, could also become frequent. Meanwhile the India, like China, is increasingly turning towards other developing countries for stable supply of energy and mineral resources, giving growing amounts of economic assistance, providing arms and military training, and seeking long-term naval access arrangements. A rising India would, then, be no longer remain immune to the many tragedies of great power politics. Finally, India, like other great powers before it, is also in the danger of falling a victim to ultranationalism and an over-determination of national interest. Tempering nationalism and balancing ends and means are two challenges that come inseparably with a rising power potential on the world stage.

# 5

# U.S.-India Defence Relations: Strategic Perspectives

India's strategic interests in Asia are two-fold: ensuring security in its immediate neighborhood and protecting India's interests, including its economic and energy needs, in the rest of Asia and the Middle East. Indian officials believe that the most likely military contingencies they face in the medium term are "Kargils and Tsunamis"—sharp, limited land engagements on their borders and broader humanitarian problems in the extended region. They seek capabilities that would equip India to make its presence felt in the area, from the Persian Gulf to Southeast Asia, and to respond if necessary to other kinds of contingencies. India's national security policy is based on the premise that its immediate neighborhood is dangerous and that regional instability from neighboring countries fuels India's internal insurgencies. India's relationship with Pakistan has been troubled from the start and has often been a sticking point for the United States. Insurgents in Kashmir have close ties with counterparts in Pakistan. Central India's "Naxalite" revolutionaries are said to have loose ties with Maoists in Nepal. India has traditionally discouraged any direct U.S. involvement in the region's geopolitics. Improved relations with the United States, however, have brought Indian and U.S. policies into closer alignment on problems in Nepal, Bangladesh, and Sri Lanka.

Beyond the immediate South Asian region, India's broader concerns in Asia include ensuring the security of India's lifelines for trade, investment, and most importantly, energy. Indian security analysts draw a distinction between the promising area to India's east and the troubled region to India's west. To the east, India has built up its political, economic, and military relations, especially with Singapore and Japan. The fact that Indian officials see their economic relations in Asia as a security issue is in itself an indication of how their view of security has broadened in the past decade. Maritime security in the Indian Ocean has become an increasingly important strategic concern as India's energy needs continue to grow.

India's defence policy in the South Asian region is essentially land-based, and the army has long been the dominant service. By contrast, security in an Asian and Indian Ocean context relies much more on the sea and the air. As a result, the bulk of India's plans for procurement of major new military systems are for the navy and air force. The Indian Navy wants to remain the predominant military force in the Indian Ocean. Its doctrine makes a distinction between areas close to India's shores, where the navy expects to be able to exclude other powers, and those further out to sea, where it recognizes that exclusion is not feasible and, implicitly at least, that it must aim to operate in cooperation with other powers. In recent years, its relations with the U.S. Navy have become closer and friendlier. The prospect of a future Chinese presence in the Indian Ocean, on the other hand, is something India's security analysts are watching uneasily. In the west, by contrast, India believes that instability and Islamic extremism could spill over from Afghanistan and Central Asia, to India's detriment. India's need for energy supplies makes the Persian Gulf a particular concern. India currently imports 70 percent of its oil needs and in the next decade expects to import almost 90 percent of its increased oil demands. In addition, India has a substantial number of its nationals working in the Persian Gulf.

## Washington's Strategic Interests

In the past, the two areas of major U.S. strategic interest were the western Pacific and the Middle East and Persian Gulf. The increasing U.S. focus on political and economic relationships in Asia and the rise of China and India have increased India's strategic importance in U.S. eyes. India's democratic heritage, impressive economic performance, and civilian control of the military are all seen as attractive factors in pursuing a closer strategic relationship. U.S. officials expect India to play a major role in shaping Asia's strategic environment. The United States would like to include India in its international efforts to prevent terrorism, stop the proliferation of weapons of mass destruction (WMDs), assist in the war on terror, and ensure the security of energy lanes in the Indian Ocean. India has joined the Container Security Initiative, which is aimed at improving the security of international trade, but has thus far not joined the Proliferation Security Initiative, a loose understanding on procedures for international cooperation to prevent the onward spread of nuclear weapons equipment and technology.

Senior U.S. naval officers have spoken of a "global maritime partnership," or a "thousand-ship navy," a framework for cooperation including both naval and civilian maritime assets of countries throughout Asia and the Indian Ocean. They see India as a uniquely valuable participant in this type of flexible structure for working together. Both this concept and the practical experience of working with India following the Asian Tsunami of 2005 lead the United States to stress the importance of interoperability in its emerging relations with India.

Common ground: Both the United States and India seek peaceful engagement with China, although both also view China as a potential long-term security concern and neither wants to see Asia dominated by a single country. Nevertheless, China is a major trading partner for both the United States and India, and neither country wants to exacerbate Chinese concerns about "encirclement" or treat China as an enemy. India, however, does not want to be regarded as an element in a U.S. strategy toward China.

The security of energy lanes in the Indian Ocean is perhaps the issue on which U.S. and Indian analysts agree most strongly. Like their Indian counterparts, U.S. security officials consider the safety of sea lanes crucial to national security. U.S. interest in the Indian Ocean is primarily motivated by a desire to protect global energy markets. Over half of the world's oil supplies travel through sea lanes in the Indian Ocean, and disruption of energy supplies would have a major impact on the United States regardless of whether U.S. supplies specifically travel through these waters.

Divergent views: The biggest contrast between U.S. and Indian security goals has to do with India-Pakistan relations. India sees

Pakistan as the principal source of terrorism, and one that affects India not just in Kashmir but also in other parts of the country. Washington sees Pakistan primarily as an ally in the war on terror, albeit one that is under U.S. pressure to deal more effectively with domestic Islamic militant groups.

In the Middle East, India and the United States share concerns about terrorism and energy supply but differ on what to do about them. India has good relations with Israel, including important military supply ties, but has generally avoided other actions that could antagonize the Arab countries. It has grave misgivings about U.S. policies in Iraq and on the Israeli-Palestinian dispute. India has also declined a U.S. invitation to send an army division to participate in the postwar management of Iraq. Another bone of contention in the Middle East is Iran. The United States would like to see Iran isolated and contained, whereas India continues to pursue energy deals with Iran and depends on Iran to provide it with land access to Afghanistan and Central Asia.

Even where U.S. and Indian strategic goals are similar, there are important differences in how they expect to achieve them. India's desire to diversify its sources of energy and its concern about Chinese activities in the Indian Ocean, for example, have led it to make overtures to the military junta in Myanmar (Burma), a contrast to the hard line Washington has maintained. Similar differences in perspective have come up over Indian oil deals in Sudan and Nigeria.

Turning strategic overlap into partnership: India and the United States have carried on a formal strategic dialogue for almost a decade. The primary regular mechanism for this conversation is the Defence Policy Group, which has focused mainly on briefings on broader U.S. policies and on discussing relatively noncontroversial issues on which India and the United States share similar views. In addition, the two countries maintain a Joint Working Group on Terrorism, which has been most successful in dealing with operational aspects of the problem and has not attempted to resolve differences over Pakistan.

Real strategic exchange is relatively new for both Indians and Americans. India's sensitivity about its relations with China and U.S. concerns about Pakistan have made it difficult for India and the United States to have candid consultations on the issues that are the most important to their future strategic interests. If the two countries are to achieve a real "strategic partnership," that kind of candor will need to develop, along with increased familiarity with each other's military practices and a nuanced understanding of strategic outlooks.

## U.S. - India Defence Relationship

The U.S. and India are working to build the architecture of a durable defence partnership that will support our common interests in maintaining security and stability, defeating terrorism and violent religious extremism, preventing the spread of weapons of mass destruction and associated materials, data and technologies, and protecting the free flow of commerce via land, air and sea lanes. Since the signing of the New Framework for the U.S.-India Defence Relationship by Secretary Rumsfeld and Minister Mukherjee on 28 June 2005, the U.S. and India have made considerable progress in enhancing the relationship, through signing foundation agreements, conducting exercises and engaging in ongoing dialogue on a variety of security issues.

President Bush and Prime Minister Singh announced their intent to increase U.S.-Indian cooperation to improve security in the maritime domain. The two countries will soon sign an agreement for mutual logistics support that will enable our militaries to cooperate more easily during combined training, exercises and disaster relief operations. In January 2006, Secretary Rumsfeld and Minister Mukherjee signed the Research, Development, Test and Evaluation Agreement which will facilitate new avenues of cooperation in the area of scientific exchanges and joint development.

The U.S. and India's Military Services are improving their interoperability through increasingly sophisticated and complex exercises. The MALABAR Naval exercise conducted in September and October 2005 was the largest naval exercise to date between the U.S. and Indian Navies, and was the first to involve both U.S. and Indian aircraft carriers. The U.S. and Indian Air Forces conducted the third Cope India air exercise in November 2005 at Kalaikunda Air Station, West Bengal, India, the first U.S.-India exercise to involve Airborne Warning and Control System aircraft. U.S. and Indian Armies held a company-size exercise – their largest ever – in the foothills of the Himalayas in January 2006. Most recently in February 2006, the U.S. and Indian Navies were able to quickly organize a passing exercise with aircraft carriers from both countries, demonstrating capabilities that can be used to respond collaboratively to future emergencies at sea.

The U.S. and India seek to expand defence trade, co-production, joint development, and technology transfer, all of which will improve interoperability and cooperation. We are working through several forums to achieve this goal. The U.S. intends to transfer the USS TRENTON amphibious transport ship to India in early 2007. U.S. firms will compete with contemporary technology in the Indian Air Force's upcoming tender for Multi-Role Combat Aircraft and a U.S. firm is competing in the Indian Army's commercial tender for a new light helicopter.

The U.S. Department of Defence and the Indian Ministry of Defence conduct ongoing dialogue on several topics of mutual interest under the auspices of the annual Defence Policy Group meetings, including counter-terrorism, missile defence cooperation, and strategic planning. A U.S. Defence Department delegation will travel to India soon to discuss the Quadrennial Defence Review with senior Indian officials and influential strategic thinkers.

U.S.-Indian defence cooperation is a force for good. The U.S. and India cooperated closely in providing aid to tsunami victims in December 2004-January 2005. In January 2006, the U.S. Navy rescued Indian mariners off the Horn of Africa whose ship had been hijacked by Somali pirates. Under the auspices of the U.S.-India disaster relief initiative, approved in July 2005, India airlifted supplies and made a contribution to the American Red Cross following Hurricane Katrina, and the U.S. and Indian militaries are working together to expand disaster relief cooperation.

## U.S-India Security Relations

Remarkable changes have taken place in the framework of US-India security relations in recent years. During the Cold War, estrangement characterized the two democracies because of India's non-aligned policy, close relations with the erstwhile Soviet Union and tensions with Pakistan, coupled with the US containment policy towards the Soviet Union, and the US alliance with Pakistan. Based on common strategic, economic and political interests after the end of the Cold War, the US and India have moved from being "estranged democracies" to "engaged democracies". Such a change is primarily due to America's adjustment of its strategy and policy toward India as well as South Asia and the Asia-Pacific. The changing US-Indian security relations will have a great impact on China's security environment. This paper focuses on the implications of these changes for China from three perspectives: the emergence of a Sino-US-India strategic triangle; the complicated security situation in South Asia; and the America factor in Sino-India relations.

The increasing attention being paid to the relationship between the Indian and the US security apparatus - particularly over the last couple of years - is no longer a matter that can be dismissed as mere speculation. Indeed, after India's five under-ground nuclear tests at Pokhran in May 1998, the US initiated a series of strict sanctions under the aegis of the US Nuclear Proliferation Prevention Act of 1994. The security relationship between Washington and New Delhi had ebbed and suspicion seemed to characterize the bilateral agenda.

President Clinton's visit to India in March 2000, which was the fourth presidential visit in the history of the two countries and the first in the last 22 years, was a turning point in the ambivalent US-India relations of yesteryears. On May 1, 2001, not long after he took office, President George W. Bush made a speech to announce his security policy and plans for developing a missile defence system India had expressed its approval of this programme earlier, and was, indeed, seen to be even more supportive than the US' traditional allies. Later, in order to win India's support in the fight against terrorism, the US lifted its sanctions on India and the two nations agreed to comprehensively co-operate in the field of the global war against terrorism. Indeed, in May 2002, US Special Forces were flown into India and took part in a two-week military manoeuvre in north India, in the historical city of Agra. This manoeuvre was the first between the two countries in 39 years and demonstrated that their military cooperation had reached a high level.

What are the changes in US-India relationship? Why are these changes occurring? What are the implications of these changes for China's security, and how will these affect Sino-India relationships and Sino-US relationships? This paper attempts to examine these questions.

## *US-India Relations: From Estrangement to Rapprochement*

With the beginning of the Cold War, the primary US goal with regard to countries in South Asia was "to orient those nations toward the United States and the other Western democracies and away from the Soviet Union." However, India's geo-strategic interests and considerations were different from those of the US.

As opposed to Pakistan, who joined the US led BTO (Baghdad Treaty Organization, later the Central Treaty Organization, CENTO) and SEATO (the South East Asia Treaty Organization), India initially supported the principles of self-government and non-alignment – resulting in its refusal to participate in the US-led strategic alliance against the Soviet Union.

India was also opposed to the setting up of a defensive alliance in order to contain China. It recognized the new Communist-led government of China in December 1949, regarded Taiwan as a part of China, and criticized the US for its official stance against the People's Republic. In January 1951, India was the only non-Communist state that voted against a resolution sponsored by the United States in the United Nations (UN) General Assembly labelling China as an aggressor.

As a third corollary, India began to receive military, political, and economic assistance from the erstwhile Soviet Union from the 1960's – an alliance which brought about further estrangement in Indo-US relations. Indeed, India still depended on Moscow for military and political support, and when the Soviet Union invaded Afghanistan in 1979 – which made the US and China stand by Pakistan's side – India complained that the US did not try to find a political method to resolve the Afghanistan crisis. On the other hand, US did not punish India for its close relationship with Soviet Union in the 1980's.

The other important factor was the India-Pakistan War of 1971. The US sent its Seventh Fleet into the Bay of Bengal and this act was regarded as a threat by India and it pushed the already ebbing Indo-US relationship to an all-time low. By supporting Pakistan, New Delhi argued that America had forced India into an unnecessary and costly arms race, that American assistance gave Pakistan the means and the inspiration to challenge New Delhi, and that the Pakistan-US relationship came to be seen as not directed against communism, but against India.

During the Cold War, America's policy toward India was different from its policy toward the two other big Asian nations - China and Japan. America did not include India as its strategic alliance partner nor did it include India as a possible containment target. And just as the United States did not approve of India attempting to balance power between United States and the Soviet Union, India did not endorse the United States' attempt to balance power between India and Pakistan. In sum, with India implementing the policy of non-alignment, maintaining friendly relations with the Soviet Union, and engaging Pakistan; and, the contrasting United States' policy of forming alliances in order to deter the Soviet Union, made it difficult for the US and India to work together.

With the end of the Cold War, myriad factors began to push the United States and India to change their relationship from estrangement to one of convergence. The United States and India are two of the largest democracies in the world and, furthermore, they have similar egalitarian values. The US also hopes that India will play an active role in the process of democratisation in Russia. Starting from the 1990s, with India beginning to implement policies to create an open market economy, the United States has been treating India as a newly developed market; United States has progressively emerged as India's greatest source for foreign investment supplies and trading partner. Up to 1998, it seemed that the two countries attempted to form a new relationship that would bring them closer and engender a more robust co-operative relationship. Even though this relationship was damaged in 1998, when India exploded its nuclear bombs and the Americans responding with an embargo, the relationship that had taken off after the Cold War had not ended. Indeed, with eight rounds of security dialogue between US Deputy Secretary of State, Strobe Talbot, and the then Indian Foreign Minister, Jaswant Singh, the security relationship between the two countries normalised.

During the Kargil crisis of 1999, India successfully won sympathy and support from the US. In stark contrast, the US initially cold-shouldered Pakistan's new regime when General Pervez Musharraf rode to power through a military coup. The two situations in 1999 led United States' South Asian policy shift to 'focusing on India and reducing on Pakistan.'

President Clinton's India visit was the first turning point in the Indo-US security relationship. During his visit, President Clinton admitted that the US had ignored India over the preceding 20 years and indicated that it would end the passive impact caused by nuclear issues in future. In a joint communiqué which was termed 'India-US relations: A Vision for the 21st Century', the Indo-US relationship was termed a 'continuous, constructive in political area, and beneficial in economic arena' style of new partnership. This new style of partnership, according to certain independent analyses, was formed on the basis of both the sides deriving mutual strategic benefits, economic benefits, and socio-political benefits.

President George W. Bush continued the policy after he took office. When the then Indian Foreign Minister, Jaswant Singh, visited Washington in April 2001, Bush told him that the new administration would continue and strengthen its predecessor's policy to promote bilateral relations. After Bush declared his new Missile Defence plan on May 1, 2001, Condoleeza Rice, then Special Assistant to the President on National Security Affairs, broke protocol and took an initiative to call Singh and introduce the U.S. missile defence policy to him; US Deputy Secretary of State, Richard Armitage, also visited India in order to muster support. This is the first time that the US has valued India as an important partner in its strategic agenda.

The September 11, 2001, attack and the war on terrorism that followed provided a chance for the US and India to forge an even closer strategic cooperation. It has become a turning point in the Indo-US security relationship. The two countries together implemented a co-operative framework of relationships based on three dimensions: democracy, economy, and security. In the security field, the United States felt that India, as a de-facto nuclear state, had co-operative potential with the US on the proliferation issue. India actively supported the US missile defence plan as well as that on counter-terrorism. With the end of the US sanctions on India, the two countries improved and increased high level leadership communications, military contact, and economic co-operation. On November 9, 2001, President Bush told the visiting Indian Prime Minister, Atal Behari Vajpayee, that his administration was committed towards developing a fundamentally different relationship with India, based upon both trust and mutual values. After the meeting of the two top leaders, in a joint statement signed by both the countries, expressed their desire to enhance bilateral co-operation in the war against terrorism, and agreed to renew the activities of the Joint Working Group on Counter-terrorism. The Joint Working Group on Counter Terrorism was established in January 2000 as a first step towards increasing exchange and technology co-operation in the field of defence and security. Thereafter, the two countries maintained a high-level contact frequently and formulated a comprehensive co-operative agenda. Mohammed Ayoob believes that the United States and India can begin close co-operation in the following security arenas: (1) improve the region's security and stability; (2) counter terrorism; (3) promote democracy; (4) prevent nuclear proliferation, and (5) contain China during the first 10 years of the new century. As Stephen Cohen, the celebrated US specialist on South Asia security issues has commented, the United States and India's relationship was 'structurally changing'.

However, the partnership between the United States and India has not developed into a possibility of creating an alliance similar to that of the US-Japan or US-UK Alliance. The reasons are as follows:

First, India's five nuclear tests in 1998 greatly damaged the US-led international non-proliferation regime. Though the United States has adjusted its non-proliferation policy to some measure after Bush's taking office, India's nuclear tests and the United State's embargo afterward continue to have some negative effects on the Indo-US relationship. After 9/11, the US pressure on India to join the Nuclear Non-Proliferation Treaty (NPT) and Comprehensive Test Ban Treaty (CTBT) has lessened, although it is still to disappear. This has been perceived as a bargaining chip for the co-operation the United States seeks from India in its fight against terrorism.

Secondly, America realized that India and South Asia is the "most dangerous region in the world". In considering facts such as territorial disputes, the ethnic and religious divergence, and the nuclear confrontation between India and Pakistan; the need for Pakistan to support the United States in its counter-terrorism campaign; and South Asian and American relationships with other major countries in the region, the United States will not create an alliance in the region with any third country. Creating such an alliance to counter a third party does not benefit US interests.

Thirdly, Americans and Indians have very different views of a just international order. These differences have led to specific Indian-American disagreements in three important areas: the limits of humanitarian peacekeeping; the make-up of the UN Security Council; and the emergence of China. Most Indians have trouble accepting the principle of humanitarian interventions and fear that the US would extend the principle to South Asia - which means the United States would support the principle of 'self-determination' and press for a plebiscite in Kashmir. Similarly, the United States is unwilling to accept the Indian demand for a UN Security Council seat. Some Americans would regard it as a 'reward' for India's nuclear programme, and fear that this would further accelerate the trend towards nuclear weapons.

Finally, India and the United States are each groping for a strategy to cope with the emergence of China as a major world power. The United States is especially concerned about China's challenge to its world leadership, while India is especially concerned about China's future relationship with Pakistan. For India, creating or joining an alliance against China does not suit its national interests. One Chinese scholar pointed out that if India does not participate in the containment of China, China's development would lighten US strategic pressure on India. If India joins forces with the United States to contain China, the future of the 21st century will not belong to India. An Indian scholar argued that, as a developing country, India's priority is economic development. India has always attached the highest value to maintaining independence in making her foreign policy and sovereignty and avoided becoming part of an US or western agenda towards China. The United States is also unlikely to be willing to underwrite the costs of guaranteeing Indian security, and it would be foolish for India to entrust her security to a superpower with global interests. Furthermore, The United States and India both have substantive interests in China. Both within the United States and India, there are significant numbers of people that believe that China is a 'threat' to the interests of the two countries. Both countries also have people that advocate close engagement.

## United States' South Asia Policy

United States and India's relationship has changed in these various ways because the US has adjusted its strategy and policy in South Asia. The adjustment is demonstrated in the following areas:

### *United States Security Policy Towards India*

In terms of non-proliferation, the US urges India not to carry out nuclear tests, not to produce fissile materials, not to deploy missiles with nuclear warheads, to stop a dangerous nuclear and missile arms race and to control the export of sensitive materials. As anti-terrorism become the United States' greatest concern, it has reduced the pressure on India in the area of halting the spread of nuclear arms. In terms of Kashmir, there is a change from supporting Pakistan's policy which is implementing United Nations policy of giving the residents of Kashmir the right of plebiscite for its future to supporting India's policy of solving the problem through negotiation while respecting Kashmir residents' view. In terms of its relations with India and with Pakistan, the United States, in accordance with its own advantage, and comparing the power of different nations in South Asia, has slowly changed its focus to India.

An article published in *Washington Times*, quoting the Executive Director of US-India Commercial Committee, Michael Clark, stated that, for an American company, the most important thing was not the rising of the Indian middle class, but undoubtedly the information technology corporations in India, which have extraordinary potential. Some scholars in China concluded that the US policy toward India had changed from 'paying equal attention to India and Pakistan' in the early period of the post-Cold War era to 'focusing on India and reducing Pakistan' during the Clinton administration. The focus was once again changed to 'raising India and curbing Pakistan' when Bush took over and 'regarding Pakistan while respecting India' after the 9/11 attacks and the Enduring Freedom campaign in Afghanistan.

## Balance of Power to Power Advantage

The advantage is demonstrated in the following manner: (1) US obtains more influence in South Asia, compared to Russia and China; and (2) India wins the dominant position in the Indian subcontinent, compared to the other South Asian countries. Zbigniew Brzezinski, the eminent American strategist, recognized India as "the strongest state in South Asia and to some extent the regional hegemon." But at the same time, he thought that, "as a geostrategic player, India is not – at least, not to the same degree as either Russia or China – a source of geopolitical concern." However, this kind of judgment undervalues India's position and capability. The US recognizes India as the largest democracy in the world. India's economy increased by six per cent annually in the 1990's and it also has a growing information technology industry. The United States is India's largest trading partner, its biggest investor and its biggest provider of advanced technology. Besides, Indian Americans are playing an important role in shaping the United States' South Asia policy. During his trip to South Asia in March 2000, President Clinton visited India for seven days while halting symbolically in Pakistan only for some hours. It is obvious that U.S. places its relationship with India on the top of its South Asia policy framework. Compared with Pakistan, which experiences economical trouble and political turbulence and has only one-seventh of India's territory, Washington regards New Delhi as the largest democracy and a potentially important economic partner. Nevertheless, the United States is unlikely to discard its Cold War ally – Pakistan. Contrarily, the United States needs Pakistani support and co-operation as an Islamic 'frontline state' in the war against terrorism.

In sum, against the backdrop of the its preferential values in favour of democracy and its long-term benefits, and the comparison of power between different countries in South Asia, the United States changed its strategic policy of focusing on the balance of power during the Cold War to define and implement a new policy in South Asia: 'Focusing on India and Reducing on Pakistan.' This new policy attempted to go beyond the balance of power. However, judgments based on past traditions, concerns regarding the anti-terrorism efforts and the dangerous situation in South Asia, have diluted this perspective to one within which there is a 'focus on India while respecting Pakistan.' Thus, despite the initial intent, the US policy has not entirely gone beyond the balance of power.

### *Security Policy for the Asia-Pacific Region*

This is primarily demonstrated in the United States' increasing focus on the Asia-Pacific region or, more accurately, in the emergence of an integrated military strategy for the Europe-Atlantic region and the Asia-Pacific region. India and the Indian Ocean are expected to play an important role in such a geo-strategy. In the closing days of the Clinton administration, the containment of China gradually increased in importance as a factor influencing America's Asia-Pacific strategy. In addition to causing trouble on the Taiwan issue, the strategy of containment included reliance on Japanese and Indian Forces, and especially on the trend of enhancing India's capabilities to contain China. Giving the fact that counter-terrorism has became the primary issue in American strategy, the United States intends to use the war on terrorism to implement its military strategy in the Asia-Pacific region in addition to strengthening homeland security. The US military strategy in the Asia-Pacific region, consequently, includes securing influence and location in Central Asia; the limiting of Western Asia's development; and a return to South East Asia. Within this context, India and the Indian Ocean constitute the bridge for the United States in its regional military strategy.

### *The Change in United States and India's Relationship is also affected by Pakistan, China, and Russia*

While Pakistan has attempted to balance Indian superiority by seeking external ties, India has perceived this as a way of upsetting the natural balance of power in South Asia. For America, Pakistan's role in the United States' military strategy is especially important when America's personal interests are in jeopardy (anti-communism, containment of the erstwhile Soviet Union, and counter terrorism). As Pakistan is a traditional ally of the United States and a frontline state in fighting terrorism, without a more normal India-Pakistan relationship, the India-US relationship will remain highly sensitive to Indian perceptions of Washington's relationship with Islamabad.

It is widely accepted both in the United States and India that China is likely to pose a long-term strategic challenge to them. How will China deal with the outer world after it consolidates its economic and technological ascent? There are different assumptions in the United States and India. Some believe that the future role of China in the Asia-Pacific region will be stable and defensive, rather than destructive and offensive. Others assume that - based on aspects of its strategic culture - China may undertake an offensive foreign policy at the point of time when Chinese leaders think the international balance of power is in their favour. The United States and India have mutual interests, but different policies, in terms the nature of their future dealings with a rising China. There are also essential divergences on issues such as Taiwan and human rights between China and the United States. There are also basic differences on issues including border problems and non-proliferation between China and India.

With the end of the Cold War, the balance of power in South Asia has been upset, and the influence of Russia in South Asia has weakened. Russia still maintains a stable co-operative relationship with India, especially in the field of defence. In the joint statement of Russia-India strategic partnership issued on October 3, 2000, the two parties claimed "democratization of international relations" which is obliviously aimed at hegemonies. During President Putin's three-day visit to India in early December 2002, both sides signed the Delhi Declaration on Further Consolidation of Strategic Partnership, which heightened the bilateral relations to a new level. In conclusion, based on the rise of the Indian power, the importance of South Asia and the emergence of an Asia-Pacific perspective, the United States has gradually changed its balance of power policy. America is using the balance of power (method) to secure a power advantage (goal).

## China's Security Environment: Opportunities and Challenges

There are two defining characteristics of the security environment in the Asia-Pacific region after the end of Cold War: (1) The United States has become the only superpower in the world today. It is also the most important external power in Asia, and plays a key role in South Asian security; (2) China and India are emerging Asian powers. Each has a population of over a billion, possess nuclear weapons and numbers among the fastest growing economies in the world. Relations among these three countries will undoubtedly dominate the course of events within the Asia-Pacific region in the 21st century. Their interactions, and how they deal with the triangle will, to a large extent, influence future peace and stability in the region.

China and India, the two largest developing countries in the world, have a commonality of history, culture, economy and social characteristics, and profiles of development. Each applies itself to internal economic development, carries out an independent foreign policy and strives for a peaceful international environment. China and India are among what Brzezinski described as "five geo-strategic players", what Henry Kissinger listed as the "six big powers", and what Samuel Huntington pointed out are "core states of seven civilizations." China is a big power in East Asia while India is a big power in South Asia. Each has advantages and influence in their respective regions. However, they are not world powers that have global influence. In terms of institution and comprehensive strength, they cannot even be ranked as strong powers. For America, China and India, at one end, are two emerging markets offering economic benefits and developing opportunities. At the other end, China and India are also two transitional countries demonstrating uncertainty, from the United States' strategic point of view. What Washington fears most is the possibility of China and India, with Russia, forming an alliance based on a common understanding and interests of a new international political and economical order and a multi-polar world.

The United States and India, the largest democracies in the world, share common political values and strategic interests. Their common geo-political, economic and socio-political interests are advancing a co-operative agenda (which their differences over nuclear proliferation may not be able to halt). With the US–India relationship moving forward over the past two years, the two countries have developed a comprehensive co-operative framework covering democracy, economy and security. The United States now pays more attention to India's role as the largest democracy than it did before. India's continuous and fast-growing economy, especially its information technology industry, attracts great investment from transnational corporations based in America. In the security arena, the U.S. leadership has gradually begun to 'forget' India's nuclear tests and has come to recognize India as a *de facto* nuclear power, as also its preponderant position in South Asia. With India's support for America's unilateral action in missile defence, the US and India moved from divergence to co-operation in the field of non-proliferation. After 9/11, counter-terrorism has been a new field of strategic co-operation for U.S. and India. In a related development, Pakistan turns out to be less of an 'obstacle' for the US–India framework of relationships.

China and the United States, the largest developing and developed countries respectively, also have comprehensive common strategic interests. Besides large potential economic cooperation, they also share broad interests in other fields such as regional stability and the role and reform of the United Nations.

What is more likely is the emergence of a "soft balance of power" system among the three countries. Alternately, at one end, a vicious competitive relationship among the three countries may emerge, and the "soft balance of power" may be changed into a "hard balance of power" similar to that in the Cold War era, if one of them regards the development of relations between the two other countries as a challenge to its national interests, or if any two in this triad forge a relationship as a means to contain the third country. At the other end, it is possible for China, the US and India to establish a relatively harmonious relationship if they can seek out common views and interests, and push their differences aside to deal with bilateral and trilateral relations within a strategic perspective.

## *China's Security Environment*

South Asia is one of the most unstable regions in world today. Focusing on the Kashmir issue, the conflict between India and Pakistan has lasted for more than half a century, during which three wars have been fought. The Kashmir issue includes many conflicting factors: territorial dispute, ethnic and religious divergence, political opposition and nuclear confrontation. One can also find in the Kashmir issue three threats for today's world:

national separatism, religious extremism and cross-border terrorism. India and, immediately thereafter, Pakistan tested their nuclear weapons and then became *de facto* nuclear powers in the year 1998. The United States has initiated a counter-terrorism campaign after 9/11, which focuses substantially on this region. These various elements are new factors in the conflict over Kashmir between India and Pakistan.

Nuclear proliferation in South Asia makes the Kashmir issue more dangerous. According to the assessment of the Institute for Science and International Security, if all of the plutonium available to it is made into nuclear weapons, India can produce 45-95 warheads; while if all of the plutonium and weapon-grade uranium available to Pakistan is converted to nuclear weapons, this could produce 30-50 warheads. A May 2002 report published in *The New Scientist* pointed out that, if a limited nuclear war were to break out between India and Pakistan, 10 small warheads used in the five biggest cities of each of these countries, respectively, would kill three million people and injure even more. The international community at large fears that a war between the two nuclear countries could open a Pandora's box and lead to the world's first nuclear war.

The struggle against terrorism makes the Kashmir issue even more complicated. After 9/11, India has sought increasingly and far more vigorously to establish the connections between terrorism and Pakistan. India has condemned the two Pakistan-based groups, the Lashkar-e-Toiba and Jaish-e-Mohammed, that led the terrorist attack on India's Parliament on December 13, 2001, and that are also responsible for cross-border terrorist activities. Pakistan, on the other hand, actively works with the United States in the military campaign against terrorism in Afghanistan and claims that it is opposed to any fundamentalist organization or individuals who engage in terrorist activity in the name of Kashmir at home or abroad. However, President Musharraf has also declared that Pakistan would continue to support the Kashmiri struggle for independence 'morally, politically and diplomatically'.

In conclusion, nuclear tests and counter-terrorism make South Asia an international hotspot and a focus of global attention. In terms of non-proliferation and anti-terrorism, China and the South Asian countries share common interests and a potential for cooperation. China borders most South Asian countries. Regional stability in South Asia is, consequently, an important guarantee for China's west and southwest security environment. China hopes that both India and Pakistan will try to solve their problems by political and diplomatic means. China's President, Jiang Zemin, recently made mention of an old Chinese saying, 'peace favours both and conflict injures either', when he attended the First Summit of the Member States of the Conference on Interaction and Confidence Building Measures in Asia (CICA) which was convened in Almaty, Kazakhstan, on June 3-5, 2002.

## *America Factor in Sino-India Relationships*

India, in the assessment of one Indian scholar, has always viewed close US-China relations with misgivings and feared that they might adversely affect her interests. Three factors dominate this evaluation: (1) During the 1971 India-Pakistan war, the US and China jointly supported Pakistan. The US had sent its Seventh Fleet into the Bay of Bengal to threaten India. (2) In India's perception, the United States was guilty by omission of ignoring China's actions in actively building up Pakistan's nuclear deterrence against India through the nineteen eighties, because both China and Pakistan were US allies in fighting the Soviet Union in Afghanistan. (3) Soon after India's nuclear tests in 1998, the United States and China issued a Joint Communiqué to condemn these.

In comparison to the up-and-down Sino-U.S. relationship framework, the US-India relationship has witnessed an upswing after the end of the Cold War. The perception that regards an 'emerging China' as a threat is beginning to dominate policy-making circles in both the US and India. This will be harmful for both Sino-US and Sino-India relations. For America, China and India are two major powers that can influence security affairs in the Asia-Pacific, especially in East Asia and South Asia. China and India are also populous, transitional and emerging big powers. Both China and India regards their relations with the US as their most important external relationship.

The economic development of China and India needs America's cooperation and support. At the same time, America needs the huge markets of the two big Asian countries. The United States could be a positive factor for Sino-India relationships – if it tries to promote regional stability in South Asia and help China and India's economic modernization. It could, as well, cast itself in a negative role – when it plays the 'India card' in its dealings with China; or plays the 'China card' in developing its relations with India.

Within China, in recent years, there has been a fundamental reassessment of South Asia and its importance in geo-politics, as well as of India and its role in regional affairs. The nature of Sino-Indian relationships should be "good neighbours in geo-politics, good friends in economic cooperation, and good partners in international affairs." Such a relationship must be established on the basis of their common sense and understanding of mutual interests. Through economic co-operation and regional stability, China, the US and India should and would be able to reach a 'win-win-win' situation.

## India-U.S. Relations: A Vision for the 21st Century

At the dawn of a new century, President Clinton and Prime Minister Vajpayee resolve to create a closer and qualitatively new relationship between the United States and India. We are two of the world's largest democracies. We are nations forged from many traditions and faiths, proving year after year that diversity is our strength. From vastly different origins and experiences, we have come to the same conclusions: that freedom and democracy are the strongest bases for both peace and prosperity, and that they are universal aspirations, constrained neither by culture nor levels of economic development

There have been times in the past when our relationship drifted without a steady course. As we now look towards the future, we are convinced that it is time to chart a new and purposeful direction in our relationship. Globalization is erasing boundaries and building networks between nations and peoples, economies and cultures. The world is increasingly coming together around the democratic ideals India and the United States have long championed and lived by.

Together, we represent a fifth of the world's people, more than a quarter of the world's economy. We have built creative, entrepreneurial societies. We are leaders in the information age.

The currents of commerce and culture that link our societies run strong and deep. In many ways, the character of the 21st century world will depend on the success of our cooperation for peace, prosperity, democracy and freedom. That presents us with an opportunity, but also a profound responsibility to work together. Our partnership of shared ideals leads us to seek a natural partnership of shared endeavors.

In the new century, India and the United States will be partners in peace, with a common interest in and complementary responsibility for ensuring regional and international security. We will engage in regular consultations on, and work together for, strategic stability in Asia and beyond. We will bolster joint efforts to counter terrorism and meet other challenges to regional peace. We will strengthen the international security system, including in the United Nations, and support the United Nations in its peacekeeping efforts. We acknowledge that tensions in South Asia can only be resolved by the nations of South Asia. India is committed to enhancing cooperation, peace and stability in the region.

India and the United States share a commitment to reducing and ultimately eliminating nuclear weapons, but we have not always agreed on how to reach this common goal. The United States believes India should forgo nuclear weapons. India believes that it needs to maintain a credible minimum nuclear deterrent in keeping with its own assessment of its security needs. Nonetheless, India and the U.S. are prepared to work together to prevent the proliferation of nuclear weapons and their means of delivery. To this end, we will persist with and build upon the productive bilateral dialogue already underway.

We reaffirm our respective voluntary commitments to forgo further nuclear explosive tests. We will work together and with others for an early commencement of negotiations on a treaty to end the production of fissile materials for nuclear weapons. We have both shown strong commitments to export controls, and will continue to strengthen them. We will work together to prevent the spread of dangerous technologies. We are committed to build confidence and reduce the chances of miscalculation. We will pursue our security needs in a restrained and responsible manner, and will not engage in nuclear and missile arms races. We will seek to narrow our differences and increase mutual understanding on non-proliferation and security issues. This will help us to realize the full potential of Indo-U.S. relations and contribute significantly to regional and global security.

The true measure of our strength lies in the ability of our people to shape their destiny and to realize their aspirations for a better life. That is why the United States and India are and will be allies in the cause of democracy. We will share our experience in nurturing and strengthening democratic institutions the world over and fighting the challenge to democratic order from forces such as terrorism. We will cooperate with others to launch an international Community of Democracies this year. The United States applauds India's success in opening its economy, its achievements in science and technology, its commitment to a new wave of economic expansion and reform, and its determination to bring the benefits of economic growth to all its people. Our nations pledge to reduce impediments to bilateral trade and investment and to expand commerce between us, especially in the emerging knowledge-based industries and high-technology areas.

We will work together to preserve stability and growth in the global economy as well. And we will join in an unrelenting battle against poverty in the world, so that the promise of a new economy is felt everywhere and no nation is left behind. That is among the fundamental challenges of our time. Opening trade and resisting protectionism are the best means for meeting it. We support an open, equitable and transparent rule-based multilateral trading system, and we will work together to strengthen it. We agree that developed countries should embrace policies that offer developing countries the opportunity to grow, because growth is the key to rising incomes and rising standards. At the same time, we share the conviction that human development also requires empowerment of people and availability of basic freedoms.

As leaders in the forefront of the new high-technology economy, we recognize that countries can achieve robust economic growth while protecting the environment and taking action to combat climate change. We will do our part to meet the global environmental challenges, including climate change and the impacts of air and water pollution on human health. We also pledge a common effort to battle the infectious diseases that kill people and retard progress in so many countries. India is at the forefront of the global effort that has brought us to the threshold of the eradication of polio. With leadership, joint research, and application of modern science, we can and will do the same for the leading killers of our time, including AIDS, malaria and tuberculosis.

We are proud of the cooperation between Indians and Americans in advancing frontiers of knowledge. But even as we unravel the mysteries of time and space, we must continue to apply our knowledge to older challenges: eradicating human suffering, disease and poverty. In the past, our cooperation helped ease mass hunger in the world. In the future, it will focus as well on the development of clean energy, health, and education.

Our partnership is not an end in itself, but a means to all these ends. And it is reinforced by the ties of scholarship, commerce, and increasingly of kinship among our people. The industry, enterprise and cultural contributions of Americans of Indian heritage have enriched and enlivened both our societies.

Today, we pledge to deepen the Indian-American partnership in tangible ways, always seeking to reconcile our differences through dialogue and engagement, always seizing opportunities to advance the countless interests we have in common.

As a first step, President Clinton has invited Prime Minister Vajpayee to visit Washington at a mutually convenient opportunity, and the Prime Minister has accepted that invitation. Henceforth, the President of the United States and the Prime Minister of India should meet regularly to institutionalize our dialogue.

We have also agreed on and separately outlined an architecture of additional high-level consultations, and of joint working groups, across the broad spectrum of areas in which we are determined to institutionalize our enhanced cooperation. And we will encourage even stronger people-to-people ties.

For India and the United States, this is a day of new beginnings. We have before us for the first time in 50 years the possibility to realize the full potential of our relationship. We will work to seize that chance, for our benefit and all those with whom we share this increasingly interdependent world.

### *Institutional Dialogue Between the United States and India*

1. During the visit of President Clinton to Delhi in March 2000, President Clinton and Prime Minister Vajpayee agreed as part of their vision for the future relationship that a regular, wide-ranging dialogue is important for achieving the goal of establishing closer and multifaceted relations between India and the United States and for the two countries to work jointly for promotion of peace and prosperity in the 21st century. The two leaders agreed on a number of steps to intensify and institutionalize the dialogue between India and the United States.
2. The President of the United States and Prime Minister of India will hold regular bilateral 'Summits' in alternating capitals or elsewhere, including on the occasions of multilateral meetings, to review bilateral relations and consult on international developments and issues. They will remain in frequent contact by telephone and through letters.
3. The two countries will also hold an Annual Foreign Policy Dialogue at the level of the Secretary of State of the United States and External Affairs Minister of India. This dialogue will be broad-based and touch upon all aspects of US-India relations, including considering the work of other groups as appropriate.
4. The two countries also consider the ongoing Dialogue on Security and Non-proliferation between the Deputy Secretary of State of the United States and External Affairs Minister of India important for improving mutual understanding on bilateral, regional and international security matters. They agreed that this dialogue should continue and take place semi-annually or as often as considered desirable by both sides. The Principals of this dialogue will establish Expert Groups on specific issues as considered desirable and appropriate.
5. Foreign Office Consultations between the Under Secretary of State for Political Affairs of the United States and Foreign Secretary of India will continue. The two leaders believe that close cooperation between the two countries is a factor of stability in the politically and culturally diverse and

rapidly transforming Asia. A Dialogue on Asian Security will also be conducted as part of the Foreign Office Consultations. The two sides will also stay in close touch and consult on international democracy initiatives.

6. The two leaders consider combating international terrorism as one of the most important global challenges. They expressed satisfaction at the establishment of the Joint Working Group on Counter-terrorism and its productive first meeting in February 2000. They agree that the Joint Working Group should continue to meet regularly and become an effective mechanism for the two countries to share information and intensify their cooperation in combating terrorism.
7. The two leaders see an enormous potential for enhancement of economic and business relations between the two countries in the Knowledge Age. They decided to institutionalize bilateral economic dialogue. They will keep themselves informed and follow developments in the bilateral economic dialogue closely through a high-level coordinating group. The coordinating group will be led on the US side by the White House with the support of the State Department, and on the Indian side by the Prime Minister's Office with the support of the Ministry of External Affairs.

The Coordinating Group will develop a common economic agenda for and undertake preparations for the Heads of Government meetings. With broad inter-agency and inter-ministerial representations at senior official levels, it would convene regularly to facilitate close coordination on the various issues raised in the ministerial dialogues and ensure that discussions therein complement and reinforce broad economic and foreign policy objectives, including the deepening of bilateral cooperation on high technology and information technology issues.

US-India Financial and Economic Forum: The US Secretary of the Treasury and the Indian Minister of Finance will host a forum on finance and investment issues, macroeconomic policy and international economic developments at regular intervals. Their meetings at the ministerial level would be supplemented by sub-Cabinet meetings and involve, as appropriate, the participation of the Securities and Exchange Commission, Federal Reserve, Council of Economic Advisors, and other officials of the US Government and the Securities and Exchange Board of India, Reserve Bank of India, and other officials of the Government of India.

US-India Commercial Dialogue: The US Secretary of Commerce and Minister of Commerce and Industry of India will lead a dialogue to deepen ties between the Indian and American Business communities. The dialogue will encompass regular government-to-government meetings to be held in conjunction with private sector meetings. Its aim will be to (a) facilitate trade, and (b) maximize investment opportunities across a broad range of economic sectors, including information technology, infrastructure, biotechnology, and services. Participation will include, as appropriate, representatives of other Cabinet agencies and ministries on both sides. Close contact will be maintained with business associations, and activities will be planned with the benefit of such private sector input, including the establishment of subcommittees to pursue specific projects or sectoral issues of mutual interest.

US-India Working Group on Trade: The United States Trade Representative and the Ministry of Commerce and other concerned Ministries/Departments of the Government of India will engage in regular discussion to enhance cooperation on trade policy. As appropriate, individual trade issues could be examined in greater depth with the participation of other agencies with corresponding responsibilities and through creation of sub-groups. The Group will serve as a locus of consultation on a broad range of trade-related issues, including those pertaining to the World Trade Organization. The Group will receive inputs from the private sector (including trade policy issues identified in the US-India Commercial Dialogue) as appropriate.

The two leaders consider cooperation between the two countries in energy and environment an important part of their vision for the future. They have agreed to set up a Joint Consultative Group on Clean Energy and Environment. The Group will hold periodic ministerial/high level meetings as desirable and appropriate and will lay emphasis on collaborative projects, developing and deploying clean energy technologies, public and private sector investment and cooperation, and climate change and other environmental issues. The Co-conveners of the Group will be the Department of State of the United States and the Ministry of External Affairs of India.

The two leaders believe that the strong scientific resources of the two countries provide excellent opportunities for scientific collaboration between them. They agree to set up a US-India Science and Technology Forum. The Forum shall promote research and development, the transfer of technology, the creation of a comprehensive electronic reference source for US-India science and technology cooperation, and the electronic exchange and dissemination of information on US-India science and technology cooperation, and other programs consistent with the previous practice of the US-India Foundation.

6

# Capability Relation Management in Defence Systems and Relation

## Introduction

"It is not the strongest of the species that survive, nor the most intelligent but the one most responsive to change."

*Charles Darwin*

Engineering activities in future defence systems and capability development vary, but all result in evolutions that occur in a context of Systems-of-Systems (SoS) where a defence organisation must maintain a sustained, sustainable and controlled SoS evolution as a whole. Change in defence is inevitable. Defence has to embrace change and manage it in order to survive and become more effective and responsive. The concept of System-of-Systems (SoS) has been extensively examined, and is broadly acknowledged as a challenging issue because of its high inherent complexity. For a SoS to achieve its desired functionality, its component systems will need to interact in a prescribed and predictable manner. Modelling these interactions, their dependencies, and the impact of changes to any system on the SoS is essential to modelling the SoS. Therefore, an important component of managing development and evolution within a SOS is managing the relations between the component systems. The inherent complexity implied by SoS translates to a similar complexity to managing relations within a SoS. The reality, that individual systems are continuously developed and evolved, only adds to this complexity. Currently, Defence lacks the capacity to manage relations systematically within a SoS during the analysis, planning and development of systems and capabilities.

The responses from capabilities and systems to evolutionary change occurring within a SoS context are determined by the ways that their relations are handled both internally and externally. Relation management is also a critical issue to those commonly used engineering disciplines and approaches, such as Systems Engineering (SE) and architectural approaches (e.g. DoD C4ISR AF). However, it has not been fully explored and addressed in terms of requirements, principles, methods or solutions. Within a SoS context, the relation management of systems and capabilities is an architecture issue that does not belong to individual systems or capabilities, but is instead shared by all involved ones. As a result, it cannot be the responsibility of developers of individual systems and should be addressed at the level of SoS or an organisation [Chen, 2003].

This paper introduces an architecture-model based approach to systems and capability relation management. It firstly classifies concepts and classes related to systems and capability management, and then explicitly defines relations between these concepts and classes. The definitions of concepts, classes and relations form a knowledge schema for establishing a body of knowledge for defence capability and systems management. The approach can let the defence develop an architecture management system that can store and manage knowledge and information of capability, systems and architecture products in context.

## Background, Challenges and Issues

Constantly changing defence requirements, capabilities and systems are challenging the ability of Defence to handle the complexity and relations of systems and capabilities, and questioning its confidence in managing future planning, development and operation. Defence experience in its efforts to achieve many new defence concepts, such as Networked Centric Warfare (NCW) and Network Enabled Capability (NEC), highlights the great difficulties in understanding, communicating, and representing these concepts. There are further substantial difficulties in migrating these concepts into operational and integrated systems and capabilities. Underpinning many of these difficulties are the difficulties in managing the changing relations between systems and capabilities, particularly within a SoS context. These difficulties and challenges face all main Defence business areas from strategic planning, capability study, acquisition and development to operation. Thus, there is an obvious need for Defence to seek better solutions.

## *Relations between Systems*

A collection of systems, with an overriding mission or purpose, is generally regarded as comprising a SoS. Various relations exist between these systems. Within a Defence SoS context, systems and capabilities are related in the following possible basic manners:

### *Structure-related*

System A and System B are structure-related if System A has one of the following relationships to System B:

- System A is a component of System B; or
- System A is a basis of System B.

#### *Function-related*

System A and System B are function-related if to perform its own functions, System A requires certain functions or services delivered by System B. Information-related System A and System B are information-related if there are requirements for information flows or information exchanges between two systems. In other words, there is a connectivity and information reach-ability between them.

#### *Operation-related*

System A and System B are operation-related if they are both used in an operation scenario to jointly fulfil a mission.

#### *Generation-related*

System A and System B are generation-related if System A will be a replacement of System B. Due to the features and complexity of systems integration and deployment, in addition to these basic manners, there are other types of relations. These include indirect relations, inheritance relations, dynamic relations, naming of relations and tightness of relations. A system may have either the same relation or different relations to a number of systems.

Relation issues exist throughout the whole life cycle of defence capability management. Different phases, stages or contexts of the life cycle face different relation issues, and deal with different relation contexts in different timeframes.

The relations between systems and capabilities change when systems or capabilities evolve. A sustained, sustainable, controlled and managed evolution of defence SoS will be difficult to achieve if capability and system relations become unmanageable. Better relation management leads to better responses to changes. To cope with the challenge of successfully managing continually evolving capabilities and systems, Defence needs to develop its ability to manage context, as well as managing relations between systems and capabilities, in terms of their structures, functions, effects and information, but also the impacts generated from their deployment, use, configuration and development plans.

### *Challenges and Issues*

The relations between systems and capabilities are complicated since they are characterised by the following features:

- Managing system and capability relations is an issue concerning the whole life cycle of SoS, including planning, development, management and operation of individual systems and capabilities to the whole SoS;
- The relations can be either conceptualised and represented explicitly or implicitly understood in people' perceptions;
- The relations can be either static and fixed or dynamic;
- The relations are kinds of binding with different degrees of looseness or tightness;
- Architecturally speaking, the relations are determined by the interfaces between systems or the manner by which they are integrated.

There are additional questions such as:

- Who should be responsible for definitions and management of the relations; and
- Where and how the relations should be defined and managed.

There are a number of challenges in capability and systems relation management. The first is the variety of contexts where issues of relation management arise and need to be addressed, Relation management is salient to all business areas from strategic planning, capability study, acquisition, systems development, from preparedness to operations, and from individual capabilities or systems and various SoS contexts to the whole force. Secondly, there is a high level complexity in capability and systems relation management since it is not only a technical issue but also a cultural and management issue. The third challenge relates to knowledge management. Knowledge of capability and systems relations currently exist in people's minds and are described and represented differently in various planning and development documents that are kept separately in different sites. This knowledge needs to be captured and maintained in a form that is accessible to other potential users. Finally, there are engineering methodologies or disciplines, such as Systems Engineering, Information Management System, and Software Engineering, which deal with relations of systems from mainly a single system development perspective but not from a viewpoint of SoS management.

The relations between systems and capabilities are important for the whole life cycle of defence capability management. Fundamentally speaking, these relations are critical features and artefacts of the defence capability architecture. They are complicated and dynamic because of the constant evolution of defence capabilities and systems stemming from on-going technological development, changing defence requirements and the increasing complexity of the defence environment. Without specifications and representations of these features and artefacts, Defence will experience great difficulties in evolving its organisation and its capabilities. The investigation into the issues related to capability and system relation management reveals two important facts. In the current practice, firstly, missing definitions and specifications of these relations indicate that there are holes in the defence capability and defence information environment architecture representation as a whole. Secondly, Defence cannot at present systematically and effectively deal with architecture features and artefacts of its whole capability because of inability in handling relations between capabilities and systems.

In the current practice, these relations are, at best, fully defined by projects that manage acquisitions of individual systems and capabilities. In other words, they are handled mainly at a project level between individual systems and capabilities. They are not considered as fundamental features of the whole defence capability architecture and are not explicitly mandated and shared by other stakeholders.

## Relation Management Rationales

This exploration of the requirements, challenges and issues regarding capabilities and systems relation management suggests a need to develop a method, drawn from both engineering and management perspectives, that can help Defence systematically manage relations of capabilities and systems, throughout their life cycles, in a context of SoS. Such a method must first help classify, identify and define concepts and their conceptual relations in the context of the planning, development and management of capabilities and systems. The method then also needs to help capture, represent and manage various these relations.

In order to address the requirements, challenges and issues, the relation management for systems and capabilities is aimed to achieve seven main objectives:

- Concept management;
- Conceptual relation management;
- Systems relation management;
- Interface relation management;
- Provision of linkage and traceability of system (and capability?) knowledge;
- Throughout the life cycle of SoS; and
- Being part of the architecture practice;

The high complexity of systems and capabilities' architectures results from its diverse applications in relation to various concepts, such as scenario, capability, platform and system, and their use throughout the whole Defence Capability Systems Life Cycle from planning, development, acquisition, operation, deployment and maintenance. This makes the concepts and relation management be one of important components and fundamental feature of defence architecture data/knowledge management. These relations should be fully explored and managed at the enterprise level from the following perspectives:

- Architecture relation
- Acquisition relation
- Operation relation

The relation management for capability and systems is established on a basis of two components: *concept and conceptual relation management,* and *object relation management.*

## *Concept and Conceptual Relation Management*

In the real world, all concepts (such as scenario, capability, platform, system, architecture, project and document) are context-based. The context of a concept is defined by the definition of its attributes and its relation to other concepts. A relation between two concepts is a kind of conceptual linkage that somehow binds the concepts together. Without context specifications, a concept can mean different things to different people Understanding a concept means an understanding of its all definitions of attributes and relations to others.

Any concept may have many "real world" instantiations. Using object-oriented terminology, an object is an instance of a concept. The distinction between two objects that belong to the same concept can also be made according to their contexts. The context of an object is specified by its relations to other objects, and understanding an object requires a full awareness of its attribute values and relations in context.

A relation between two concepts is defined as a characterised linkage with a specific meaning. A relation between objects is an instance of the relation defined between two concepts, or, using object-oriented terminology, two classes). Knowledge of conceptual relations is sometimes documented but often exists only in individual's minds, and is incomplete and inconsistent depending on their understandings. Given a lack of suitable artefacts, methods or mechanisms, it is hard for people to share their knowledge concerning these relations. There has been no method or mechanism to manage them. Fundamentally speaking, concept management in large organisations like Defence, is an issue of knowledge management.

There is, however, an important issue to address when considering concept management. There are often situations where two real world objects, which are quite different things, are mistakenly said to represent the "same" concept. The situation often arises because of a lack of a suitably clear terminology and a general lack of precision in the use of language. Within Defence, confusion often arises when discussions are related to scenarios, capability, systems or architecture. The approach to this issue is to introduce subclasses under the concept class. This mirrors the situation in the real world, where, for example, a communications system is a type of system, and Link 11 is an instance of a communications system. In other words, a class representing a concept may have a number of subclasses;. Hence a concept can be viewed as a super class for these classes. The motivation to define and manage concepts as class hierarchies is to better capture the semantics within the form of the concept model, through the exploration and definition of the attributes and relations of the subclasses. For the remainder of the paper, a concept is treated as a class in order to avoid possible confusion.

Concept modelling, therefore, needs to distinguish between different concepts (for instance, a system and a project) and where necessary, to define different classes for the same concept (for example, operational architecture view and system architecture view are different classes of the same concept "architecture view") in a concept hierarchy. In other words, the initial stage of concept management requires the establishment of concept taxonomies large concept hierarchies are organised into class packages. There is an analogy with good software engineering practice. The classes within a package should be cohesive, and the classes between packages should only be loosely coupled.

## *Relation Management*

In order for the relation management for capability and systems to succeed, the relations between concepts/classes must be systematically studied, explored and explicitly defined. The definitions of relations between concepts or classes can be seen as the establishment of a kind of ontology among the taxonomical structures of class definitions. The class and relation definitions achieved in such a combination of taxonomical structures and ontology linkage lay a foundation for relation management. This approach makes it feasible to specify, maintain and systematically manage the relations between classes, and that the relations between classes can eventually be used correctly and successfully.

A requirement to achieve good relation management is the development of an environment or system that can serve as a basis for: managing concepts and objects in context; conducting analysis, synthesis and evaluation of values and relations of objects; handling complexity; exploring and studying dependency; maintaining traceability; and visualising concepts, objects and their relations and dependencies. Hence relation management will be achieved through two main activities, that is, conceptual (or class) relation definitions and object context management.

*Class relation Definition*

The relations defined between the concepts of the conceptual models are explicit descriptions and representations of organisational knowledge. They serve as an ontology that underpins the overall conceptual model. Through knowledge engineering of the concept relations, the conceptual model can become a knowledge schema that can support organisation and management of architecture features and artefacts concerning relations between capabilities and systems. Neither the knowledge nor the resulting architecture features and artefacts are currently properly captured and managed.

Through defining and modelling concepts and their relations, the conceptual model becomes a foundation for a sharable body of defence capability architecture knowledge. The model by itself, however, does not directly handle relations between objects although they are defined in it.

*Object Context Management*

From a modelling perspective, an object's potential relations are defined according to the relation definitions of the class that the object belongs to. They may be created either when the object is created or subsequent to its creation. From a user's perspective, it must also be possible to modify an object's relations when there is a need. Object context management requires an environment that is an object store, developed on the basis of the elicited conceptual model, that can enable the desired relation management features. In such an environment, all stored objects require that their full context descriptions, in terms of relations to other objects, are stored as well. Through specifying the relations between capabilities and systems, these architecture features and artefacts, which are currently missing in the defence capability and defence information environment management as a whole, will be captured and managed.

## Approaches to the Relation Management

Based on the investigation into the features, requirements, and rationales of the relation management, this paper introduces a concept, called the Defence Architecture Information Model (DAIM), which provides a model-based solution for Defence to establish the relation management for systems and capabilities and enhance its systems engineering, software engineering and architecture practice.

In order to ensure the success in the relation management, DAIM is designed, as expected, to have a joint power of knowledge presentation and organisation that is usually delivered from three separate methods, that is, taxonomy, ontology and metadata. The approach to DAIM development has been to use an object-oriented modelling language that meets the requirements not only for concept and conceptual relation management. It may also serve as the basis of an object context management system based on the development of an object store which in turn may be based on an object-oriented database.

A class is defined in DAIM because:

- It represents a concept (e.g. scenario, project, system, and architecture) which there are real world objects associated with, and
- It has its unique features in terms of attributes, relations and methods or rules that jointly defined its context in DAIM, and
- A concept or class and its associated objects needs to be managed by DAIM, and
- A class is considered to be useful in managing systems relation and architecture data.

There are different ways to define and model real world concepts and classes even using the same approach. In order to ensure that DAIM can play the roles discussed earlier, the main objectives of the development team were:

- Firstly, class hierarchies defined in DAIM should cover all information / knowledge entities related to major platforms, systems, scenarios, capabilities and their requirements, projects and architecture resources. In other words, all these concepts will be represented within DAIM such that objects of the relevant classes can then be created to represent real world objects (or entities).
- Through DAIM, secondly, the relations between classes are defined explicitly such that its objects can be linked to other objects defined in the relevant classes.
- Finally, DAIM was developed in the Unified Modelling Language (UML), to serve as a logical data model for the architecture repository development.

## *Systems and SoS Context*

A system can be broadly defined as an integrated set of elements that accomplish a defined objective. People from different disciplines or business interests have different perspectives of what a "system" is. Due to a diversity of use of the term, it is suggested that a system class in the DAIM is an abstraction of a real world system with the following features:

- A clearly defined system boundary;
- Based on a grand design;
- With a system life cycle from planning to retirement/ disposal; and
- Has the general features of a system (e.g. lifecycle, component systems, interfaces).

The issues and interests concerned from a system perspective are:

- Internal design of a specific system;
- Interfaces to other systems;
- Development process.

System class is taxonomically further defined with a number of subclasses:

- Business system
- Military operation system
- Platform system
- Information-based system
- Business support system
- C2 support system
- Intelligence support system
- Reconnaissance system
- Surveillance system
- Infrastructure system
- Federation system

There are a variety of relations defined between these system classes. These relation definitions will be used to help specify relations that exist between real world systems when their associated objects are created in the object store. The relations specified between real world system objects will fill a gap in current defence capability architecture descriptions.

The federation system is a site-based federation of all C4ISREW systems, bound to deliver joint functions. Such a site can be either a capability platform, like a warship, or a command centre, where required C4ISR component systems work together. As a communication infrastructure system, each individual C4ISR system, if it is a distributed systems, can be used or integrated into different federation systems on different sites. In other words, a federation system is structured-related to individual C4ISR systems. Or, individual C4ISR systems can be part of a federation system or many different federation systems. Capturing these system relations should enable and support many system and architecture analysis activities.

Also included in the System Package is a SoS Context Class. There are a lot of debates on whether a SoS should be considered as "a system".

In DAIM, we choose to define a SoS context that has the following features. It:

- Has a context of interests;
- Involves a collection of systems, nodes and objects;

- Has no grand design;
- Has no life cycle for the context, but each system has its own life cycle;
- Has a common purpose or function when all involved systems, nodes and objects are working together;
- Has a context evolution resulting from systems evolution;
- May be described in the form of an architecture.

Unlike the systems classes, the issues concerned from a SoS context perspective include:

- Joint effects
- Interoperability levels and analysis
- Information sharing;
- Planning, coordination and management of systems evolution.

There are sub-classes of the SoS Context class. These include:

- C2 information environment;
    - o Force domain (e.g. Army, Navy,..);
    - o Operation domain;
    - o Region domain;
- Capability information environment;
- Business information environment;

There are strong and important relations between instances (or objects) of *System Class* and *SoS Context Class*. A system instance is:

- defined and studied;
- operated, used and deployed;
- managed and maintained;
- planned, evolved, improved, designed and developed in the context of one or more objects of SoS context class.

A SoS context object is about:

- a shared understanding or common interests among
- shared requirements for
- a joint effort or function/ capability of;
- a shared environment/situation of;

- an agreement among a number of systems involved in the context.

A system class object can be associated with a number of objects in different subclasses of the SoS context class.

A SoS context (object) can be considered as a system if:

- all relations among involved systems are defined and stable; and
- all involved systems share a common life cycle; and
- there is an authority of control or ownership; and
- there is a need.

## *System Classes and Relations Management*

The System and SoS context class hierarchies, together with relation management, should strengthen architecture management for the Defence capability process. It has the potential to capture the supplementary system knowledge regarding SoS architectures required to support Defence's architecture activities and concurrent engineering practice.

The taxonomical structure captured in the System Package can help users to identify system types and their relations to other system objects in the context of capability and system development. The exercise of creating system objects with its context information and managing this information throughout a system's life cycle can significantly improve the awareness of its relations and impact on other components of DAIM.

The DAIM-based repository will have a rich repertoire of systems relations, including *pattern-with, component, based-on, part-of, interoperate-with,* and *used-by*. These relation often have different impacts on evolutions of SoS and require different strategies in development and management. The pattern-with relation, for example, defines a binding or collaborative relation of two systems that is not as strong as the interoperate-with relation, which requires detailed specifications and interface design. The System Class package is one of the six main class packages included in the DAIM. As a result, the relation management achieved through the DAIM is established across all these class packages. All knowledge relating to the core concepts (scenario, capability, system, architecture and project) can be integrated through relation management and form a body of knowledge on systems and capabilities throughout their life cycles. With the support of such a systematically established body of knowledge, capability planners, analysts and other stakeholders can, easily and effectively access relevant information and knowledge linking strategic scenarios, operation or exercise scenarios, capability development scenarios, to systems, capabilities or platforms involved. In the current practice, unfortunately, these relations across concepts are not defined, specified and managed. They are also missing components of SoS architecture.

In traditional practices of Systems Engineering and architecture development, systems relations are addressed in the activities of design and development. In the phase of design, systems relations must be fully investigated and defined. The issues related to interfaces and composition then need to be addressed through design and represented in the form of architecture that guides the implementation and evolutions of SoS. The relation management can effectively enhance the applications of Systems Engineering and architecture practice.

## Benefits and Applications

The DAIM is a foundation to generate an integrated architecture capability for planning and managing Defence capability and its information environment. Through using the well-developed mechanism for the relation management, DAIM can play a number of important roles in defence capability knowledge engineering and supporting systems and capability management.

With the established knowledge schema that can manage complicated relations among concepts such as operation scenarios, capabilities, systems, and architectures, and their real world objects, DAIM provides the basis for a solution for enterprise-wide architecture knowledge integration and management, that addresses three important issues, that is, defence scenario management, systems and capability relation management, and architecture data management, in an integrated manner. As discussed earlier, relation management requires an object store as a solution for implementation of the object context management. DAIM can then be used as a data schema for architecture repository development. Based on an object store, it would provide a facility to enable traceability, dependency analysis, synthesis, visualisation, simulation, SoS analysis and experimentation, and capability analysis and development. The repository can provide context descriptions of all DAIM objects and can help generate, understand and synthesize "big pictures" of various SoS contexts of interest from capability and systems planning and development. The dependency is a kind of relations that exists between two objects of the same class or different classes. Dependencies can be classified into the following categories:

- Function dependency;
- Structure dependency;
- Information dependency
- Effect dependency;
- Time dependency; and
- Financial dependency.

One of the great challenges in planning, managing and developing SoS is to develop an ability to handle traceability when dealing with "big pictures" of defence capability in various contexts and for different purposes.

The establishment of mechanisms for the relation definition and object context management provides a basis and support for highly desirable functions or activities in relation to analysis and visualisation of dependence and traceability. The traceability, as one of main benefits from the relation management, hopefully achieved through the DAIM and its associated object store is characterised as follows:

- Captured in an architecture repository (an object store);
- In a context of the whole defence capability and system architecture space or across concepts, projects and business areas, including:
  - o Inter-system
  - o Inter-capability
  - o Inter-project
  - o Inter-architecture
  - o Inter-process
  - o Inter-business area.

With the ability to effectively handle dependency and traceability in the whole defence information environment (DIE) SoS context through relations defined between concepts (or classes) and specified between objects, DAIM offers an opportunity to develop a knowledge management system and process for Defence capability architecture practice.

The benefits to Defence's many business areas should be substantial, enabling knowledge to be captured, applied at the appropriate time and reused. The consequence should be that Defence should derive substantial additional benefits from its architecture investments.

Through systematic definitions of concepts and relations, in summary, DAIM becomes a conceptual model that describes the entire architecture space of capability and systems It provides:

- A method for concept management (taxonomies and an ontology for scenarios, capabilities, projects, systems and architectures).
- A method also for relation management that covers
    - Scenarios relations;
    - Systems relations;
    - Capability relations;
    - Projects relations;
    - Architecture relations; and
    - Relations across concepts.
- A foundation to enable important architecture activities, such as:
    - Architecture planning;
    - Architecture analysis and evaluation; and
    - Architecture management.
- An environment to deal with issues concerning "big pictures" of defence capability and DIE. It will, in a SoS Context, support :
    - Traceability;
    - Visualisation;
    - Dependency analysis;
    - Interoperability analysis.

With the mechanism of concept and relation management in the architecture repository, capability planners, analysts, architects, developers or even war-fighters can query, search and trace various relations and dependencies. All real world objects captured in the repository are searchable with their attributes and relations and can be visualised with its full context in terms relations to other objects in the same class of different classes. If the relation definitions can be further formalised, it should be possible to explore more semantics and rules that can be used to develop automatic reasoning functions related to capability and system relation analysis, synthesis and visualisation.

Another advantage of developing the systems and capability relation management solution in the context of DAIM is that it allows the extension of the relation management coverage to include other related concepts, such as scenarios, projects, architecture and references. Consequently, it also supports the traceability of relations and dependence to be linked with associated scenarios and architecture descriptions. Theses advantages prove the improvement of integrated knowledge management for the defence systems and capability management as a whole.

## Conclusions

Dynamic changes of defence war-fighting requirements and constant evolutions of technologies require systematic and effective relation management for its systems and capabilities. The approach discussed in this paper presents both concepts and solutions for achieving the relation management that enables context-aware systems and capability planning, development, deployment and management. The systems and capability relation management is introduced as part of the defence architecture data management solution. It adds a new element to the architecture of defence SoS, which is currently missing and difficult to manage. Through systematic and effective capability and systems relation management, a defence organisation can become more confident and capable in the evolution of the organisation and its capability and systems.

7

# Special Relationship

The Special Relationship is a phrase often used to describe what some believe to be exceptionally close political, diplomatic, cultural and historical relations between the United States and the United Kingdom, following its use in a 1946 speech by British statesman Winston Churchill. While both countries maintain close relationships with many others, the level of cooperation in military planning, execution of military operations, nuclear weapons technology and intelligence sharing with each other was often described as "unparalleled" among major powers. The special relationship was most recently demonstrated by British support for the US-led invasion of Iraq.

### *Churchillian Creation*

The existence of a special relationship between the two governments was recognized since the nineteenth century, not least by rival powers. Their troops had been fighting side by side—sometimes spontaneously—in skirmishes overseas since 1859, and the two democracies shared a common bond of sacrifice in World War I.

However, as David Reynolds observes: 'For most of the period since 1919, Anglo-American relations had been cool and often suspicious. America's "betrayal" of the League of Nations was only the first in a series of US actions—over war debts, naval rivalry, the 1931-2 Manchurian crisis and the Depression—that convinced British leaders that the United States could not be relied on.' Equally, as President Truman's secretary of state, Dean Acheson, recalled: 'Of course a unique relation existed between

Britain and America—our common language and history insured that. But unique did not mean affectionate. We had fought England as an enemy as often as we had fought by her side as an ally.'

Arguably, 'the fall of France in 1940 was decisive in shaping the pattern of international politics', leading the special relationship to displace the entente cordiale as the pivot of the international system. During World War II, as an observer noted, 'Great Britain and the United States integrated their military efforts to a degree unprecedented among major allies in the history of warfare.' 'Each time I must choose between you and Roosevelt,' shouted British Prime Minister Winston Churchill at General Charles de Gaulle, leader of the Free French, in 1945, 'I shall choose Roosevelt.'

Churchill's mother was American, and he felt keenly the links between the English-speaking peoples. He first used the term 'special relationship' in 1945 to describe not the Anglo-American relationship alone but the United Kingdom's relationship with both the United States and Canada. The New York *Times Herald* quoted Churchill in November 1945:

We should not abandon our special relationship with the United States and Canada about the atomic bomb and we should aid the United States to guard this weapon as a sacred trust for the maintenance of peace.

Churchill used the phrase again a year later, at the onset of the Cold War, this time to note the special relationship between the United States on the one hand, and the English-speaking nations of the British Commonwealth and Empire under the leadership of the United Kingdom on the other. The occasion was his 'Sinews of Peace Address' in Fulton, Missouri, on 5 March 1946:

Neither the sure prevention of war, nor the continuous rise of world organization will be gained without what I have called the fraternal association of the English-speaking peoples...a special relationship between the British Commonwealth and Empire and the United States. Fraternal association requires not only the growing friendship and mutual understanding between our two vast but kindred systems of society, but the continuance of the intimate relationship between our military advisers, leading to common study of potential dangers, the similarity of weapons and manuals of instructions, and to the interchange of officers and cadets at technical colleges. It should carry with it the continuance of the present facilities for mutual security by the joint use of all Naval and Air Force bases in the possession of either country all over the world. There is however an important question we must ask ourselves. Would a special relationship between the United States and the British Commonwealth be inconsistent with our over-riding loyalties to the World Organisation? I reply that, on the contrary, it is probably the only means by which that organisation will achieve its full stature and strength.

In the opinion of one international relations specialist: 'the United Kingdom's success in obtaining US commitment to cooperation in the postwar world was a major triumph, given the isolation of the interwar period. A senior British diplomat in Moscow, Thomas Brimelow, admitted: 'The one quality which most disquiets the Soviet government is the ability which they attribute to us to get others to do our fighting for us... they respect not us, but our ability to collect friends.' Conversely, 'the success or failure of United States foreign economic peace aims depended almost entirely on its ability to win or extract the co-operation of Great Britain'. Reflecting on the symbiosis, a later champion, former prime minister Margaret Thatcher, declared: 'The Anglo-American relationship has done more for the defence and future of freedom than any other alliance in the world.'

### *Military Cooperation*

The intense level of military co-operation began with the creation of the Combined Chiefs of Staff in December 1941, a military command with authority over all American and British operations. This cooperation has increased steadily since the early 1950s when military contacts were re-established.

### *Shared Military Bases*

Since the Second World War and the subsequent Berlin Blockade, the United States has maintained substantial forces in Great Britain. In July 1948, the first American deployment began with the stationing of B-29 bombers. Currently, an important base is the radar facility RAF Fylingdales, part of the US Ballistic Missile Early Warning System, although this base is operated under entirely

British command and has only one USAF representative for largely administrative reasons. Several bases with a significant US presence include RAF Menwith Hill (only a short distance from RAF Fylingdales), RAF Lakenheath and RAF Mildenhall. During the Cold War critics of the special relationship jocularly referred to the United Kingdom as the "biggest aircraft carrier in the world."

Following the end of the Cold War, which was the main rationale for their presence, the number of US facilities in the United Kingdom has been reduced in number in line with the US military worldwide. Despite this, these bases have been used extensively in support of various peacekeeping and offensive operations of the 1990s and early 21st century. The two nations also jointly operate a military facility on Diego Garcia in the British Indian Ocean Territory and on Ascension Island, a dependency of Saint Helena in the Atlantic Ocean.

## *Nuclear Weapons Development*

The Quebec Agreement of 1943 paved the way for the two countries to develop atomic weapons side by side, the United Kingdom handing over vital documents from its own Tube Alloys project and sending a delegation to assist in the work of the Manhattan Project. The United States later kept the results of the work to itself under the postwar McMahon Act, but after the United Kingdom developed its own thermonuclear weapons, the United States agreed to supply delivery systems, designs and nuclear material for British warheads through the 1958 US-UK Mutual Defence Agreement.

The United Kingdom purchased first Polaris and then the American Trident system which remains in use today. The 1958 agreement gave the United Kingdom access to the facilities at the Nevada Test Site, and from 1963 it conducted a total of 21 underground tests there before the cessation of testing in 1991. The agreement under which this partnership operates was updated in 2004; anti-nuclear activists claimed renewal may breach the 1968 Nuclear Non-Proliferation Treaty. The United States and the United Kingdom jointly conducted subcritical nuclear experiments in 2002 and 2006, to determine the effectiveness of existing stocks, as permitted under the 1998 Comprehensive Nuclear Test Ban Treaty.

### *Military Procurement*

The United Kingdom is the only collaborative, or Level One, international partner in the largest US aircraft procurement project in history, the F-35 Lightning II program. The United Kingdom was involved in writing the specification and selection and its largest defence contractor BAE Systems is a partner of the American prime contractor Lockheed Martin. BAE Systems is also the largest foreign supplier to the United States Defence Department and has been permitted to buy important US defence companies such as Lockheed Martin Aerospace Electronic Systems and United Defence.

Other joint projects include the RAF Harrier GR9 or United States Marine Corps AV-8B Harrier II and the US Navy T-45 Goshawk. The UK also operates several American designs, including the Javelin anti-tank missile, M270 rocket artillery, the Apache gunship, C-130 Hercules and C-17 Globemaster transport aircraft.

## Other Areas of Cooperation

### *Intelligence Sharing*

A cornerstone of the special relationship is the collecting and sharing of intelligence. This originated during World War II with the sharing of code breaking knowledge and led to the 1943 BRUSA Agreement, signed at Bletchley Park. After WWII the common goal of monitoring and countering the threat of communism prompted the UK-USA Security Agreement of 1948. This agreement brought together the SIGINT organizations of the USA, UK, Canada, Australia, and New Zealand and is still in place today. The head of the CIA station in London attends each weekly meeting of the British Joint Intelligence Committee.

One present-day example of such cooperation is the UKUSA Community, comprising the USA's National Security Agency, the United Kingdom's Government Communications Headquarters, Australia's Defence Signals Directorate and Canada's Communications Security Establishment collaborating on ECHELON, a global intelligence gathering system. Under classified bilateral accords, UKUSA members do not spy on each other.

Following the discovery of the 2006 transatlantic aircraft plot, the CIA began to assist the Security Service (MI5) by running its own agent networks in the British Pakistani community. Security sources estimate 40 per cent of CIA activity to prevent a terrorist attack in the United States involves operations inside the United Kingdom. One intelligence official commented on the threat against the United States from British Islamists: 'The fear is that something like this would not just kill people but cause a historic rift between the US and the UK.'

## *Economic Policy*

The United States is the largest source of foreign direct investment to the British economy; likewise the United Kingdom is the largest single investor in the US economy. British trade and capital have been important components of the American economy since its colonial inception. In trade and finance, the special relationship has been described as 'well-balanced', with London's 'light-touch' regulation in recent years attracting a massive outflow of capital from New York. The key sectors for British exporters to the United States are aviation, aerospace, commercial property, chemicals and pharmaceuticals, and heavy machinery. British ideas, classical and modern, have also exerted a profound influence on US economic policy, most notably Adam Smith on free trade and John Maynard Keynes on counter-cyclical spending, while the British government has adopted workfare reforms from the United States. American and British investors share entrepreneurial attitudes towards the housing market, and the fashion and music industries of each country are major influences on their counterparts. Trade ties have been strengthened by globalisation, while both governments agree on the need for currency reform in China and educational reform at home to increase their competitiveness against India's developing service industries. In 2007 the US ambassador suggested to British business leaders that the special relationship could be used 'to promote world trade and limit environmental damage as well as combating terrorism'.

## *Personal Relationships*

The relationship often depends on the personal relations between British prime ministers and US presidents. The first example was the close relationship between Winston Churchill and Franklin Roosevelt who were in fact distantly related. Prior to their collaboration during World War II Anglo-American relations had been somewhat frosty. President Woodrow Wilson and Prime Minister David Lloyd George in Paris had been the only previous leaders to meet face-to-face, but had enjoyed nothing that could be described as a special relationship, although Lloyd George's wartime Foreign Secretary, Arthur Balfour, got on well with Wilson during his time in the United States and helped convince the previously skeptical president to enter the war.

Churchill spent much time and effort cultivating the relationship which paid dividends for the war effort though it cost Britain much of her wealth and ultimately her empire. Two great architects of the special relationship on a practical level were Field Marshal Sir John Dill and General George Marshall, whose excellent personal relations and senior positions (Roosevelt was especially close to Marshall) oiled the wheels of the alliance considerably.

The links that were created during the war—such as the UK military liaison officers posted to Washington—persist. However for Britain to gain any benefit from the relationship it became clear that a constant policy of personal engagement was required. Britain starting off in 1941 as somewhat the senior partner had quickly found itself the junior. The diplomatic policy was thus two pronged, encompassing strong personal support and equally forthright military and political aid. These two have always operated in tandem, that is to say the best personal relationships between British prime ministers and American presidents have always been those based around shared goals. For example, Harold Wilson's government would not commit troops to Vietnam. Harold Wilson and Lyndon Johnson did not get on especially well.

Peaks in the special relationship include the bonds between Harold Macmillan (who like Churchill had an American mother) and John F. Kennedy, and between Margaret Thatcher and Ronald Reagan. Nadirs have included Dwight D. Eisenhower's opposition to UK operations in Suez under Anthony Eden and Wilson's refusal to enter the war in Vietnam.

### *Macmillan and Kennedy*

Macmillan famously quipped that it was Britain's historical duty to guide the power of the United States as the ancient Greeks had the Romans. He endeavoured to broaden the special relationship beyond Churchill's conception of an English-Speaking Union into a more inclusive Atlantic Community. His key theme, 'of the interdependence of the nations of the Free World and the partnership which must be maintained between Europe and the United States', was one that Kennedy subsequently took up.

On the prime minister's retirement in October 1963, the president declared: 'In nearly three years of cooperation, we have worked together on great and small issues, and we have never had a failure of understanding or of mutual trust.' For his part, Macmillan confided to Kennedy's widow in February 1964: 'He seemed to *trust* me—and (as you will know) for those of us who have had to play the so-called game of politics—national and international—this is something very rare but very precious.'

However, even in the celebrated 'golden days' of the Kennedy-Macmillan partnership, the special relationship was tested, most severely by the Skybolt crisis of 1962, when Kennedy and his secretary of defence, Robert McNamara, ignoring the British contribution to the development of the atomic bomb and reneging on a promise made by Eisenhower, tried to divest the United Kingdom of its nuclear deterrent by unilaterally cancelling a joint project without consultation. Dean Acheson, a former US Secretary of State, also chose this moment to challenge publicly the special relationship and marginalise the British contribution to the Western alliance in his West Point speech of 1962:

Great Britain has lost an empire and has not yet found a role. The attempt to play a separate power role—that is, a role apart from Europe, a role based on a 'Special Relationship' with the United States, a role based on being the head of a 'Commonwealth' which has no political structure, or unity, or strength and enjoys a fragile and precarious economic relationship—this role is about played out.

On learning of Acheson's attack, Macmillan thundered: In so far as he appeared to denigrate the resolution and will of Britain and the British people, Mr. Acheson has fallen into an error which has been made by quite a lot of people in the course of the last four hundred years, including Philip of Spain, Louis XIV, Napoleon, the Kaiser and Hitler. He also seems to misunderstand the role of the Commonwealth in world affairs. In so far as he referred to

Britain's attempt to play a separate power role as about to be played out, this would be acceptable if he had extended this concept to the United States and to every other nation in the Free World. This is the doctrine of interdependence, which must be applied in the world today, if Peace and Prosperity are to be assured. I do not know whether Mr. Acheson would accept the logical sequence of his own argument. I am sure it is fully recognised by the US administration and by the American people.

The looming collapse of the alliance between the two thermonuclear powers forced Kennedy into an immediate volte-face at the Anglo-American summit in Nassau, where he agreed to sell Polaris as a replacement for the cancelled Skybolt. Richard E. Neustadt in his official investigation concluded the crisis in the special relationship had erupted because 'the president's "Chiefs" failed to make a proper strategic assessment of Great Britain's intentions and its capabilities'.

The Skybolt crisis with Kennedy came on top of Eisenhower's wrecking of Macmillan's policy of détente with the Soviet Union at the May 1960 Paris summit, and the prime minister's resulting disenchantment with the special relationship contributed to his decision to seek an alternative in British membership of the European Economic Community (EEC). According to a recent analyst: 'What the prime minister in effect adopted was a *hedging strategy* in which ties with Washington would be maintained while at the same time a new power base in Europe was sought.' Even so, Kennedy assured Macmillan 'that relations between the United States and the UK would be strengthened not weakened, if the UK moved towards membership.'

### *Wilson and Johnson*

Prime Minister Harold Wilson recast the alliance as a 'close relationship', but neither he nor President Lyndon B. Johnson had any experience of foreign policy, and Wilson's attempt to mediate in Vietnam, where the United Kingdom was co-chairman with the Soviet Union of the Geneva Conference, was unwelcome to the president, who was rumoured to have called the prime minister a 'creep'. 'I won't tell you how to run Malaysia and you don't tell us how to run Vietnam,' Johnson snapped in 1965. However relations were sustained by US recognition that Wilson was being criticised at home by his neutralist Labour left for not condemning US involvement in the war.

Despite US Defence Secretary Robert McNamara's insistence that the United Kingdom should 'pay the blood price' by sending troops to Vietnam as 'the unwritten terms of the Special Relationship', Wilson refused to commit regular forces, only special forces instructors. His stance was consistent with a burden-sharing arrangement agreed by Macmillan, whereby British forces had been concentrated against the Communist insurgency in Malaya. 30,000 British troops were still defending Malaysia in 1964 in an undeclared war with Indonesia. Australia and New Zealand were Commonwealth allies that did commit regular forces to Vietnam.

The Johnson administration's support for IMF loans delayed devaluation of sterling until 1967. The United Kingdom's subsequent withdrawal from the Persian Gulf and East Asia 'came as a shock to the United States', where it was strongly opposed, British forces being especially valued for their out-of-area contribution. In retrospect Wilson's moves to scale back Britain's global commitments and correct its balance of payments contrasted favourably with Johnson's overexertions which accelerated the United States' relative economic and military decline.

### *Heath and Nixon*

A Europeanist, Prime Minister Edward Heath preferred to speak of a '"natural relationship", based on shared culture and heritage', and stressed that the special relationship was 'not part of his own vocabulary'.

The Heath-Nixon era was dominated by the United Kingdom's 1973 entry into the European Economic Community (EEC). Although the two leaders' 1971 Bermuda communiqué restated that entry served the interests of the Atlantic Alliance, American observers voiced concern that the British government's membership would impair its role as an honest broker, and that, because of the European goal of political union, the special relationship would only survive if it included the whole Community.

Critics accused President Richard M. Nixon of impeding the EEC's inclusion in the special relationship by his economic policy, which dismantled the postwar international monetary system and sought to force open European markets for US exports. Detractors also slated the personal relationship at the top as 'decidedly less than special'; Prime Minister Edward Heath, it was alleged, 'hardly dared put through a phone call to Richard Nixon for fear of offending his new Common Market partners.'

The special relationship was 'soured' during the Arab-Israeli War of 1973 when Nixon failed to inform Heath that US forces had been put on DEFCON 3 in a worldwide standoff with the Soviet Union, and US Secretary of State Henry Kissinger misled the British ambassador over the nuclear alert. Heath, who learned about the alert only from press reports hours later, confessed: 'I have found considerable alarm as to what use the Americans would have been able to make of their forces here without in any way consulting us or considering the British interests.' The incident marked 'a low ebb' in the special relationship.

### *Callaghan, Ford and Carter*

While President Gerald Ford never visited England, the British government saw the US bicentennial in 1976 as an occasion to celebrate the special relationship. Political leaders and guests from both sides of Atlantic gathered in May at Westminster Hall to mark the Declaration of Independence. Prime Minister Jim Callaghan presented a visiting US Congressional delegation with a gold-embossed reproduction of Magna Carta, symbolising the common heritage of the two nations. British historian Esmond Wright, of the Institute of US Studies, noted 'a vast amount of popular identification with the American story'. A year of cultural exchanges and exhibitions culminated in July in a state visit to the United States by the Queen.

Ties between Callaghan and President Jimmy Carter were cordial but not emotional. When Carter came to London on his first foreign trip in May 1977 he described the relationship as 'very special' but, with both left of centre-governments being preoccupied with economic malaise, diplomatic contacts remained low key. US officials characterised relations in 1978 as 'extremely good', with the main disagreement being over trans-Atlantic air routes.

### *Reagan and Thatcher*

After a period of disengagement and drift in the 1970s, the personal friendship between President Ronald Reagan and Prime

Minister Margaret Thatcher, often described as 'ideological soul-mates', reinvigorated what she affirmed as the 'extraordinary alliance'. They shared a commitment to the philosophy of the free market, low taxes, limited government, and a strong defence; they rejected détente and were determined to win the battle of ideas with the Soviet Union.

Thatcher summed up her understanding of the special relationship at her first meeting with Reagan as president in 1981: 'Your problems will be our problems and when you look for friends we shall be there.' Celebrating the 200th anniversary of diplomatic relations in 1985, she enthused: 'There is a union of mind and purpose between our peoples which is remarkable and which makes our relationship a truly remarkable one. It is special. It just is, and that's that.' The president acknowledged: 'The United States and the United Kingdom are bound together by inseparable ties of ancient history and present friendship... There's been something very special about the friendships between the leaders of our two countries. And may I say to my friend the Prime Minister, I'd like to add two more names to this list of affection—Thatcher and Reagan.'

In 1982 Thatcher and Reagan reached an agreement to replace the British Polaris fleet with a force equipped with US-supplied Trident missiles, and Reagan became only the second foreign leader to address both Houses of Parliament (the first was de Gaulle in 1960). The confidence between the two principals was momentarily strained by Reagan's belated support in the Falklands War, but this was more than countered by the Anglophile US Defence Secretary, Caspar Weinberger, who provided communications intercepts and approved shipments of the latest weapons to the massing British task force. Thatcher later stood alone among Western allies when she returned the favour by letting US F-111s take off from RAF bases for the bombing of Libya, justifying it as an overdue move to help Reagan 'turn the tide against terrorism'.

Feathers were ruffled over the US invasion of the Commonwealth island of Grenada, and the potential risk to Britain's deterrent and security posed by the Strategic Defence Initiative and Reagan's proposal at the Reykjavik Summit to eliminate of all ballistic nuclear weapons despite large conventional disparities.

Even so, an observer of the period concludes: 'Britain did indeed figure more prominently in American strategy than any other European power'. A leading historian singles out the personal dynamic of 'Ron' and 'Margaret' in this success:

At crucial moments in the late 1980s, her influence was considerable in shifting perceptions in President Reagan's Washington about the credibility of Mr Gorbachev when he repeatedly asserted his intention to end the Cold War. That mercurial, much-discussed phenomenon, 'the special relationship,' enjoyed an extraordinary revival during the 1980s, with 'slips' like the US invasion of Grenada in 1983 apart, the Thatcher-Reagan partnership outstripping all but the prototype Roosevelt-Churchill duo in its warmth and importance. ('Isn't she marvellous'?' he would purr to his aides even while she berated him down the 'hot line.')

### *Clinton and Major*

The special relationship waned for a time with the passing of the Cold War, despite intensive co-operation in the Gulf War. Thus, while it remained the case that: 'On almost all issues, Britain and the US are on the same side of the table. You cannot say that for other important allies such as France, Germany or Japan', it was also acknowledged: 'The disappearance of a powerful common threat, the Soviet Union, has allowed narrower disputes to emerge and given them greater weight.'

Republican administrations had enjoyed strong links with the Conservative governments, and the new Democratic President Bill Clinton said he intended to maintain the special relationship, avowing: 'I'm a great Anglophile', but he and Prime Minister John Major were 'an odd couple', who 'got off on the wrong foot'. Their personal relationship was described as 'especially awful', with the two leaders once refusing to speak to one another while dining side-by-side. Both the Conservatives and Labour had sent advisers to the United States to aid the rival candidates in the 1992 presidential election, and it emerged that the Conservative government had allowed Home Office press officers to search files for evidence that Clinton had applied for British citizenship to avoid the Vietnam draft while a Rhodes scholar at Oxford in 1969; no evidence was found that he had.

Major stood accused of letting the special relationship become a personal relationship with the losing candidate, President George H. W. Bush, and of having 'bet on the wrong horse in the presidential race'. *The Economist* predicted: 'the special relationship, declared dead scores of times since Suez, will soon face another burial'. The Clinton administration did little to rebut a report in the *New York Times* in January 1993 that Major topped a 'Clinton enemies list'. The president afterwards explained: 'I was determined there would be no damage but I wanted the Tories to worry about it for a while.' At Clinton's first meeting with Major in February 1993 Clinton joked that he was 'grateful that I got through this whole campaign with most of my time in England still classified.'

The nuclear alliance—'the heart of the special relationship'—was weakened when Clinton extended a moratorium on tests in the Nevada desert in 1993, and pressed Major to agree to the Comprehensive Nuclear Test Ban Treaty. The freeze was described by a British defence minister as 'unfortunate and misguided', as it inhibited validation of the 'safety, reliability and effectiveness' of fail-safe mechanisms on upgraded warheads for the British Trident II D5 missiles, and potentially the development of a new deterrent for the twenty-first century, leading Major to consider a return to Pacific testing, and the Ministry of Defence to turn to computer simulation. One analyst accused the United Kingdom of using safety and reliability as cover for testing a replacement warhead for the WE.177 free-fall bomb. The moratorium weakened the case for British reliance on Trident, resulting in the *entente nucléaire* with France in 1995 under a Joint Nuclear Commission.

A genuine crisis in transatlantic relations blew up over Bosnia. London and Paris resisted relaxation of the UN arms embargo, and discouraged US escalation, arguing that arming the Muslims or bombing the Serbs could worsen the bloodshed and endanger their peacekeepers on the ground. US Secretary of State Warren Christopher's campaign to lift the embargo was rebuffed by Major and President Mitterrand in May 1993. After the so-called 'Copenhagen ambush' in June 1993, where Clinton 'ganged up' with Chancellor Kohl to rally the European Community against the peacekeeping states, Major was said to be contemplating the death of the special relationship. The following month the United States voted at the UN with non-aligned countries against Britain and France over lifting the embargo. By October 1993 Christopher was bristling that Washington policy makers had been too 'Eurocentric', and declared that Western Europe was 'no longer the dominant area of the world'. The US ambassador to London demurred, insisting it was far too early to put a 'tombstone' over the special relationship. A senior US State Department official described Bosnia in the spring of 1995 as the worst crisis with the British and French since Suez. By the summer US officials were doubting whether NATO had a future.

The nadir had now been reached, and, along with NATO enlargement and the Croatian offensive in 1995 that opened the way for NATO bombing, the strengthening Clinton-Major relationship was later credited as one of three developments that saved the Western alliance. The president acknowledged: 'John Major carried a lot of water for me and for the alliance over Bosnia. I know he was under a lot of political pressure at home, but he never wavered. He was a truly decent guy who never let me down. We worked really well together, and I got to like him a lot.'

A rift opened in a further area. In February 1994 Major refused to answer Clinton's telephone calls for days over his decision to grant Sinn Féin leader Gerry Adams a visa to visit the United States to agitate. Adams was listed as a terrorist by London. The US State Department, the CIA, the US Justice Department and the FBI all opposed the move on the grounds that it made the United States look 'soft on terrorism' and 'could do irreparable damage to the special relationship'.

Under pressure from Congress, the president hoped the visit would encourage the IRA to renounce violence. While Adams offered nothing new, and violence escalated within weeks, the president later claimed vindication after the IRA ceasefire of August 1994. To the disappointment of the prime minister, Clinton lifted the ban on official contacts and received Adams at the White House on St. Patrick's Day 1995, despite the fact the paramilitaries had not agreed to disarm. The rows over Northern Ireland and the Adams affair reportedly 'provoked incandescent Clintonian rages'.

In November 1995 Clinton became only the second US president ever to address both Houses of Parliament, but by the end of Major's premiership disenchantment with the special relationship had deepened to the point where the incoming British ambassador banned the 'hackneyed phrase' from the embassy.

### *Blair, Clinton and Bush*

The election of British prime minister Tony Blair in 1997 brought an opportunity to revive what Clinton called the two nations' 'unique partnership'. At his first meeting with his new partner, the president said: 'Over the last fifty years our unbreakable alliance has helped to bring unparalleled peace and prosperity and security. It's an alliance based on shared values and common aspirations.' The personal relationship was seen as especially close because the leaders were 'kindred spirits' in their domestic agendas. New Labour's Third Way, a moderate social-democratic position, was partly influenced by US New Democratic thinking.

Co-operation in defence and communications still had the potential to embarrass Blair, however, as he strove to balance it with his own leadership role in the European Union (EU). Enforcement of Iraqi no-fly zones and US bombing raids on Iraq dismayed EU partners. As the leading international proponent of humanitarian intervention, the 'hawkish' Blair 'bullied' Clinton to back diplomacy with force in Kosovo in 1999, pushing for deployment of ground troops to persuade the president 'to do whatever was necessary' to win.

The personal diplomacy of Blair and Clinton's successor, US president George W. Bush, further served to highlight the special relationship. Despite their political differences on non-strategic matters, their shared beliefs and responses to the international situation formed a commonality of purpose following the September 11 Attacks in New York and Washington DC. Blair, like Bush, was convinced of the importance of moving against the perceived threat to world peace and international order, famously pledging to stand 'shoulder to shoulder' with Bush:

> This is not a battle between the United States of America and terrorism, but between the free and democratic world and terrorism. We therefore here in Britain stand shoulder to shoulder with our American friends in this hour of tragedy, and we like them will not rest until this evil is driven from our world.

In a 1997 Harris poll published after Blair's election, 63% of Americans viewed Britain as a close ally, up by one percent from

1996, 'confirming that the long-running "special relationship" with America's transatlantic cousins is still alive and well'. Britain came second behind its colonial offshoot Canada, on 73%, while another offshoot, Australia, came third, on 48%. Popular awareness of the historical link was fading in the mother country, however. In a 1997 Gallup poll, while 60% of the British public said they regretted the end of Empire and 70% expressed pride in the imperial past, 53% wrongly supposed that America had never been a British possession.

In 1998, 61% of Britons polled by ICM said they believed they had more in common with Americans than they did with the rest of Europe. 64% disagreed with the sentence, 'Britain does what the US government tells us to do.' A majority also backed Blair's support of Bill Clinton's strategy on Iraq, 42% saying action should be taken to topple Saddam Hussein, with 24% favouring diplomatic action, and a further 24%, military action. A majority of Britons aged 24 and over said they did not like Blair supporting Clinton over the Lewinsky scandal.

A 2006 poll of the US public showed that the United Kingdom, as an 'ally in the war on terror' was viewed more positively than any other country. 76% of Americans polled viewed the British as an 'ally in the War on Terror' according to Rasmussen Reports. According to Harris Interactive, 74% of Americans viewed Great Britain as a 'close ally in the war in Iraq', well ahead of next-ranked Canada at 48%.

A June 2006 poll by Populus for *The Times* showed that the number of Britons agreeing that 'it is important for Britain's long-term security that we have a close and special relationship with America' had fallen to 58% (from 71% in April), and that 65% believed that 'Britain's future lies more with Europe than America.' 44% agreed that 'America is a force for good in the world.' A later poll during the 2006 Israel-Lebanon conflict found that 63% of Britons felt that the United Kingdom was tied too closely to the United States. A 2008 poll by *The Economist* showed that Britons' views differed considerably from Americans' views when asked about the topics of religion, values, and national interest. Indeed, it has been argued that Britons are more closely aligned with other Western Europeans, especially the Germans and Dutch. *The Economist* remarked:

For many Britons, steeped in the lore of how English-speaking democracies rallied around Britain in the second world war, [the special relationship] is something to cherish. For Winston Churchill... it was a bond forged in battle. On the eve of the war in Iraq, as Britain prepared to fight alongside America, Tony Blair spoke of the 'blood price' that Britain should be prepared to pay in order to sustain the relationship. In America, it is not nearly so emotionally charged. Indeed, American politicians are promiscuous with the term, trumpeting their 'special relationships' with Israel, Germany and South Korea, among others. 'Mention the special relationship to Americans and they say yes, it's a *really* special relationship,' notes sardonically Sir Christopher Meyer, a former British ambassador to Washington.

## *1967 Letter*

In 1967 a group of prominent Americans sought to reaffirm the importance of close ties in a letter published in *The Times* of London, saying that the special relationship should remain a fundamental bilateral policy even if the United Kingdom entered the European Economic Community. They suggested that the two governments 'begin to consider contingent means, including mutually beneficial trade and fiscal reforms, for saving and strengthening the historic relationship between our nations, whatever the outcome of the E.E.C. negotiations'. Signers included 10 senators, 29 members of the House of Representatives and a number of university presidents. *The Times* proposed a 'wide Atlantic-based free trade area' as one possibility of a broader economic grouping.

## *Friendly Fire*

More British servicemen were killed in the 1991 Gulf War by US fire than by Iraqi soldiers. A public controversy arose after US military authorities refused to allow USAF pilots to give evidence at a 1992 British inquest into the deaths of nine British soldiers killed in a US air strike, saying they had already supplied all the relevant information. The inquest jury returned a verdict of unlawful killing. Families of those killed accused the United States of 'double standards' after three US military officers were reprimanded for negligence after a separate incident involving the similar death of a US soldier. Tammy Groves, solicitor for the families, said: 'We have been denied any inquiry in the US; there have been no reprimands; and the pilots have not been named. The contrast could not be greater.' Anne Leech, whose son was one of the British soldiers killed, said: 'They are supposed to be a friendly country, but it shows it only goes as far as they want it to... Unless people are made accountable for what they do in these situations it will continue to happen.'

President George H. W. Bush responded: 'My heart goes out to their families. But I see no reason in going beyond what we've already done to fully account for this terrible tragedy of war.' Peter Atkinson, whose son was also killed, said: 'We met George Bush. He was trying to slide out of meeting us so I ran after him, collared him and told him what I thought. He said to me "You want the facts?... Right, you'll get them." Months later they sent us a report. It was rubbish. All the relevant details had been censored out.'

Further friendly fire incidents in the 2003 Iraq War brought assurances from officers and politicians that they would not hurt the close alliance: 'A situation like this does not mean anything of harm to the coalition, but in many ways it brings us closer together,' said RAF Group Captain Jon Fynes. However the US government again refused to co-operate with the coroner's investigations.

This culminated in the United States attempting to prevent the release of cockpit videos—later leaked to *The Sun*—showing events leading to the death of Lance-Corporal Matty Hull of the Household Cavalry, and threatening newspapers that published them with prosecution.

The coroner slammed US 'intransigence', and the British press accused the Pentagon of operating 'in a no-fault zone', with the *Daily Telegraph* commenting: 'This will reaffirm the view of many in the British military that while the US has the best kit, it does not necessarily have the best training... Uninhibited by the risk of any sanction, is it any wonder that they go about their lethal business with such apparent insouciance?' *The Spectator* described the British forbearance towards American evasiveness as "a bleak parable of the flaws at the heart of the U.S.-U.K. 'special relationship'."

### *Iraq*

Following the 2003 invasion of Iraq, senior British figures criticized the refusal of the US Government to heed British advice regarding post-war plans for Iraq, specifically the Coalition Provisional Authority's de-Ba'athification policy and the critical importance of preventing the power vacuum in which the insurgency subsequently developed. British defence secretary Geoff Hoon later stated that the United Kingdom 'lost the argument' with the Bush administration over rebuilding Iraq. Speaking on the same topic, Prince Andrew said there were "occasions when people in the UK would wish that those in responsible positions in the US might listen and learn from our experiences", that there was 'healthy skepticism' in the United Kingdom toward what was said in Washington DC, and a feeling of 'why didn't anyone listen to what was said and the advice that was given'. CNN acknowledged that the Prince's views were widely shared in the U.K.

### *Extraordinary Rendition*

Assurances made by the United States to the United Kingdom that 'extraordinary rendition' flights had never landed on British territory were later shown to be false when official US records proved that such flights had landed at Diego Garcia repeatedly. The revelation was an embarrassment for British foreign secretary David Miliband, who was obliged to apologise to Parliament, describing the incidents as 'a most serious matter'.

Legal and moral doubts also arose over the US government's extraordinary rendition process, which ignored extradition treaties and officially sanctioned the kidnap and extrajudicial transfer of people (some of them British citizens) from one country to another, sometimes to one of their covert CIA-run prisons, known as black sites, other times to Guantanamo Bay detention camp. The United Kingdom's Intelligence and Security Committee stated that America's failure to heed British concerns had 'serious implications' for future intelligence relations.

### *Criminal Law*

In 2003 the United States pressed the United Kingdom to agree to an extradition treaty which, proponents claimed, allowed for equal extradition requirements between the two countries. Critics argued that the United Kingdom was obligated to make a strong prima facie case to US courts before extradition would be granted, and that, by contrast, extradition from the United Kingdom to the United States was a matter of administrative decision alone, without prima facie evidence. This had been implemented as an anti-terrorist measure in the wake of the September 11, 2001 attacks. Very soon, however, it was being used by the United States to extradite and prosecute a number of high-profile London businessmen (e.g. the Natwest Three and Ian Norris ) on fraud charges. Contrasts have been drawn with the United States' harboring of Provisional IRA terrorists in the 1970s through to the 1990s and repeated refusals to extradite them to the UK.

On 30 September 2006 the US Senate unanimously ratified the 2003 treaty. Ratification had been slowed by complaints from some Irish-American groups that the treaty would create new legal jeopardy for US citizens who opposed British policy in Northern Ireland. *The Spectator* condemned the three-year delay as 'an appalling breach in a long-treasured relationship'. The United States also refused to accede to another priority of the Blair government, the treaty setting up the International Criminal Court.

### *Trade Policy*

Trade disputes and attendant job fears have sometimes strained the special relationship. The United States has been accused of pursuing an aggressive trade policy, using or ignoring WTO rules; the aspects of this causing most difficulty to the United Kingdom have been a successful challenge to the protection of small family banana farmers in the West Indies from large US corporations such as the American Financial Corporation, and high tariffs on British steel products. In 2002 Blair denounced Bush's imposition of tariffs on steel as 'unacceptable, unjustified and wrong', but although Britain's biggest steelmaker Corus called for protection from dumping by developing nations, the Confederation of British Industry urged the government not to start a 'tit-for-tat'.

### *Diplomacy*

In October 2007 The United Kingdom's first Muslim government minister, Shahid Malik, rebuked US authorities after having been detained and searched for explosives at a Washington airport on his way home from a meeting with the US Department of Homeland Security. This was the second occasion on which this Member of Parliament had been detained and searched, having received the same treatment at JFK airport during a visit to the United States in November 2006. Mr Malik remarked: 'The abusive attitude I endured last November I forgot about and I forgave, but I really do believe that British ministers and parliamentarians should be afforded the same respect and dignity at USA airports that we would bestow upon our colleagues in the Senate and Congress.'

The ongoing refusal of the US embassy in Grosvenor Square to pay the London congestion charge has also been a minor source of controversy. Embassy officials claimed they did not have to pay the congestion charge because it was a tax, from which diplomats were exempt. London officials asserted that the congestion charge was no different from the toll charges paid by drivers to travel into US cities such as Manhattan via bridges and roads. US embassies paid similar congestion charges in Singapore and Oslo.

### *Current Status*

Although British Prime Minister Gordon Brown stated his support for the United States on assuming office in 2007, he appointed ministers to the Foreign Office who had been critical of aspects of the relationship or of recent US policy. A Whitehall source said: 'It will be more businesslike now, with less emphasis on the meeting of personal visions you had with Bush and Blair.' Present British policy is that the relationship with the United States remains the United Kingdom's 'most important bilateral relationship'.

Prior to his election as US president in 2008, Barack Obama, suggesting that Blair and the UK had been let down by the Bush administration, declared: 'We have a chance to recalibrate the relationship and for the United Kingdom to work with America as a full partner.'

After her first ministerial-level talks with British Foreign Secretary David Miliband in early February 2009, US Secretary of State Hillary Clinton declared: 'It's often said that the United States and Great Britain have long enjoyed a special relationship.

It is certainly special in my mind, and one that has proven very productive. Whoever is in the White House, whichever party in our country, this relationship really stands the test of time.' Miliband spoke of a commitment 'to renew and refresh the special relationship'.

On meeting Brown as president for the first time in March 2009, Obama reaffirmed that 'Great Britain is one of our closest and strongest allies and there is a link and bond there that will not break... This notion that somehow there is any lessening of that special relationship is misguided... The relationship is not only special and strong but will only get stronger as time goes on.' Commentators, however, noted that the recurring use of 'special partnership' by White House Press Secretary Robert Gibbs could be signaling an effort to recast terms. One commentator noted the new term in a review of the HMS *Gannet*-pen holder which Brown presented to the president, and other gifts exchanged at the time. Obama presented Brown with 25 DVDs of American movies.

The following week British Cabinet Secretary Sir Gus O'Donnell, trying to plan the G-20 London summit, said it was hard to deal with US Treasury officials because they were 'unreachable'. The special relationship was also reported to be 'strained' after a senior US State Department official criticised a British decision to talk to the political wing of Hezbollah, complaining the United States had not been properly informed. The protest came after the Obama administration had said it was prepared to talk to Hamas and at the same time as it was making overtures to Syria and Iran. A senior Foreign Office official responded: 'This should not have come as a shock to any official who might have been in the previous administration and is now in the current one.'

In June 2009 the special relationship was reported to have 'taken another hit' after the British government was said to be 'angry' over the failure of the US to seek its approval before negotiating with Bermuda the resettlement to the British overseas territory of four ex-Guantanamo Bay inmates wanted by China. A Foreign Office spokesman said: 'It's something that we should have been consulted about.' Asked whether the men might be sent back to Cuba, he replied: 'We are looking into all possible next steps.' The move prompted an urgent security assessment by the

British government. Shadow Foreign Secretary William Hague demanded an explanation from Miliband, as comparisons were drawn with his previous embarrassment over the US use of Diego Garcia for extraordinary rendition without British knowledge, with one commentator describing the affair as 'a wake-up call' and 'the latest example of American governments ignoring Britain when it comes to US interests in British territories abroad'.

In August 2009, while America was engaged in a heated debate regarding President Barack Obama's healthcare reform proposals in the United States, American media outlets asked Daniel Hannan MEP to describe the healthcare in the United Kingdom on their programmes and television stations. Hannan's reply to the questions was that he wouldn't wish the NHS on anybody what so ever and repeatedly lambasted the NHS. Conservative leader David Cameron disavowed Hannan's comments and called the MEP 'a man with eccentric views', this incident angered many in the United Kingdom and thousands took to micro-blogging site Twitter to voice their outrage.

In August 2009 the special relationship was again reported to have 'taken another blow' with the release of Abdelbaset Ali Mohmed Al Megrahi, the man convicted of the 1988 Lockerbie Bombing on compassionate grounds, Hillary Clinton said 'it was absolutely wrong to release Abdelbaset al-Megrahi' adding 'We are still encouraging the Scottish authorities not to do so and hope they will not', President Barack Obama also commented that the release of al-Megrahi was a 'mistake' and 'highly objectionable', Colonel Gaddafi of Libya expressed his gratitude towards Prime Minister Gordon Brown and Scottish Justice Secretary Kenny MacAskill for the release.

# 8

# Indo-Russian Defence Co-operation Relation

The jointly developed Indo-Russian anti-ship cruise missile, which was successfully test-fired from Chandipur interim test range in Orissa recently is a crucial step forward in India's defence efforts. This technological achievement places India among a small group of countries to acquire the capacity of producing cruise missiles. What, however, makes the jointly produced cruise missile distinguishable from others is that it travels at a supersonic speed i.e. more than twice the speed of sound. Almost all other contemporary anti-ship missiles fly at subsonic speed. Its other distinguishing feature is that the Indo-Russian cruise missile is a state-of-the-art product.

Its unmatchable speed is its high point, making it invincible. The supersonic speed imparts it a greater strike-power as well. Possessing stealth characteristics, the 6.9-metre cruise missile weighing three tonnes has a range of 280 km. Its another outstanding feature is that it is highly accurate and can be guided to its target mainly with the help of an onboard computer. This has been established by the test-flight. The computer and the guidance system have been designed by India whereas Russia has provided the propulsion system. The missile has been designed and manufactured by a team of Indian and Russian scientists and technologists who worked under the aegis of a joint venture company named *Brahmos* which stands for Brahmaputra and the river from which Moscow derives its name.

The test-firing of the cruise missile which took place in the middle of June this year was described as an unqualified success.

The *Brahmos* recorded its performance as having met cent per cent technical parameters, both in terms of the flight range and hitting accuracy. Defence Minister Jaswant Singh who was present at Chandipur along with Indian and Russian scientists and technologists described the launch as a "landmark in technology partnership".

The Chandipur launch was the first in a series of test-flights of the cruise missile planned to demonstrate the capabilities of the system. A series of other test-flights will take place before the missile is simultaneously inducted into the Indian and Russian arsenals in about two years. It will also be sold to third countries in due course of time.

One of its special features is that this essentially anti-ship missile can be launched from ground, ship, submarine or air. Defence analysts underline that the eventual addition of this strategic missile is a logical follow-up of the goal set as per the country 's nuclear philosophy. Stated in plain terms, it is essential for the fulfilment of India's minimum nuclear deterrent profile as outlined in the draft nuclear doctrine prepared by the Vajpayee Government. The acquisition of the cruise missile which can be tipped with a nuclear warhead has obvious implications for our nuclear weapons' delivery system. Though it is a weapon of offence that increases the range of targets in the regional theatre, the Prime Minister, Mr Atal Behari Vajpayee has sought to reassure the world that India will continue to preach and adhere to the doctrine of universal peace.

In order to avoid heat and controversy, both India and Russia have taken care to ensure that the production of the cruise missile did not violate obligations under the US-sponsored Missile Technology Control Regime (MTCR) or any of the international agreements related to proliferation. That is why the missile range is well within the 300 km limit stipulated under the MTCR.

It is a triumph of India's defence diplomacy that its reinforced strategic partnership with Russia envisaging the acquisition of sophisticated weapon systems and their joint production has caused little offence to the United States. This is so because New Delhi has taken steps to strengthen its ties with Washington, burying several fathoms deep its bitter Cold War days memory. The US too no longer considers Russia as an adversary. This is evident from the May Day speech of President George Bush. What is more, the Americans understand Russia's economic compulsions which have forced it to sell its sophisticated weaponry.

Meanwhile, both India and Russia have welcomed the joint development of the supersonic cruise missile with great exuberance. Elated at the successful test flight from Chandipur, the state-owned Russian collaborating company, *Mashinostroyenie*, is putting up the cruise missile on display at the Moscow annual air show. *Mashinostroyenie* has designed the missile and its propulsion system leaving the all-important software and the guidacec system to its Indian counterpart— the Defence Research and Development Organisation (DRDO) of the Defence Ministry. The Russian media has greeted the collaboration heartily arguing that it has helped tilt the strategic balance in the region in India's favour.

New Delhi has described the missile test as an"outstanding example of Indo-Russian joint endeavour". The President, Mr KR Narayanan and Prime Minister Mr Vajpayee have termed it as a symbol of defence cooperation between the two countries. The development of the cruise missile takes their decades-old defence cooperation and the revived post-Cold War strategic partnership to a new high. It may be recalled that during the Russian President, Mr Vladimir Putin's visit to India last October, a Joint Declaration of Strategic Partnership was issued. During the Defence Minister, Mr Jaswant Singh's visit to Moscow a few days before the Chandipur launch, this strategic relationship was further reinforced. On these two occasions, the two countries signed a series of agreements on the acquisition of sophisticated weapon system and for a joint production of some of them including missiles. Indeed, the revived defence relationship is seeking to attain a level higher than what it was during the erstwhile Soviet era. Defence analysts feel that this could even be an indication of the emerging strategic realignment in the region. It may be noted that India's strategic interests spread across the Indian Ocean are with the Persian Gulf at one end and the Malacca Straits at the other. Another point to note is the qualitative breakthrough in the Indo-Russian defence relationship which is evident from the two sides moving away from a mere buyer-seller equation to that of a partnership in designing and producing new generation weapon system.

A point to note is that the newly developed cruise missile is more than a match to similar anti-ship missiles available with China. The latter has mounted *Moskit* anti-ship missiles on its recently acquired Soverameny-class warships. Beijing is also planning to mount its aerial version of the *Moskit* on its SU-27 planes. According to defence experts, the Indian cruise missile with its supersonic speed will be able to check movements by the Chinese warships, especially in the Indian Ocean area. Besides, its extraordinary accuracy and speed increases the range of its targets. In any case, the acquisition of the new missile will make India's position unchallenged in the regional theatre for a long time to come.

## India, Russia Aim to Take their Defence Ties

During a meeting between Defence Minister A K Antony and his Russian counterpart Anatoly Serdyukov here, both sides agreed to reassess bilateral defence ties in the light of new global realties. From a buyer and a seller relationship, the Indo-Russian relation has evolved to be one of "mutual cooperation of joint production", Antony said at a joint press briefing following his discussions with Serdyukov.

"One of the most important projects which are underway in terms of bilateral military technical cooperation is the production of the Sukhoi 30 MKI fighter, the MT 90 tanks, as well as the implementation of the Brahmos project and the implementation of the counter additional free Project 11356," said Serdyukov.

Citing instances of evolving ties with Russia, Antony said "Our joint effort in the production of the Brahmos and plan to co-develop FGFA (Fifth Generation Fighter Aircraft) are some of the examples," adding that "these projects could be the harbinger of the newer heights that our defence relations can achieve." Earlier, Antony ruled out ignoring Russia at the cost of a deepening military and strategic relation with the US.

"When we are improving our relations with US and other countries, it does not mean at the cost of our old friendship. Friendship with Russia will continue, and it will further increase and defence relations with Russia will further develop," said Antony ahead of the Seventh India-Russia Inter-Governmental

Commission on Military Technical Cooperation talks here on Wednesday. He said the very fact that there is joint inter-governmental Commission between India and Russia is demonstrative of the special relations between the two old friends.

"Important projects such as the licenses projects of T 90 tanks, multi-road fighter aircrafts, SU 30 MKI, repair and refurbishment of aircraft carrier Abmiral Bosky, along with supply of the base fighter aircraft Mi 29k are evidence of successful implementation of the programme," said Antony. Antony is on a four-day visit to Russia. Talks relating to the development of Fifth Generation Fighter Aircraft are likely to dominate the visit.

The seventh meeting of the India-Russia Inter-Governmental Commission on Military Technical Cooperation (IRIGC-MTC) focussed on issues, including the further revamping of bilateral military ties, additional purchase of Russian defence hardware and cost escalation in deals that have already been inked.

Antony and Serdyukov co-chaired the IRIGC-MTC meeting. India is the biggest market for Russian weaponry worldwide, with armament sales touching almost 10 billion dollars annually.

Moscow is keen on retaining the Indian market in the face of growing competition from the US, French and Israeli armaments majors.

Antony's trip sets the stage for Prime Minister Manmohan Singh's visit to Moscow in November for his annual summit meeting with Russian President Vladimir Putin. External Affairs Minister Pranab Mukherjee had visited Moscow last week.

This is Antony's first visit to Russia and only his second abroad since assuming office a year ago. He had visited Singapore in June for a meeting of the Shangri-La Dialogue regional security grouping. (ANI)

## India Russia: Strategic Relations

The India-Russia strategic relations with its embedded military ties have been, in the past 15 years, buffeted by the turbulence of international upheavals and domestic events. The collapse of the Soviet Union and the end of the cold war have quite dramatically altered the dynamics of this strategic relationship. The emergence of a unipolar world with the USA as the sole superpower impinged adversely on a once 'special' relationship and forced both Russia and India to review their geo-political calculations in the light of a changed geo-political environment.

Having earlier claimed for itself a leading role in the non-aligned movement(NAM) as a counterweight to the two superpower-led blocs, India found itself searching for identity and place in international affairs with the demise of one superpower. India had neither the economic clout nor any other attribute of power to be reckoned with in the world political arena. The rise of insurgency and secessionistic tendencies, both within the country and in its neighbourhood, shifted the focus of defence and security to internal stability. A fortress-mentality protectionist economic model, based on the Soviet pattern, was abandoned and India reached out to global donors for economic rejuvenation. In a suddenly unfamiliar scenario, India began to address its own economic vulnerabilities which stood out in stark contrast to the success of the Asian Tigers. Its somewhat diminished stature forced India to assess the world through the prism of its own interests.

At the same time the Russian domestic scene underwent major convulsions. The high residual costs of the collapsed Soviet model manifested itself with the economy in disarray and starvation on the streets. The Russian leadership abandoned its ideology based foreign policy and the special relations with India became a casualty. Russian leadership, dominated by 'west' oriented members, adopted a neutral stance towards India. Two schools of thought emerged. One comprising academics and defence industry professionals, were for continuing the special relations with India, which they argued, could stem the wave of Islamic fundamentalism sweeping across the Central Asia. Additionally, the income accruing from India's import of Russian arms would be crucial to Russia's transition to a free market economy. The other school of thought, comprising foreign ministry incumbents, were of the opinion that Pakistan had a vital role in fulfilling Russia's immediate concerns of foreign policy and security, and that Islamic fundamentalism, boiling over in Russia's southern flank would be best tackled by working closely with Pakistan, Iran and Turkey. That the second school prevailed was demonstrated by the change of policy by Russia in supporting the Pakistan sponsored UN resolution calling for the establishment of a nuclear-free zone in South Asia. This policy somersault was followed by Russia severing all support to Najibullah in Afghanistan, much to the consternation of India. The strain in Indo-Russian relations was again manifest in Russia reneging on the cryogenic engine and transfer of technology deal under intense pressure from the USA. The huge debt run up by India for purchase of arms from the erstwhile Soviet Union, amounting to over $16 billion became another issue of dispute. The rupee-ruble exchange rate and the repayment scheduling developed into irritants in the relations and it was much later that a mutually agreeable deal was hammered out.

The demise of the Soviet Union resulted in many defence plants closing down in Russia and CIS countries and the impact on Indian armed forces was severe. Product support, just satisfactory in the good times, was completely curtailed. Spare parts and consumables like tyres and split-pins were in short supply and the Indian military had to drastically cut down on operational training to conserve available stocks for any contingency. While a brave front was kept up, the reality was that the capability of the Indian armed forces with 80% of its hardware from Soviet Union, remained severely compromised for an unacceptably long period. Many delegations from India went to Russia and the CIS countries, carrying suitcases filled with dollars and searching for spares and equipment urgently required to raise the availability of tanks, ships and aeroplanes from the alarmingly low levels of 25-30% to an operationally acceptable minimum of 50%. In Russia however, a near chaotic situation obtained, and the cash-strapped country arbitrarily raised the cost of spares by as much as 500-1000%. The Indians had to make emergency calls to South Block, Delhi, for release of additional funds to meet these inflated dollar demands.

During this period of uncertainty, no new weapon systems were procured by India. With an inherent lag in the procurement process of 3-4 years, items ordered in 1991-92 materialised only in 1996-97. While some indigenisation was attempted in India, success was limited and later, this attempt came under attack by Russia for infringement of the IPR convention. However there were some positives also during this difficult period. While Russia went along with other permanent members of the UN Security

Council in condemning India's nuclear tests in 1998, Russia did not impose any sanctions against India. Russia also progressed the deal to build two light water 1000 mega-watt nuclear reactors at Kudankulam, Tamil Nadu. This was despite the USA putting pressure on Russia to scuttle the deal. This move helped in restoring some confidence among Indians that Russia still valued its relations with India. Again, during the Kargil operations in 1999, Russia set aside red tape to fly urgently required military spares and equipment into India.

Vladimir Putin as the PM and then as the President has regrouped and revamped the splintered military industrial complex in Russia. Russia has once again emerged as a major arms exporter. Putin also reinvigorated the India-Russia relations. During his visit to India in October 2000, major weapon deals worth over $3 billion-under negotiations for a long time-were finalised. The India-Russia Intergovernmental Commission was upgraded from the level of defence secretaries to the level of Defence Minister on the Indian side and the Deputy Prime Minister in charge of defence exports on the Russian side. In the last five years the major weapon systems acquired or contracted for include the Su-30 MKI multi-role fighters, IL-78 aircraft as platforms for the Indian AWACS, Mi-171V helicopters, Kilo-class submarines, frigates, Ka-31 AEW helicopters, aircraft carrier Admiral Gorshkov now renamed as INS Vikramaditya, MiG-29K carrier compatible fighters, T-90 tanks, AAMs, anti-tank and anti-ship missiles and various types of radars. The value of the projects under the defence cooperation programme till 2010 is $10 billion +. It is estimated that nearly 800 Russian defence production facilities would be kept in operation by Indian defence contracts. It is entirely another matter that an ageing manpower, obsolescent machinery and dependence on exports, mainly to India and China are pointers to looming problems in the making, both for the Russian military industrial complex and for countries largely dependent on Russia for weapon systems. Before analysing the current situation it would be instructive to examine the background that gave rise to the special military relationship between India and Russia.

Pakistan has been a beneficiary of US benevolence for a long time. The doctrinaire approach of Eisenhower and Dulles gathered Pakistan into the ambit of SEATO and CENTO. Weapon systems from the Western bloc flowed into Pakistan, ostensibly to counter the communist threat. Military linkages strengthened between Pakistan and the USA. Despite Pakistan's known animosity and its so-called 'unfinished agenda' of wresting control over the state of J&K, India's protests to the USA were dismissed, and assurances given that these weapons would not be used against India. India's stand that no gun has yet been fabricated that would shoot only in one direction was vindicated by later events. And the USA was reluctant to sell weapons to India for fear of offending Pakistan. Britain and France laid down unacceptable conditionalities for transfer of arms and technology to India. Left with no other alternative India turned to the Soviet Union for its requirements of weapons, immediately attracting criticism for having allegedly abandoned its non-aligned status. The Soviet Union willingly gave Mi-4 helicopters, AN-12 and IL-14 transport aircraft and later agreed to set up MiG-21 production facilities in India at Nasik for airframes, at Koraput for aero-engines and Hyderabad for avionics. The military debacle of 1962 underscored the requirement for better war preparedness and modern weapon systems. The USA established a chain of radars along the northern belt, but its offer of a 'defence umbrella' was not acceptable to India. A request for F-104 Starfighter jets was turned down by the USA.

India once again turned to the Soviet Union for its requirements of weapons. More variants of the MiG-21 were inducted and over a period of time the IAF's combat force included the Su-7, the MiG-23, MiG-25, MiG-27 and the MiG-29. The helicopter force comprised Mi-4, Mi-8, Mi-17, Mi-24/35 gunships and the heavy lift Mi-26. IL-14, AN-12, AN-32 and the IL-76 constituted the transport segment. The army got the T-54 and T-55 tanks, the amphibious PT-22 and PT-76. Later the T-72 tanks were inducted. 130 mm artillery guns, multi-barrel rocket systems for short range area saturation and a host of other infantry weapons were operationalised by the army. Pechora and OSA SAMs, Kvadrat misiles, Schilka tracked AA guns and the twin barrel Zu guns were procured for air defence. The Indian Navy inducted Soviet submarines, OSA missile boats, Petya patrol crafts, Nanuchka corvettes, Kashin class destroyers, landing crafts and motor torpedo boats. The Soviet military supplies programme included transfer of technology in various fields and has helped Indian scientists, engineers and technicians in creating a defence industrial base in the country. But one of the drawbacks has been the over-dependence on imported design with consequential negative effects on our own research and development sector and the stunting of indigenous genius.

The Soviet largesse towards India was not based on any altruism but grounded in realpolitik and cold logic. A friendly India meant greater credibility with, and easier access to, many developing third world countries. A strong India could become a significant counter-weight to China with whom Soviet Union had developed major differences. A dependable India could be an important bulwark against the US-Pakistan, China-Pakistan and US-China strategic and quasi-strategic alliances. And a dependent India in an economic partnership where the advantage lay with the Soviets could be a profitable long term investment. It can be seen that in this special relationship, India's needs were matched by Soviet Union's strengths and Soviet Union's requirements were matched by India's strengths. As long as the international geo-political equilibrium was not unduly disturbed, this relationship was destined to flourish.

The acme of this relationship between the two countries was the signing of the Treaty of Peace, Friendship and Cooperation in August 1971. One of the provisions of the Treaty was the determination of the two powers to repel aggression and for immediate mutual consultations in case either country was subjected to external attack. Some analysts have argued that this particular provision dissuaded China from 'leaning' on our northern borders when almost the entire Indian military was engaging the Pakistanis during the 1971 war. There were many occasions during the war when aeroplane loads of war-waging material was flown into our airbases as replenishments. India accomplished its war objectives and it did so by employing weapons which were predominantly of Soviet origin. The propaganda value of Soviet weapons having humbled western arms was immense and came as a big boost to the Soviet military industrial complex.

A symbolic but powerful gesture of the closeness of relations came in the form of an offer to send an Indian cosmonaut into space. Two IAF pilots were trained in the Soviet Union and on 4th April 1984, the first, and till now only, Indian cosmonaut, Sqn

Ldr Rakesh Sharma was launched into space aboard a Soviet spacecraft. It was a thrilling experience for the Indian population to hear in real-time an Indian cosmonaut out there in space engaging the Indian Prime Minister in a lively conversation.

Before the collapse of the Soviet Union, all weapon systems and military equipment were sold to India at 'friendship' prices that were substantially lower than the cost of similar systems available in the western market. Product and spares support, however, was less than efficient. The Soviet system of production, with factories and facilities spread far and wide, neccesitated a long lead time for Indian demands to be centrally collected, vetted and despatched. The Soviets were strong in standardisation of equipment but similar parts/equipment fitted on different aircraft had different part numbers. This resulted in over-accumulation of such stocks in India. In later years this led to items for, say MiG-23 being located in MiG-21 equipment depots and many more such instances. The quantum of 'dead' or non-moving stocks in our inventory was high and even at 'friendship' prices, a lot of money went waste. And as regards time delays in getting spares, our own system of procurement, mostly inflexible and procedure driven, also contributed in keeping our aeroplanes on the ground. The Army and the Navy also probably have similar experiences.

All Soviet aircraft were extremely robust and airframes could withstand a lot of aerodynamic punishment. While the aero-engines were powerful, their fuel efficiency was lower than engines of western design. The Sukhoi-7 ground attack aircraft which was the mainstay of the IAF during the 1971 war, had an engine which developed 9600 kgs of thrust with afterburner, but guzzled fuel. In avionics the Soviets lagged behind Western countries. 'Ergonomics' as applied to making the cockpit comfortable for the pilot, was not high on the Soviet designers priorities. 'Tropicalisation' of the cockpits appeared to be an afterthought in most Soviet aircrafts. In 1970 an IAF doctor's study revealed that pilots flying the Su-7, on an average lost 1000-1500 gms of body mass after a 1hour flight in summer conditions. The Soviets, however, were willing to make changes to suit Indian requirements. They were quick to respond to operational needs also. In September 1971, the IAF realised that the Su-7 did not have any armament to attack concrete structures. A message was apparently sent to

Moscow. On the night of 6/7 December, a transport aircraft unloaded large boxes at Adampur airbase. These boxes contained a number of brand new S-24 rockets which the IAF had not trained with earlier. The necessary literature regarding release conditions and other firing parameters was included. The next morning, a Su-7 aircraft loaded with the S-24 rockets attacked the Sulaimanke barrage on Sutlej river across the border from Fazilka. Many in the IAF came to know about these potent weapons only after the war. Similar such examples can be found in the Army and Navy also when the Soviets went out of their way to extend assistance. The only discordant note would be that it was an entirely one-sided give and take relationship with India always at the receiving end. But it was a warm relationship. Things are a bit different now.

The fundamental changes in the world balance of forces have had a direct bearing on the India-Russia relations. Russia is struggling to regain its lost status and stature. India strives to emerge as a major player in its own right. Both countries have established or are in the process of establishing new equations with other major players, but in the new world order all the equations are influenced by the only superpower's omnipresence. In this matrix of relationships the underlying factor is that no country can achieve its objectives in confrontation with the USA. And the USA can be ruthless if challenged.

Russia today has a growth rate of 6-7%, a GDP nearing $ 1.5 trillion and the worlds largest energy reserves including 13% of proven oil finds, 34% of natural gas and 25% of all coals. But because of the perma-frost conditions that obtain, it costs $14 to extract a barrel of oil in Russia as compared to $4 in Kuwait. And Russian economy is over-reliant on extracting energy and other natural resources. With a land mass five times the size of India, Russia has a population of only 142 million and that too is shrinking at the rate of 350,000 every year. Russia is headed for a demographic catastrophe. Russia fears that Siberia and the far east would soon be over-run by migrant Chinese labour and no immediate solutions are in sight.

India has a vibrant economy but poor imple-mentation of policy has led to a distorted development pattern with a sizeable segment of the the population still denied basic health, education and infrastructure. But a new India is emerging, harder and more self-assertive, a young India more open to new ideas, having divested itself of the baggage of anti-colonialism which was etched deep in the psyche of earlier generations, a confident India able to take a more pragmatic view of the world.

New India and new Russia search for new paradigms to accommodate an old relationship. The warmth of 1971 has long faded and circumstances that obtain now have injected a Moscow chill into the relations.

Russia, outmanoeuvred by the USA, and apprehensive of the creeping NATOisation of its former republics, is forging a strategic coalition with China, unmindful of Indian interests. The Su-30 MKI technology, funded by India, has been transferred to China, which has become a major importer of Russian hi-tech weaponry. China, with ex-Soviet Union scientists and engineers working in its defence facilities is producing fighter aircrafts, now being fitted with Russian engines, and exporting them to Pakistan in a clear violation of an earlier understanding with India. All major weapon deals between India and Russia have run into cost and time over-runs. The INS Vikramaditya still languishes in Russian waters and a firm delivery date is yet to materialise with Russia citing earlier underassessment of refurbishment costs as the cause of delay. The Akula-II nuclear submarine will take considerably longer to join the Indian Navy on lease for 10 years. The upgrade of two IL-38 aircrafts was delayed by nearly 2 years and the final product arrived in India minus the avionics and the weapon systems. India has had to agree to raise the annual cost escalation for all major deals including the Su-30 project, from 2.8% to 5 %. The Ayni airbase near Dushanbe, Tajikistan, developed by India, probably will be denied to India at Russia's behest. An element of coercion is evident.

A recent trend is jointness in defence production. Brahmos has been a success story, indicating that joint design and production is the way ahead. However in the 5th generation fighter deal, supposed to be a joint design and production programme, India came on board only after the design was frozen. The medium lift transport aircraft will also be a joint effort. Memorandums of Understanding have been signed for additional nuclear reactors at Kudakulam. Agreement has been reached by the two countries on India's access to the navigational signals of the Russian Global

Navigation Satellite System(GLONASS) as also to a part of the GLONASS radio frequency spectrum. The two countries will also co-operate in the joint satellite project "YOUTHSAT". Russian help will be available for India's moon mission 'CHANDRAYAN'.

There are compulsions on both sides, Indian and Russian to continue the strategic relationship, but in a changed environment, the contours of the relations must also harmonise with India's national interests. While India has expressed many times over, her gratitude for Russian arms and equipment and Russia's support for the Indian cause in Kashmir and now India's quest for permanent membership of the UN Security Council, Russia has been indicating its displeasure over India's improving relations with the USA. India's relations with other countries and events like the nuclear dialogue with the USA are matters sovereign to India and cannot brook interference from any third country. And while Russia has been the predominant supplier of arms to India, this level of dependency is not in India's national interest. The steps in progress to diversify our weapon sources, are steps in the right direction and can be considered to be, one can state with the luxury of hindsight available to us now, the rectification of a six decade old strategic defect. This strategic defect has also been one of the causes for our DRDO's less than satisfactory performance till now. It can only be hoped that the Rs 15,0000 crores that the DRDO has asked for over 10 years, at the rate of Rs 15,000 crore per year starting 2010, will put India on a track to achieve substantial self-reliance in our military requirements. Joint ventures with Russia ought to give impetus in our efforts towards self-reliance. Technology transfers have to be a mandatory provision for any future defence deal.

The much delayed LCA programme and the shrinking combat aircraft holdings of the IAF has compelled India to float global request for proposals for 126 fighter aircrafts in an expected mega deal of $ 7 billion. Russia, realizing it is not a front runner to clinch this deal, has indicated its displeasure by downgrading the visit status of our senior ministers. The Russian aircraft contending for this fighter deal is an upgraded version of an outdated design. Should the Russian aircraft be short-listed, India will have to carefully analyse Russia's capability to provide product support over its life-cycle, given the direction in which Russia;s military industrial complex is headed. Had the design of the Russian aircraft been contemporary, joint production would have been a win-win situation.

As and when the 126 aircraft deal is finalised, and if Russia is not the supplier, the reverberations will impact on the India-Russia strategic relationship and both the Indian and Russian establishments will have to employ all their diplomatic skills to manage the fallout. In the new world order, both India and Russia will have to learn to manage their strategic relationship in consonance with their national interests.

From a military viewpoint it is strategically imperative for India to diversify the sourcing of imported weapon systems and therefore vital to progressively reduce dependency on Russia without adversely affecting the operational preparedness of our armed forces. The India-Russia strategic relations can continue to be energised through jointness in defence production, space, nuclear and scientific co-operation and energy research.

# 9

# India-Israel Defence Nexus Deepens

The launching of an Israeli made satellite on April 20, 2009 came close on the heels of an opaque missile deal of India with an Israeli company under investigation both in India and Israel, raising further questions about India's Israeli ties and its implications. A.K. Antony, India's Defence Minister, found it hard to answer questions related to these deals while campaigning for the Congress party in the Parliament elections in his home State of Kerala.

India signed a massive US $ 1.4 billion deal with the Israeli Aerospace Industries (IAI) for the supply and joint development of medium-range surface-to-air missiles (MRSAM). The deal signed on February 27, 2009, just two days prior to the notification of elections to Parliament, was wrapped in secrecy till the Israeli Aerospace Industries officially announced it. The company explained that "early disclosure was liable to cause material difficulties in execution of the contract and even result in its cancellation", according to the Israeli business daily Globes. The company has claimed that the Indian Government wanted the signing of the contract to be kept secret.

Once the deal became public, a host of questions has been raised. A number of defence experts believe that there was no need for such a missile deal, as India already possesses a more powerful missile in the same class—the advanced air defence (ADD) missile, part of India's anti-ballistic shield. The deal ignores the success of the ADD missile, which could be deployed as a SAM and used exactly like the Israeli MRSAM. There is criticism this will adversely affect research and development of this indigenous technology. Procedural and legal questions are raised in the light of the guidelines established by the Ministry of Defence itself regarding Israeli arms companies, especially the IAI. India's Central Bureau of Investigation (CBI) is continuing its probe into dealings with the company especially related to the purchase of the Barak missile system in 2000 from IAI and Rafael, another Israeli arms firm, naming former Defence Minister George Fernandes and then Navy Chief Sushil Kumar. It is known that bribes were paid to clinch the Barak interceptor deal and there is evidence of remittances paid by the Israeli IAI. But the CBI has been going slow on the case apparently under political pressure.

An order issued on October 3, 2008 "with the approval of the Hon'ble RM (Raksha Mantri, Defence Minister)" laid down details about how to handle the IAI and Rafael. In dealing with them, the Defence Ministry order said: "Tenders in which the two firms were the only competitors should be withheld. Tenders in multi-vendor deals could be given to the two firms but they should have to be withdrawn if the CBI files any chargesheet."

In giving contract to the IAI, these are precisely the guidelines that have been breached, as the IAI was the only competitor for the MRSAM deal. From the beginning only the IAI was considered for the deal, clearly violating the guidelines. Washing his hands off the decision not to invite global tenders for the deal with the IAI, Minister Antony, in an interview to a local TV channel India Vision in Kerala, seemed to suggest that the procedure was laid down by his predecessor Pranab Mukherji, currently the Foreign Minister. Even at his evasive best, he had to admit that there was tremendous pressure on him from the armed forces to clear the deal.

In fact the two firms should have been blacklisted. In the past when allegations of corruption and about the involvement of arms dealers have cropped up, the government moved quickly to blacklist the firms involved. That was what was done with Bofors, HDW and Denal even before FIRs (First Information Reports) were filed against them. The CBI lodged an FIR in October 2006 naming the IAI as accused besides naming the Delhi-based arms dealer, Suresh Nanda, and his family members as agents of the Israeli IAI and Rafal corporations. The question —why was the IAI not barred from further contracts till the case was disposed of?—remains unanswered. In an exclusive report Haaretz the Israeli daily on April 5 ("The man who bribed Indians for Israeli arms sales") said: "Recent reports claimed that Sudhir Choudrie and another Indian arms dealer, Suresh Nanda, shared a nine per cent commission of the latest arms deal, for 2000 ground based version of the Barak missile." Rules in India forbid commission to agents and all deals are expected to be conducted directly without middlemen between companies and government.

As the controversy on the deal raged in India, an article in the Israeli daily Jerusalem Post on April 2 came out with a strange explanation for the opposition to the deal, quoting senior defence officials in Israel. "Muslim political parties in India as well as Russian and American defence companies are suspected of working behind the scenes to torpedo a $ 1.4 billion deal signed recently between Israeli Aerospace Industries and India for the development of a missile defence system." The defence officials said: "It appeared that pro-Muslim political opponents of the New Delhi Government as well as competing defence companies from around the world were spreading rumours of financial irregularities to damage Israeli-Indian defence ties." Israeli officials said that it was possible that Russian companies were also working behind-the-scenes to scuttle the deal.

The unnamed high officials of the Israeli defence establishment found an Iran factor also. "The Muslim opposition to the deal," the officials said, "could be backed by Iran which last year tried to thwart the launch of an Israeli spy satellite from India." While there is no evidence of any Muslim opposition in India being supported by Iran, it is true that Iran legitimately raised questions about the implications of the spy satellite.

Israel's spy satellite, launched by India in the third week of January 2008, has considerably enhanced Israel's intelligence gathering capacity. The launch of the Tecsar satellite, also known as Poliaris, opened a new stage in India-Israeli strategic relations and added a new factor in the complex security scenario in the Middle East. In reporting on the event, the Israeli media highlighted the strategic significance of the satellite in relation to Iran. The Haaretz reported on January 21, 2008: "The sophisticated new spy satellite could boost intelligence gathering capabilities regarding Iran." The satellite "enables Israel to establish a new point of view in space allowing it photographic angles and reception of Iranian communications which were unavailable in prior satellite launches", the daily continued. Indeed Iran had every reason to complain but it was ignored by New Delhi, playing its assigned role in the US strategy to contain Iran.

India lauched an Israeli-made spy satellite from Sriharikota near Bangalore city in the southern State of Karnataka on April 20. It is in a bid to keep a twentyfour-hour surveillance on its international borders, news agencies quoted Indian defence officials. The 300 kg radar-imaging Israeli satellite was launched via India's indigenous Polar Satellite Launch Vehicle (PSLV) and it will be positioned 500 km above the Earth. The satellite will help India track infiltration of militant movements on its borders with Pakistan and inside the country. It could capture the images even under clouds and transmit them to the country.

As in the case of the Israeli satellite launched in January 2008, the Indian Space Research Organisation (ISRO), responsible for the launch, has officially labelled the satellite a tool for "disaster management", an innocuous exercise.. The launching of the satellite in January 2008 had been explained by the same agency as "utilising its advanced technological capacity to place satellites in orbit". The ISRO deliberately had underplayed the strategic and political impli-cations of the launch. The reluctance of the ISRO to reveal security related aspects is understandable, especially at the time of elections, but on dealings with Israel it appears that the Indian public has to rely on Israeli sources to know what is happening.

In this case Israeli sources clearly stated that it is a "radar imaging espionage satellite made by Israel". "The launch will mark a new phase in the alliance between Israeli Aerospace Industries and New Delhi," it is claimed. Again, it is the same company which is under investigation both in Israel and India. The acquisition of the spy satellite was fast-tracked after the Mumbai siege last November. The Indian security establishment was impressed by the Tecsar and wanted for itself a satellite capable of monitoring developments especially in its neighbourhood. In this case also Antony skirted questions, declined to identify his Ministry as the end-user and suggested that questions may be directed to the ISRO. The Leftist parties in the country have mounted a fierce attack not only on these particular deals with Israel but the whole gamut of India-Israel strategic, defence, counter-terrorism and intelligence cooperation much to the embarrassment of the Congress party during the elections.

In 2008 Israel surpassed Russia as the main defence supplier to India after breaking the $ I billion mark in new contracts signed annually over the past years. Israel is not, as Minister Antony claims, just one among 45 countries with which India has defence deals. A Jerusalem Post article on February 15, 2009 had a screaming headline: "Israel now India's top defence supplier".

"We have a very special intense relationship with India. It is now moving toward joint development of equipment. There are several projects in the pipeline," Major General Udi Shani, Head of the Defence Ministry's SIBAT, Defence Export and Cooperation Agency said in an interview to the Indian press in the second week of February. "There is close cooperation and the Indians respect Israeli systems and our experience in fighting terror."

In fact the opposition in India to the new missile deal is not only because it is dubious but also because of widespread concern about India's burgeoning support to the war economy of Israel, the chief victims of which are Palestinians. The spy satellite, also made by the controversial Israeli Aerospace Industries fits into this. The defence and intelligence nexus between India and Israel has strategic implications not only for West Asia but also for South Asia especially through their collaboration in the US-led war on terror. While continuing to pay lip service to the Palestinian cause India is subsidising Israel's war against Palestinians.

10

# NATO-EU Relations

At the British-French Summit at St. Malo, in December 1998, France and Britain agreed that the European Union "*must have the capacity for autonomous action, backed up by credible military forces, the means to decide to use them, and a readiness to do so, in order to respond to international crises*" and issued a Joint Statement outlining their determination to enable the European Union to give concrete expression to these objectives. This decision represented a profound change in the policies hitherto adopted by the United Kingdom with regard to this issue and opened the way for the adoption of practical measures within the European Union to put it into effect.

In the new climate that prevailed after the St. Malo meeting, further progress could be made. Following the entry into force of the Amsterdam Treaty on 1 May 1999, the European Council met in Cologne in June 1999 and agreed to give the EU itself the means and capabilities needed for the implementation of a common European security and defence policy (ESDP). The role previously undertaken by the WEU was progressively assumed by the European Union.

In the intervening period, NATO continued to work with the WEU to complete and implement arrangements to facilitate cooperation between the two organisations in the event of a WEU-led crisis management operation making use of NATO assets and capabilities. Further work was undertaken to refine arrangements for the use of such assets and for information-sharing. Joint testing and evaluation of procedures were undertaken. A joint NATO-WEU crisis management exercise was held in February 2000. At their meeting in Marseilles in November 2000, WEU Ministers decided to suspend routine NATO-WEU consultation mechanisms, apart from those that would be required during the transition period.

With the transfer of responsibilities from the WEU to the EU, the relationship between NATO and the EU took on a new dimension, reflected in developments within both organisations. The Helsinki meeting of the Council of the European Union held in December 1999 established a "Headline Goal" for EU member states in terms of their military capabilities for crisis management operations. The objective of the Headline Goal is to enable the EU, by the year 2003, to deploy and sustain for at least one year, military forces of up to 60 000 troops to undertake the full range of the so-called Petersberg tasks set out in the Amsterdam Treaty of 1997. These consist of humanitarian and rescue tasks; peacekeeping tasks; and tasks of combat forces in crisis management, including peacemaking. Their role will be to undertake military operations led by the EU in response to international crisis, in circumstances where NATO as a whole is not engaged militarily, in line with the EU's resolve to develop a common European policy on security and defence which would underpin its Common Foreign and Security Policy militarily. EU member states have stated their intention to avoid unnecessary duplication with NATO structures and have emphasised that these decisions do not imply the creation of a European army.

In addition, the EU decided to create permanent political and military structures, including a Political and Security Committee, a Military Committee and a Military Staff, to ensure the necessary political guidance and strategic direction for such operations. The EU also decided to develop arrangements for full consultation, cooperation and transparency with NATO and to ensure the necessary dialogue, consultation and cooperation with European NATO members which are not members of the EU on issues related to European security and defence policy and crisis management.

The dialogue between the Alliance and the European Union has steadily intensified in accordance with the decisions taken at Washington and thereafter, and in the light of developments within the EU. Meetings of the European Council in Nice and of the North Atlantic Council in Brussels in December 2000 registered further progress. Alliance Foreign Ministers stated that they shared the goal endorsed by EU member states for a genuine partnership in crisis management between NATO and the EU. Both organisations agreed that consultations and cooperation will be developed between them on questions of common interest relating to security and effective defence and crisis management, so that crises can be met with the most appropriate military response.

An exchange of letters took place in January 2001, between the Secretary General of NATO and the Swedish Presidency of the EU, providing for joint meetings at Ambassadorial level and Ministerial level. The arrangement envisages at least three meetings at Ambassadorial level and one meeting at Ministerial level every six months (i.e. during each EU Presidency). Both organisations are committed to stepping up consultations in times of crisis. Since February 2001, regular meetings of the EU Political and Security Committee and the North Atlantic Council take place. The first formal meeting of NATO and EU Foreign Ministers took place in Budapest in May 2001 in the margins of the Ministerial meeting of the North Atlantic Council.

Joint NATO-EU Ad Hoc Working Groups have also been meeting since mid 2000 to discuss security issues such as procedures for the exchange of classified information and intelligence; modalities for EU access to Alliance assets and capabilities; capability goals (including issues relating to the Alliance's defence planning system); and permanent consultation arrangements, taking into account all relevant factors including those relating to participation. In spring 2001, the Secretary General of NATO was invited for the first time to brief the EU General Affairs Council on NATO policy.

In July 2000, NATO and the EU Council Secretariat established an interim security agreement between the two organisations governing the exchange of classified information and both organisations are working towards the conclusion of a permanent NATO-EU security agreement. In the second half of 2000, Alliance experts began contributing military and technical advice to the work of EU experts on the establishment of a catalogue of forces and capabilities for the EU Headline Goal, in preparation of the EU's Capabilities Commitment Conference held in November 2000. Within NATO, work on the principal issues facing the further development of ESDI has continued during 2001 and 2002, in particular the identification of a range of European command options; the presumption of availability of pre-identified assets and capabilities; the adaptation of Alliance defence planning; and NATO-EU consultations in times of crisis.

Cooperation between NATO and the European Union has been developed in a number of specific fields and specifically in relation to the campaign against terrorism. Direct contacts have increased and, in the wake of the terrorist attacks of 11 September, the Secretary General of NATO participated in the deliberations of the EU General Affairs Council held on 12 September to analyse the international situation following the attacks.

Cooperation between the two organisations has also contributed to the security situation in the former Yugoslav Republic of Macedonia*, where NATO is providing security for EU and OSCE monitors of the peace plan. Regular contacts have taken place between the two organisations as well as the OSCE to maximise international support for political reforms in the country and the maintenance of the political process. A joint delegation consisting of the NATO Secretary General, the EU High representative, the Chairman in Office of the OSCE and the Supreme Allied Commander Europe visited Skopje on 18 October 2001 for discussions with President Trajkovski and other political leaders.

Discussions of the situation in the Western Balkans has become a regular feature of meetings of the North Atlantic Council and the Political and Security Committee of the EU. Foreign Ministers of NATO and the EU also met in Brussels on 6 December 2001 to review cooperation across the board, and underlined their continued engagement in strengthening the peace process in the former Yugoslav Republic of Macedonia* as well as elsewhere in the Western Balkans. Further contacts between the NATO Secretary General and the EU High Representative have continued to contribute to cooperation and, in May 2002, Foreign Ministers of both organisations met again in Reykjavik reaffirming their commitment to achieve a close and transparent relationship.

The situation in southern Serbia has also been the subject of consultations and cooperation, following the need for international intervention in 2001 to defuse the risk of civil conflict in the area and to help to broker a ceasefire. Closer proximity between the Serb and Federal Yugoslav governments and European institutions continues to manifest itself and has been reflected, for example, in the interest shown by the Federal Republic of Yugoslavia in participation in the Partnership for Peace programme. The strengthening of the political process, for example through the successful conduct of municipal elections in southern Serbia in July 2002, has continued to be a priority concern of both NATO and the EU, each of which has acted to defuse set-backs when these have occurred.

## Defence Policy, including EU/NATO Relations

*The European Parliament,*

A. recalling that the development of the European Security and Defence Policy (ESDP) and the creation of structures allowing the European Union to implement a policy of conflict prevention and civil and military crisis management were undertaken with the intention of lending credibility to a coherent Common Foreign and Security Policy (CFSP) which serves the global interest and universal values, as these have been expressed in the Charter of the United Nations, B. recognising that NATO is the military security organisation for collective defence and that European states need to make a greater and more effective contribution in sharing the burden of allied security and defence responsibilities,

C. having regard to the declaration of the Laeken European Council on the operational capability of ESDP, which should enable the European Union to analyse and plan, to take decisions and, where NATO as such is not involved, to launch and carry out military crisis management operations, D. noting that, for effective crisis management by the Union, the balanced development of military and civilian capabilities is necessary, which implies close coordination between all resources and instruments, both civilian and military, available to the Union, E. aware of the considerable shortfalls in key military capabilities and assets that would ensure that the whole range of the Petersberg tasks could be carried out by easy deployment, full mobility, secure and interoperable communications and sustainability in the field, F. noting that key capability gaps highlighted by the Capability Improvement Conference of 19 November 2001 include strategic shortfalls in air transport systems and in the field of C 3-I systems (command, control, communication and intelligence) as well as tactical shortfalls in other areas, G. whereas the Union's crisis management capability has been strengthened by the recent development of close consultation and cooperation between the EU and NATO in crisis management in the Western Balkans,

H. concerned, however, that the security arrangements with NATO and agreements on guaranteed access to the Alliance's operational planning, presumption of availability of pre-identified assets and capabilities of NATO, and identification of a series of command options made available to the Union, have still not been concluded,

I. alarmed at the widening technological gap, as highlighted in the Kosovo crisis and the war in Afghanistan, between American and European forces, as a result of which European troops tend to lose the ability to work in coalitions with US forces and therefore even coherence within the Atlantic Alliance is threatened,

J. welcoming the advances made in defining concrete targets for the civilian aspects of crisis management, especially in the areas of police, the rule of law and civil protection; recognising that further work is needed to define qualitative requirements in these areas and the scope and nature of the EU's civil administration capacity,

K. noting that the further development of the EU's civilian crisis management capabilities will require a thorough needs assessment to identify other areas in which the EU should develop its capabilities, and improved mechanisms to ensure that civilian crisis management is compatible with Community activities and contributes to the capacities of the EU to prevent conflicts,

Wednesday 10 April 2002 L. recognising that in the post-11 September world the fight against international terrorism has become a major objective of the ESDP which, however, cannot be carried out by military means alone, and that the prevention and repression of terrorism requires a whole range of non-military measures such as intelligence-sharing and police and judicial cooperation, for which full interinstitutional and interpillar cooperation will be needed, or the building of democratic institutions, infrastructure and civil society in failed or failing states, M. whereas this fight against international terrorism should not impinge on the political, social and human rights of citizens, and should not be a pretext for supporting massive repressive acts by governments against their citizens; also stressing that the EU's greatest contribution to preventing international terrorism will be its capacity to be effective in the building or rebuilding of democratic institutions, social and economic infrastructure, good governance and civil society,

1. Welcomes the progress made so far on the establishment of EU crisis management structures and procedures, as well as the commitments by Member States on military and civilian capabilities which will enable the EU to carry out police missions and limited military crisis management operations at the lower end of the Petersberg tasks such as humanitarian and rescue tasks and peace-keeping tasks;
2. Supports therefore the Council's decision of 18/19 February 2002 on an EU police mission (EUPM) in Bosnia-Herzegovina to start by 1 January 2003 as the follow-on to the United Nations International Police Task Force (IPTF);
3. Considers the EUPM in Bosnia-Herzegovina to be an important civilian crisis management intervention within the framework of ESDP and the broader approach of the stabilisation and association process for the whole region;
4. Is of the opinion that the start-up costs of EUR 14 million for 2002, as well as the larger part of EUR 20 million out of the EUR 38 million yearly running costs for 2003 _ 2005, should be financed through the CFSP budget on condition that there is proper consultation of the European Parliament within the framework of the budgetary procedure; this also includes an agreement between the two arms of the budgetary authority on a general flexibility instrument within the EU budget for financing civilian crisis management operations;
5. Supports the declaration of intent of the Barcelona European Council to deploy the EU Rapid Reaction Force for its first peace-keeping mission in the Former Yugoslav Republic of Macedonia by taking over NATO' s operation 'Amber Fox', which already consists only of European troops;

6. Considers such a mission, which would depend on access to NATO's planning (Shape) and command capacities (D-Saceur), to be of great symbolic and practical importance for the EU's credibility in crisis management;
7. Is of the opinion that in the case of an EU-led operation in the Former Yugoslav Republic of Macedonia the required recourse to NATO's planning and command structures should not prejudice any general agreement on the involvement of non-EU NATO countries;
8. Considers that the first attempt to reach an agreement with Turkey has been made outside the EU decision-making procedures, and expects that an overall EU-NATO agreement on the use of NATO assets and capabilities will not undermine the decision-making autonomy of the Union; calls on the Commission and the Council to make a statement to Parliament on the negotiating mandate for this issue;
9. Underlines that expenditure on operations with military or defence implications should be shared between Member States and the Community; C 127 E/580 Official Journal of the European Union EN 29.5.2003 Wednesday 10 April 2002.
10. Urges the governments of Member States to give absolute priority in their defence procurement to fulfilling the requirements of the Rapid Reaction Force by focusing on equipment and technology that would improve its capacities to carry out Petersberg-type missions; this would imply the need for more interoperability and standardisation of the military equipment of European forces, which can be used both within an EU-ESDP context and in a NATO context;
11. Urges the Member States to assign importance to the quality of the EU military and police forces and to ensure that persons who participate have a deep and thorough understanding of their task;
12. Welcomes the creation of 14 multi-disciplinary working groups under the Spanish Presidency to examine the most crucial shortfalls in the 40 areas where deficiencies in military equipment have been identified;

13. Is of the opinion that improving military capacities is not only a question of adequate defence budgets but can primarily be achieved by rationalising defence efforts, by increasing synergy between national and multinational projects and by further abolition of obsolete Cold War structures and forces; considers that the establishment of the Capability Development Mechanism as agreed at the Göteborg European Council signifies that now is the time to relaunch action in this area as an integral element of the European Capability Action Plan;
14. Expresses its view that a strong, efficient and viable European armament industry, including research and development capacities, and an effective procurement policy are vital to the development of the ESDP and are a prerequisite if the European defence industry is to compete on more equal terms with the US industry; is concerned, in this connection, about the substantial investments which some Member States plan to make in research and development by American arms companies;
15. Calls on the Commission, in this respect, to present to the Council and Parliament a revised version of its 1997 Action Plan, a revision which is to mention, inter alia, whether the Commission could finance feasibility studies on the procurement of support equipment of non-military origin to be deployed by Member States' armed services, for example the adaptation of existing civil aircraft to perform the in-flight refuelling tanker role;
16. Considers in this context the development and purchase of the A 400 M aircraft by eight European countries to be an essential element in deployment capability, to ensuring the full mobility of European troops;
17. Believes that defence standardisation is imperative and calls on the governments of the Member States to assign higher priority to the creation of a European Armament Agency and to envisage the possibility of purchasing military equipment in a pool and to facilitate its joint use;
18. Calls on the Council, in the implementation of its European Capabilities Action Plan, to establish within the existing bodies, notably the Military Committee and the Headline Goal Task Force, a systematic procedure for reviews and

consultations at EU level concerning all national long-term defence procurement and planning programmes, with a view to seeking maximum efficiency and economies of scale from the outset, for instance with the UK's 'Future Offensive Air System' programme;

19. Reiterates its view that the control and restraint of arms exports, as well as an efficient policy to counter the global proliferation of small arms to regions of tension and to all types of official and less official combatants, should be considered an integral part of the ESDP and the EU's trade policy;
20. Shares the view that after the declaration of the Laeken European Council on the operability of the European Rapid Reaction Force it is time to formalise the meetings of EU defence ministers at Council level and regular reports to the European Parliament;
21. Recalls Belgium's initiative of drawing up a White Paper on European security in close coordination with NATO and calls on the Spanish Presidency to proceed with this project as a matter of urgency; 29.5.2003 EN Official Journal of the European Union C 127 E/581 Wednesday 10 April 2002.
22. Stresses the need to examine to what extent the full range of Petersberg missions should be redefined to include appropriate countermeasures against international terrorism and, as necessary, to adapt the headline goal and the civilian aspects of crisis management; points out that such a redefinition should not extend to the possibility of pre-emptive strikes against third parties;
23. Calls on the Presidency to report back to Parliament's responsible committee on the experiences it will gain from the EU military exercise in May 2002 which will involve command-and-control procedures rather than troops in the field;
24. Demands that the Commission undertake, in cooperation with the Presidency, a comprehensive needs-based study on civilian crisis management capabilities, to enable the EU to define its goals in the areas of civil administration, to refine and extend its capability goals in other areas of civilian crisis management, and to ensure that identified

crisis management needs can be met by coherent and concerted deployment of Member States' capabilities and Community instruments, and that these efforts are integrated with and support longer-term conflict prevention initiatives;

25. Calls further on the Presidency to report in full, in its proposed report on conflict prevention (Seville), on all progress that has been made in line with the recommendations of the Göteborg Action Plan, the Commission communication and Parliament's resolution of 13 December 2001 on conflict prevention (1), in particular, on the issues of mainstreaming of conflict prevention in all EU external relations, the involvement of international and local civil societies in activities for conflict prevention and management, and intensified cooperation with the UN and the OSCE; recalls that crisis prevention and civil crisis management are a first-pillar issue with clear responsibilities for the Commission and the European Parliament;
26. Recalls that responsibility for parliamentary monitoring of European security and defence policy is shared between the European Parliament and the national parliaments on the basis of their respective rights and duties under relevant treaties and constitutions; reiterates its view that in this perspective the WEU Parliamentary Assembly should be discontinued;
27. Notes that military expenditure and the deployment of national armed forces continue to fall within the exclusive competence of the national parliaments but that the running costs of EU joint actions for crisis management should be covered by the Community budget and therefore controlled by the European Parliament;
28. Calls therefore for closer relations and an intensified exchange of information between the European Parliament and national parliaments in relation to questions concerning the CFSP and the ESDP, in order to make more extensive dialogue between the parliaments possible;
29. Instructs its President to forward this resolution to the Commission, the Council and the governments of the Member States.

11

# History of the Australia – Malaysia Defence Relationship

## Introduction

The Australian Defence Force's commitment to the security of Malaysia is longstanding. It began with Malayan Campaign in World War II, followed shortly after by the Malayan Emergency and Confrontation. Since those conflicts, the defence relationship between Australia and Malaysia has continued to develop under the auspices of the Five Power Defence Arrangements and the Malaysia Australia Joint Defence Program. These historical links form the foundation of the continuing close defence cooperation between the two nations.

## WWII-The Malayan Campaign, Captivity and Liberation

Japan's devastating opening blows in the Second World War on 7 December 1941 were massive land, sea and air onslaughts on six widely separated points in the Pacific. They were Malaya, Pearl Harbour, Guam, Wake Island, Hong Kong and the Philippines. Before the Japanese attacked Pearl Harbour, No 1 Squadron of the Royal Australian Air Force flew Hudson aircraft into action against a Japanese invasion force at Kota Bahru on the northeast coast of Malaya. The Japanese attack was launched two hours ahead of the Pearl Harbour attack, when they began shelling shore defences at Kota Bahru soon after midnight on 8 December.

No 1 Squadron bombed the invasion convoy, caused heavy casualties and sank the Awagisan Maru, a 9700-tonne troopship, the first Japanese merchant ship to be sunk in the Pacific war. However, the success of No 1 Squadron was to be short lived. Next day, Japanese squadrons based in Thailand attacked the airfield at Kota Bahru, destroying most of the Australian Hudsons and forcing the squadron's withdrawal to Kuantan. Another Australian Squadron, No 21, was attacked at Sungei Patani and seven of its Buffalo fighters were put out of action. Later in the same day two Australian pilots were sent to Singora in Thailand but were attacked by 12 Zero fighters and were unable to complete their mission. On 10 December Britain suffered one of her worst blows of the war at sea when the capital ships Prince of Wales and Repulse were attacked and sunk by Japanese naval aircraft of the Japanese Navy's 22nd Air Flotilla then based at Saigon. The warships, accompanied by the Australian destroyer HMAS Vampire and other escorts, had sortied from Singapore into the South China Sea to seek out and destroy Japanese invasion convoys. No 453 Squadron, RAAF, was standing by at Sembawang to give fighter protection to the warships, but they were called to the scene too late. Vampire and HMS Electra rescued 796 survivors, however 840 officers and men died.

Meanwhile, a three-pronged thrust into Malaya by Japan's 25th Army was succeeding on all fronts as it pressed down the Malayan peninsula towards Singapore. By 19 December, Penang Island was occupied.

On 7 January the Japanese Army destroyed an Indian brigade and crippled a second in a crucial battle on the Slim River, the last natural barrier on the road to Kuala Lumpur. Five days later the Japanese 25th Division entered the city after its defenders were ordered to withdraw. Maintaining their momentum, the Japanese divisions pressed southwards to Johore State, which is separated from Singapore Island only by the narrow Straits of Johore.

The Australian 8th Division was deployed in Johore and on 14 January was sent into action for the first time. Its 2/30th Battalion ambushed and killed a large number of bicycle-riding Japanese soldiers at Gemas. After two days of fighting, the battalion had lost 81 killed, wounded or missing compared with an estimated 1000 enemy casualties. It withdrew in good order. On 15 January, the partly trained 45th Indian Brigade was attacked by the veteran Japanese Guards Division on the Maur River line, and were defeated. Two battalions of the 27th Australian Brigade were sent to strengthen them and at Bakri. The 2/29th Battalion destroyed eight tanks while the 2/19th routed the Japanese force to their front. However, Japanese forces cut their escape route leaving the Australians and Indian forces with no choice but to fight their way out. Lieutenant Colonel C.G.W Anderson led the breakout with lorries and all available weapons on the morning of 20 January. The column fought southwards overcoming numerous roadblocks but sustaining heavy casualties. To their despair, when the survivors reached the bridge at the river at Parit Sulong on the morning of the 21 January, they found it blocked. Anderson's force held its ground on the northern side of the river, surrounded by the enemy while the British 53rd Brigade made a failed rescue attempt from the South. A request to allow the vehicles carrying the wounded through was rejected by the Japanese. Throughout the night, the force withstood artillery shelling, tank attacks, machine gunning, mortars, snipers and bayonet charges. On the morning of 22 January, Anderson, realizing his force faced annihilation, ordered every man who was able to walk to break out in small groups and attempt to reach the Allied lines. Most of the wounded left behind were later killed by the enemy. The two battalions lost over 75 per cent of their men. For his courage and leadership during these actions Lieutenant Colonel C.G.W. Anderson, commanding officer of the 2/19th, earned the Victoria Cross.

A new threat developed on 25 January when a Japanese force landed from the sea at Endau, on the east coast of Johore, less than 100 miles from Singapore. Australian Buffalo and Hudson aircraft opposed the landing but were overwhelmed by a force of 50 enemy fighters.

A Japanese column on the east coast was ambushed at Jemalaung on 26 January by the Australians of the 22nd Brigade. The Australians lost 89 killed or missing in this bitter fight but inflicted heavy casualties on the enemy.

After the crushing defeat in Johore, all forces were ordered to immediately fall back on Singapore. The withdrawal from Johore took 4 days and was successful. The Australian 22nd Brigade, reinforced by Gordon Highlanders, had covered the approaches to the Johore causeway and early on 31 January, they were piped out of Johore by the only two surviving pipers of the Argyll and Sutherland Highlanders. The northern end of the causeway was then wrecked with demolition charges. Singapore, with its population swollen to a million people by refugees from the North, was now under siege. From January, large formations of Japanese bombers had pounded Singapore's four airfields, forcing the withdrawal of all but a few fighter aircraft. Most Australian Hudson bombers were sent south to Sumatra. Thereafter Japanese aircraft dominated the skies and their long range artillery maintained a constant barrage over the island from Johore. With no serviceable aircraft left, No 21 Squadron was ordered back to Australia.

The Japanese were not long in coming. On 8 February after heavy artillery and air bombardments lasting several days, assault troops crossed the narrow straits in assault craft propelled by outboard motors and attacked the western side of the island defended by the Australian 22nd Brigade. Although they inflicted heavy casualties, the Australian forces were thin on the ground and were forced to retreat. The brigade received reinforcements but by 6am the next day the situation was desperate. Next to come under attack was the Australian 27th Brigade when a third Japanese division, the Guards, also attacked the western area, ignoring the northern area where the bulk of the forces were deployed, including the 3rd Indian Corps and the newly arrived British 18th Division. Thus the main weight of the Japanese attack fell on the Australians.

Late on 10 February, a counter attack was ordered to regain the Krangi line. It was a hopeless mission by numerically weak forces against two Japanese divisions. Inevitably it failed, resulting in further losses. Widespread fighting continued on 11 February and on 12 February, Japanese tanks advancing towards the Bukit Timah Road were turned back. With the enemy enjoying control of the seas and of the skies over Singapore, General Percival withdrew his forces to a 40km arc around the city. A million civilians were in jeopardy and water supplies disrupted. Churchill was consulted on the 'ugly' decision that had to be made. On 15 February, Percival was given discretion to end resistance. Later that day he met General Yamashita and at 8.30pm fighting ceased.

Australia had suffered a grievous blow. Of the 18,000 AIF, 1100 RAAF and 1500 RAN personnel who served in the Malaya/ Singapore campaign, more than 1800 men and 33 women were lost and over 15,000 others were taken prisoner to suffer brutal and degrading forms of captivity which, before the war ended, resulted in the deaths of one third of their number. The most infamous example of inhumane treatment of Allied troops by their Japanese captors on what was to become Malaysian soil occurred at the POW camp at Sandakan and on the subsequent death marches to Ranau. Of the 2428 Allied service men (1787 Australians and 641 British) held at Sandakan Carp from 18 July 1942 to 15 August 1945 only six Australian soldiers escaped to survive the War. The remainder were either killed by their captors or died as a result of illness or starvation in the POW camp or on the subsequent "Death Marches" to Ranau.

The first British territory in South East Asia to be liberated was Labuan Island. On 10 June 1945, an allied invasion force of 29,000, spearheaded by the Australian 9th Division, landed in Brunei Bay. In securing the Island, Australia lost 34 men. A total of 138 Australians were killed in the liberation of Labuan, Sabah and Sarawak.

### *Malayan Emergency*

The Malayan Emergency was declared on 18 June 1948 after three estate managers were murdered in Perak, northern Malaya, by guerrillas of the Malayan Communist Party (MCP), an outgrowth of the anti-Japanese guerrilla movement which had emerged during the Second World War. Despite never having had more than a few thousand members, the MCP was able to draw on the support of many disaffected Malayan Chinese, who were upset that British promises of an easier path to full Malayan citizenship had not been fulfilled. The harsh post-war economic and social conditions also contributed to the rise of anti-government activity. The Colonial government was slow to react to the MCP at first and did not appoint a director of operations to counter the insurgency until March 1950. The new director planned to address the underlying economic, social and political problems facing the Chinese community while at the same time bringing government control to the fringe areas where the MCP received much of its support. Before this plan was fully implemented, however, the situation deteriorated further with the assassination of the British High Commissioner in October 1951. The attack galvanised British resolve to meet the threat posed by the MCP, and the Malayan government, in turn, stepped up counter-insurgency measures. Prolonged operations were undertaken against the communists in an effort to destroy their base of support in local communities and to drive them into the jungle, where it would be difficult for them to receive supplies from supporters.

Australia's involvement in the Emergency began in 1950 with the arrival of RAAF aircraft and personnel in Singapore. Dakotas from 38 Squadron were deployed on cargo runs, troop movements and paratroop and leaflet drops in Malaya, while six Lincoln bombers of 1 Squadron provided the backbone of aerial operations. As the capacity of army and police units operating against the communists improved, however, the need for air power decreased and, by 1952, Lincolns were increasingly used as part of combined air-ground assaults against the communists. One of the major military successes of the conflict was one such coordinated operation in July 1954, east of Ipoh in Perak. In Operation Termite, five RAAF Lincolns and six from a Royal Air Force squadron made simultaneous attacks on two communist camps, followed by paratroop drops, a ground attack and further bombing runs ten days later. The operation destroyed 181 camps and killed thirteen communists; one communist surrendered.

By October 1955, when the 2nd Battalion, Royal Australian Regiment (2 RAR), arrived in Penang, the outcome of the Emergency was no longer in doubt, although a lengthy "mopping up" stage followed, largely undertaken by Australian troops. 2 RAR crossed to the mainland in January 1956 to begin anti-communist operations. Over the next 20 months, as part of 28 Commonwealth Brigade, 2 RAR participated in a variety of operations, mainly in Perak, one of the main areas of communist activity.

Their work consisted of extensive patrolling, watching for contacts in the rubber plantations and mounting a perimeter guard on the New Villages, settlements which the government had established to provide infrastructure and services in outlying areas in the hope of denying the guerrillas access to their support base. Contacts were rare, however, and the battalion had a mixed record, killing two communists in an ambush on 25 June 1956 but losing three of its own troops.

2 RAR left Malaya in October 1957 and was replaced by 3 RAR in the same month. After six weeks of training in jungle warfare, 3 RAR began driving the insurgents into the jungle in Perak and Kedah, separating them from food and other supplies. Early successes for the battalion confirmed the growing ascendancy of the security forces over the communists, and by April 1959 Perak was declared secure. By late 1959, operations against the communists were in their final phase and many communists had crossed Malaya's northern border into Thailand. 3 RAR left Malaya in October 1959 to be replaced by 1 RAR. Although operating in the border region, 1 RAR made no contact with the enemy and were forbidden to move in Thailand, even when the presence and location of communists was known.

As the threat continued to dissipate, the Malayan government officially declared the Emergency over on 31 July 1960, though 1 RAR remained in Malaya until October the following year, when 2 RAR returned for a second tour. In August 1962 the battalion was committed to anti-communist operations in Perlis and Kedah, completing its tour in August 1963. In addition to air and infantry forces, Australia also provided artillery and engineering support, and an air-field construction squadron built the main runway for the air force base at Butterworth. Ships of the Royal Australian Navy also served in Malayan waters, and Australian ships had occasion to fire on suspected communist positions in 1956 and 1957. Australian ground forces in Malaya formed part of Australia's contribution to the Far East Strategic Reserve, which was set up in April 1955 primarily to deter external communist aggression against countries in south-east Asia, especially Malaya and Singapore.

Lasting 13 years, the Malayan Emergency was the longest continuous military commitment in Australia's history. Thirty-nine Australian servicemen were killed in Malaya, although only 15 of these deaths occurred as a result of operations, and 27 were wounded, most of whom were in the Army.

## *Confrontation with Indonesia*

Between 1963 and 1966, Indonesia and Malaysia fought a small, undeclared war which came to involve troops from Australia and Britain. The conflict resulted from a belief by Indonesia's

President Sukarno that the creation of the Federation of Malaysia, which was declared on 31 August 1963, represented an attempt by Britain to maintain colonial rule behind the cloak of independence granted to its former colonial possessions in south-east Asia. .

The term "Confrontation" was coined by Indonesia's Foreign Minister, Dr Subandrio, in January 1963, and it has come to refer to Indonesia's efforts at that time to destabilise the new federation, with a view to breaking it up. The actual war began when Indonesia launched a series of cross-border raids into Malaysian territory in early 1963.

The antagonism that gave rise to Confrontation was already apparent in December 1962, when a small party of armed insurgents, with Indonesian backing, attempted to seize power in the independent enclave of Brunei, only to be defeated by British troops from Singapore. By early 1963 military activity had increased along the Indonesian side of the border in Borneo, as small parties of armed men began infiltrating Malaysian territory on propaganda and sabotage missions. These cross-border raids, carried out by Indonesian "volunteers", continued throughout 1963; by 1964 Indonesian regular arm units had also become involved.

Australian units which fought during Confrontation did so as part of a larger British and Commonwealth force under overall British command. Australia's commitment to operations against Indonesia in Borneo and West Malaysia fell within the context of its membership in the Far East Strategic Reserve. At first, the Australian government kept its troops from becoming involved in Confrontation, not least because of fears that the conflict would spread to the long-and difficult to defend-border between Papua New Guinea and Indonesia. Requests from both the British and Malaysian governments in 1963-64 for the deployment of Australian troops in Borneo met with refusal, though the Australian government did agree that its troops could be used for the defence of the Malay Peninsula against external attack. In the event, such attacks occurred twice, in September and October 1964, when Indonesia launched paratroop and amphibious raids against Labis and Pontian, on the south-western side of the peninsula. Members of the 3rd Battalion, Royal Australian Regiment (3 RAR) were used in clean-up operations against the invading troops. Although these attacks were easily repelled, they did pose a serious risk of escalating the fighting; the Australian government relented in January 1965 and agreed to the deployment of a battalion in Borneo.

The military situation in Borneo thus far had consisted of company bases located along the border between Indonesia and Malaysia to protect centres of population from enemy incursions. By 1965 the British government had given permission for more aggressive action to be taken, and the security forces now mounted cross-border operations with the purpose of obtaining intelligence and forcing the Indonesians to remain on the defensive on their own side of the border. Uncertain where the Commonwealth forces might strike next, the Indonesians increasingly devoted their resources to protecting their own positions and correspondingly less on offensive operations, although these continued on a much reduced scale.

The first Australian battalion, 3 RAR, arrived in Borneo in March 1965 and served in Sarawak until the end of July. During this time the battalion conducted extensive operations on both sides of the border, were engaged in four major contacts with Indonesian units, and twice suffered casualties from land mines.

Its replacement, the 28th Brigade, 4 RAR, also served in Sarawak-from April until August 1966. Although it had a less active tour, the 28th Brigade also operated on the Indonesian side of the border and was involved in clashes with Indonesian regulars. Altogether, two squadrons of the Special Air Service, a troop of the Royal Australian Signals, several artillery batteries and parties of the Royal Australian Engineers were involved in Borneo, in addition to the two infantry battalions. Ships of the Royal Australian Navy served in the surrounding waters and several RAAF squadrons were also involved in the Confrontation.

Continuing negotiations between Indonesia and Malaysia ended the conflict, and the two sides signed a peace treaty in Bangkok in August 1966. Twenty-three Australians were killed during Confrontation, seven of them on operations, and eight were wounded. Because of the sensitivity of the cross-border operations, which remained secret at the time, Confrontation received very little coverage in the Australian media.

## The Five Power Defence Arrangements

In 1967, as part of its 'East of Suez' policy, Britain announced its intention to withdraw its military forces from Malaysia and Singapore during the 1970s. The announcement caused considerable concern for Malaysia and Singapore as they had relied heavily on Britain to guarantee their security. Britain's subsequent decision to complete the withdrawal of around 26,000 troops by the end of 1971 gave greater urgency to find a solution.

Those efforts would lead to the formation in November 1971, of the Five Power Defence Arrangements (FPDA), involving Britain, Australia, New Zealand, Singapore and Malaysia. The cornerstone of the FPDA was the Communique in which the five powers agreed that in the event of any form of armed attack externally organized or supported, or the threat of such attack against Malaysia or Singapore, their Governments would immediately consult together for the purpose of deciding what measures should be taken jointly or separately in relation to such an attack or threat.

The longevity, relevance and evolution of the FPDA is well illustrated by Australia's commitment of forces under the arrangement. On 11 February 1971, Headquarters Integrated Air Defence System (IADS) was formed at Butterworth with Australia providing the Commander. On 1 September 1971 IADS assumed operational responsibility for the air defence of Malaysia and Singapore.

Under the FPDA, an ANZUK force of some 7,100 men, including 3,400 Australians with 1500 stationed at Butterworth was established to support the defence of Malaysia and Singapore. In line with the changing strategic and defence environment in the region, including the end of the war in Vietnam, ANZUK force was disbanded in 1975 and the function of IADS has subsequently evolved. Although the number of Australian defence personnel in Malaysia has also reduced during subsequent years to it's current strength of 186 personnel, Australia's commitment to regional security under the FPDA is today still evident in its strong support of IADS, its permanent P3-C maritime patrol aircraft detachment and the Australian Army Rifle Company at Butterworth, and its strong commitment and participation in frequent multi-lateral Exercises.

The FPDA arrangements were intended to be transitional, providing security for Malaysia and Singapore for a few years while they developed their own national capabilities. Instead, while there have been fluctuations in the level of involvement of its members, FPDA, as the only multi-lateral security arrangement in South-East Asia, is still in good shape. For over thirty years the FPDA has progressively evolved to form a key element of relations between the five members and continues to provide a stabilising influence in the region.

## *Malaysia Australia Joint Defence Program*

The last major development in the history of Australia's close defence relationship with Malaysia occurred in 1992 with the signing of the Malaysia Australia Joint Defence Program (MAJDP), aimed at enhancing the effectiveness of the bi-lateral defence relationship between Malaysia and Australia. Under the program, ADF officers have the opportunity of undertaking long-term attachments with the MAF while similar numbers of Malaysian officers are attached to ADF Units. Significant numbers of MAF personnel also undertake military training courses in Australia at institutions such as Centre for Defence and Strategic Studies, Australian Command and Staff College, Australian Defence Force Academy and the Duntroon Royal Military College while Australian officers attend the Maktab Turus Angkatan Tentera. Australia and Malaysia also conduct frequent bi-lateral exercises to improve interoperability, promote understanding of each other's unique operational environments and to strengthen the military skills and capabilities of both forces.

12

# National Missile Defence Options and the Bush Administration

## Introduction

In the last few years of the Clinton administration, the United States appeared to be moving towards the deployment of a limited National Missile Defence (NMD) system, intended to protect the entire country from small-scale attacks by long-range ballistic missiles armed with chemical, biological, or nuclear weapons. Under pressure from the Republican Congress, it seemed quite possible that by the end of his administration, President Clinton would begin NMD deployment, and a formal deployment decision was scheduled for the summer of 2000. However, in a September 1, 2000 speech, Clinton announced that he would not begin deployment – in effect passing the deployment decision onto the next president. This decision appeared to be influenced by a number of factors, including two recent test failures, continued Russian opposition to NMD and Russian unwillingness to modify the ABM Treaty to permit NMD deployment, lack of support from key allies, and technical criticisms of the NMD system's likely effectiveness.

With the election of George W. Bush as president, the probability of a near-term NMD deployment has greatly increased. Bush and his key advisors appear to be strong NMD supporters and as a presidential candidate Bush made it clear that he favored a rapid deployment of NMD. Moreover, the Republican-controlled Congress, long frustrated by what it saw as endless delaying tactics on NMD by the Clinton administration, will continue to push hard for a rapid NMD deployment, emphasizing that existing legislation requires NMD deployment as soon as technologically feasible.

While President Bush will probably spend some time reviewing NMD options and attempting to persuade Russia and key allies to accept an NMD deployment, it seems quite likely that by or before the end of the first year of his administration Bush will decide to begin NMD deployment.

This paper will not focus on whether or not deploying NMD is a good idea. (Its author believes that the NMD system proposed by Clinton is not needed, is unlikely to work, and will have serious and adverse international consequences that far outweigh any benefits it can provide, and that a Bush NMD system is unlikely to be much better.1) Instead, it will focus on the technical options for NMD deployment in the Bush Administration.

This paper will first review the status of NMD and its key technologies at the end of the Clinton administration. It will then consider in more detail four key technical issues relevant to a potential NMD deployment: (1) the real-world effectiveness of Clinton's proposed NMD system; (2) the NMD testing program; (3) the relationship between NMD and theatre missile defences (TMDs); and (4) potential boost-phase approaches for NMD. Finally, it will discuss what is known about President Bush's views on NMD, and review the range of NMD options open to him. Although Bush's plans cannot be predicted with any certainty, it is speculated here that his most likely approach would be to deploy a reconfigured and expanded version of Clinton's ground-based NMD system, which would be eventually supplemented by sea-based interceptors and possibly also by a boost-phase system.

## The Clinton Administration Plan

In 1996, under intense pressure from the Republican-controlled Congress, the Clinton administration announced its so-called "3+3" plan for NMD. Under this plan, NMD technology would be developed for three years, at the end of which (in 2000), a deployment decision could be made. If the decision was then made to deploy, an initial NMD capability could then be operational in another three years (by 2003).

Otherwise, development would continue, so that the NMD system would remain deployable in three years. Prior to President Clinton's decision not to begin NMD deployment, it was already clear that the earliest possible deployment date had slipped to 2005. In his September 1 speech, Clinton stated that the earliest realistic operational date for the first phase of his proposed system was actually 2007.

The primary official justification for the Clinton NMD program was the possible emergence of a missile threat from countries such as North Korea, Iran or Iraq. An important, but secondary justification, was the possibility an accidental or unauthorized launch of missiles from Russia. Although China's nuclear missile force is not part of the Clinton administration's justification for a potential NMD deployment, these missiles are prominently cited as a threat by many NMD supporters outside of the administration.

As is discussed below, if President Bush wants to rapidly deploy an NMD system, then his system will almost certainly have to be built up out of the same basic components (interceptors, radars, etc.) as Clinton's proposed system. Unless Bush entirely abandons the Clinton approach in favour of a technologically different approach (such as a boost phase system), which would involve a substantial delay in initial operational capability, his NMD system will share not only the same components, but also many of the strengths and weaknesses of the Clinton Administration's proposed system.

Thus it is useful to review how Clinton's proposed system would have worked.

In the Clinton administration plan, the NMD system would have been built up out of a small number of components, including:

- Ground-based interceptors (GBIs) equipped with infrared-homing Exo-atmospheric Kill Vehicles (EKVs);
- X-band missile defence radars;
- Upgraded early warning radars;
- Space-based Infrared System—Low Earth Orbit (SBIRS-Low) missile tracking satellites;
- Early warning satellites;
- Command and control facilities and communication relays.

These components, most of which are well along in development and testing, could be could be assembled in various configurations to produce the NMD system. The "weapon" of the NMD system is the GBI, which would use its high-speed booster rocket to propel its EKV payload towards incoming missile targets. The EKV, which can operate only above the atmosphere, would use infrared and possibly visible light sensors to home in on its target. It would then attempt to destroy the incoming missile's warhead in a direct, high-speed collision.

The NMD command and control system would use information from a number of sensors to track and discriminate potential targets, and to guide the interceptors to these targets. The primary NMD sensor is the X-band radar ("X-band" refers to the radar's 10 GHz operating frequency). The X-band radar (which is very similar to, albeit much larger, than the radar for the THAAD TMD system) is a large, phased-array radar that has been specifically designed for NMD use, and is optimized for precision tracking and discrimination.

The X-band radars would be supplemented by a number of Upgraded Early Warning Radars (UEWRs). These radars are upgraded versions of the United States' five existing large phased-array early warning radars. Relatively minor improvements in these radars' processing hardware and software would give them the ability to track missile targets accurately enough to guide to interceptors, a capability they do not have now. However, although the UEWRs are large and powerful radars, both their range and azimuth resolution are far inferior to that of the X-band radars, and they thus have little ability to discriminate missile warheads from decoys or other false targets.

The other primary NMD sensor system is the SBIRS-Low space-based missile tracking system. The system, expected to use a constellation of as many as 24 satellites, would use infrared and visible light sensors to track missiles and their warheads. The tracking accuracy would be high enough to guide interceptors in the absence of radar data. SBIRS-Low is also expected to play a role in discriminating warheads from decoys, since its infrared and visible sensors provide very different information about target characteristics than do the X-band radars. SBIRS-Low is unlikely to be ready in time to be part of an initial NMD deployment.

However, once operational it will provide almost complete global coverage of missiles through their entire flight trajectories. SBIRS-Low is also intended to support upper tier theatre missile defence systems such as Navy Theatre Wide and the Theatre High-Altitude Area Defence (THAAD) system. Under the Clinton administration's plan, the NMD system would have been deployed in phases. The initial system, the C-1 system, would deploy 20 interceptor missiles (this number would be increased to 100 soon thereafter) in central Alaska and a single X-band radar at Shemya, at the western end of the Alaskan Aleutian island chain.

These locations are ideally suited for defence against missiles from North Korea or China. However, the X-band radar at Shemya cannot see missiles approaching U.S. territory from other directions, such as from the Middle East. In the initial phase of Clinton's system, this problem would be solved by using Upgraded Early Warning Radars in Alaska, California, Massachusetts, Greenland and Britain to provide sensor coverage for missiles approaching from other directions. The stated goal of this C-1 system is to defend the entire United States from a few tens of warheads equipped with "simple" countermeasures from North Korea, or a smaller number of warheads from the Middle East (the number is smaller due to the limited discrimination and tracking limited capabilities of the UEWRs).

Under the Clinton administration's plan, the full NMD system, the C-3 system, would not be operational until sometime after 2010. According to a notional architecture released by the Ballistic Missile Defence Organization (BMDO) in the spring of 1999, the C-3 system would add a second interceptor site at the former Safeguard site in North Dakota, with a total of 200-250 interceptors up divided between the two launch sites. The C-3 system would also deploy up to eight more X-band missile radars and the SBIRS-Low space-based missile tracking system. An April 2000 estimate by the Congressional Budget Office was that this C-3 system would cost about $60 billion.3

## Some Technical Issues Relevant to NMD Deployment

If the United States deploys an NMD system, it is important that that system work, and work very well. Moreover, it is also important that US political and military leaders have a clear and accurate understanding of how effective the defence will be if it is ever actually used.

Supporters of Clinton's proposed NMD system claim that it will be highly effective against small-scale missile attacks. Indeed, until perhaps a year ago, it seemed to be widely assumed, even by many NMD opponents, that the system would work.

However, test failures and increased scrutiny of the ability of the NMD system to deal with steps taken by an adversary to defeat it have revived the question of whether the system will actually work.

The key issue here is the operational effectiveness of the NMD system. That is, how well it will work in the real world, where an attacker would likely attempt to defeat the system. The issue is NOT whether it is possible to "hit a bullet with a bullet" or whether it is possible to hit warhead targets on a test range. There is little doubt that, with enough time and money, the U.S. could build a system that could reliably hit an ICBM warhead under controlled circumstances on a test range. However, the problem of achieving effective defence against an adversary that attempts to defeat the system is a qualitatively different and much more difficult problem.

The operational effectiveness of the NMD system will be determined primarily by its ability to deal with steps – "countermeasures" – that an attacker takes to defeat the system. Countermeasures have been the fundamental problem for ballistic missile defences from the beginning, and still are. Every country that has developed and deployed intercontinental-range ballistic missiles has had a parallel (and highly classified) program to develop missile defence countermeasures. President Clinton specifically cited the problem of countermeasures in his September 1 announcement deferring the deployment decision.

There are many possible countermeasures and to be reliable and effective, a defence must be effective against all plausible countermeasures. However, Clinton's proposed NMD system – which now has a relatively well defined overall design comprised of specific components – appears to be vulnerable to a number of specific countermeasures. The recent report *Countermeasures: A Technical Evaluation of the Operational Effectiveness of the Planned US*

*National Missile Defence System* sponsored by Union of Concerned Scientists and the MIT Security Studies Program surveyed a range of countermeasures and analyzed three in detail:4

- Biological submunitions. A missile attacker using biological weapons could package them in numerous small submunitions that would be released shortly after the end of the missile's boost phase. This tactic would overwhelm the defence with too many targets to fire at.
- Anti-simulation decoys. If the appearance of the warhead is disguised, then almost any object with a volume larger than a warhead can be a credible decoy, since both heavy and light objects move on identical trajectories in outer space, where the defence interceptor operates. In particular, the warhead could be put inside a light-weight balloon covered with a thin layer of metal and released along with numerous similar, but empty, balloons.
- Cooled shroud. Covering the warhead with a thin shroud cooled with liquid nitrogen would make it effectively invisible to the heat-seeking interceptors the defence uses.

The *Countermeasures* report found that each of these countermeasures appeared to be able to defeat the planned NMD system and were within the means of countries able to develop nuclear-armed intercontinental-range ballistic missiles (ICBMs). It therefore argued that it did not make sense to deploy the system unless it could be demonstrated through testing that the system could in fact defeat such countermeasures.

The primary response to the *Countermeasures* report made by NMD supporters is that it underestimates the difficulty of actually implementing the countermeasures it discusses. They argue that these countermeasures are too difficult for emerging missiles states such as North Korea to deploy, at least for many years.

However, the best way to judge if an emerging missile state such as North Korea could build such countermeasures is by comparison to the problems they would have already had to solve in order to pose a missile threat to the United States. An emerging missile state able to attack the US with nuclear-armed ICBMs would have already solved much harder problems - building ICBMs, building nuclear weapons small enough to be delivered by such missiles, solving reentry heating problems, etc. – than are involved with putting a warhead inside a balloon or putting a cooled shroud around a warhead. Any country capable of building long-range nuclear-armed ballistic missiles is clearly capable of building such countermeasures. Moreover, the September 1999 National Intelligence Estimate (NIE) on the Ballistic Missile Threat to the United States through 2015 stated that emerging missile states could have countermeasures technologies such as reentry vehicle (RV) separation, RV reorientation, simple (balloon) decoys, RV spin-stabilization, chaff, low-power jammers, booster fragmentation, and radar absorbing materials available by the time they test-flight their missiles. 5

NMD supporters have also argued that the *Countermeasures* report assumes a static defence configuration, but that the NMD system will evolve and adapt to observed countermeasure developments.

However, the *Countermeasures* report analyzed the complete NMD system planned by the Clinton administration, which it has stated can defeat even complex countermeasures, and showed that this claim is not correct. Moreover, the NMD system cannot adapt to changes it cannot observe. Countermeasures can be tested on the ground, and since emerging missile states have no facilities with which to observe flight tests, they have no reason to test fly their countermeasures. For example, the US didn't even know that North Korea's Taepodong missile had a third stage until it was flown over Japan on its only flight. Moreover, the changes required to defeat proposed countermeasures are not minor and will require extensive development and testing, and potential attackers will also be able to respond to these changes.

### *The NMD Testing Program*

How will it be known if an NMD system will be effective in the real world? Although simulation will necessarily play a vital role, the only way to determine whether the planned NMD system will work in the real world is through a program of tests against realistic threats. However, a testing program against only cooperative targets (no effective countermeasures, complete advance knowledge) may tell you very little about how the defence will work in the real world.

This situation is illustrated by the only actual use of a ballistic missile defence – the Patriot in the 1991 Gulf War. Prior to the Gulf War, Patriot had 17 tests against ballistic missile targets, and every one was successful. But against the Iraqi missiles it failed completely, although it was a political success. Unlike the test range targets, which flew on smooth, predictable trajectories, the Iraqi missiles broke apart and maneuvered vigorously, and Patriot had almost no chance of destroying such targets.

This example illustrates that it is essential the defence be tested against realistic targets if a correct understanding of its real-world effectiveness is to be obtained. However, there has NEVER been an intercept test of a missile defence such as the planned US NMD system against targets employing credible countermeasures. And under current plans, by the time the initial US NMD system could be deployed and operational, no such realistic tests will have occurred.

The NMD program has had three intercept tests so far. In the first test, held in October 1999, the kill vehicle hit its target, however, the second and third intercept tests, in January and July 2000 respectively, failed. These three intercept tests all used the same target set: a conical warhead and a larger, spherical balloon (the final stage of the missile used to boost these targets was also in the field of view). The infrared signal from the balloon was about seven times larger than that of the warhead, and the defence had complete advance knowledge of the characteristics of both the target and decoy. Tests against such targets do not demonstrate discrimination, much less real world effectiveness, they only establish basic functioning in a very controlled environment.

NMD supporters argue that it is appropriate to start with such simple targets, because you must "walk before you run." This is true. But these tests in no way demonstrate that the system can work against a real-world attack – one that actually attempts to defeat it. This might not be a concern if subsequent tests used realistic target sets and if a deployment decision was not made until after these realistic tests. However, this is far from being the actual situation. Under current plans, realistic tests would not occur until AFTER the defence is deployed and operational, if ever. As of mid-2000, plans called for a series of 19 intercept tests to be carried out through the end of 2005. However, this testing program is already well behind schedule, and is unlikely to be completed before the 2007 date by which the NMD system could be operational.

Each of these 19 tests will be against targets representing the "defined C-1 threat.6 (Recall that the initial phase of NMD deployment is known as the C-1 system.) The C-1 system is only intended and required to counter threats that use no countermeasures or have only "simple" countermeasures (the C-1 threat).

Administration and contractor statements make it clear the C-1 threat includes no credible countermeasures.

For example, according to Major General William Nance, the NMD Program Manager, the mock warhead and large balloon target set used in the first three intercept tests was "more than representative" of the decoys and countermeasures an emerging missile state might use.7 Similarly, John Peller (then the NMD program manager at Boeing, the NMD Lead System Integrator) stated that "the target suite was equal to, if not more challenging than, the current projected rogue threat."8 In June 2000 Congressional testimony, BMDO Director Lt. General Kadish said that the defined C-1 threat does not include "many" of the countermeasure technologies that the September 1999 National Intelligence Estimate says will be available to emerging missile states by the time they flight test their missiles.9 This situation does not change qualitatively throughout the entire projected series of 19 flight tests, all of which feature an undisguised warhead and spherical balloon decoys. By requiring the C-1 system only to be effective against attackers using no countermeasures (or completely ineffective ones), BMDO has in effect defined away the countermeasures problem until *after* the initial deployment has occurred.

However, even a few successful intercepts against such unrealistic targets are taken as demonstrating the technical feasibility of the NMD system.

The next phase of deployment is then supposed to be able to deal with "complex" countermeasures. But the apparent availability of effective countermeasures against this system indicates that while the planned NMD system may be able to "walk" on the test range it will not be able to "run" in the real world. The combination of a rush to deployment with an unrealistic testing program raise the likelihood that the US will incur the worst possible NMD outcome: suffering substantial international diplomatic and security costs for the deployment of an NMD system that does not work.

To avoid such an outcome, the NMD system should be tested realistically against a range of plausible countermeasures. This could be done by establishing an independent countermeasures "red team," with expertise and resources equivalent to that believed to be held by emerging missile states, to develop, construct, and test countermeasures. Once this red team determined which countermeasures were feasible, they should be tested against the planned NMD system. These tests should be conducted without the defence having complete advance information on the nature of the threat it will face. Ideally, this testing should be done before committing to deployment. At a minimum, analysis should demonstrate that the planned defence could defeat such plausible countermeasures before beginning deployment.

In response to criticisms of the NMD testing program, BMDO has reportedly modified the test program. According to Major General Nance, the NMD Program Manager, future tests will now include multiple threats ands targets with multiple interceptors and that the NMD program will work with the test community to create a task force that combines developmental and operational testers for planning and execution of the NMD test base.10

Although General Nance has stated that these changes will greatly improve the realism of the NMD test program, the limited publicly available information about these changes suggest that they are minor ones that do not change the fundamental problems with the testing program. In particular, they do not appear to involve either credible countermeasures or an independent countermeasures red team.

### *The Relationship Between NMD and TMD*

In addition to its NMD program, the United States is also developing a number of TMD systems. These systems can be divided into three groups: low-altitude systems capable of covering relatively small areas, high-altitude systems capable of covering much larger areas, and boost-phase systems.

The United States is currently developing three low-altitude TMD systems. These are the U.S Army's Patriot PAC-3 system, the Navy Area Defence system, and the Medium Extended Air Defence System (MEADS) being developed jointly with Italy and Germany. The U.S. is also supporting Israel in the development of its Arrow system. All of these systems are intended to cover relatively small areas from relatively short-range (perhaps 1,500 km or less) missiles, and all of them use interceptors that rely on atmospheric forces for maneuvering. None of these systems are regarded as having any significant capabilities against long-range strategic ballistic missiles or as being violations of the ABM Treaty. However, these systems could also be deployed independently of the NMD system to defend US allies or overseas forces from short and medium range missiles. In this restricted way, at least for countries for which the missile threat is seen as being due to shorter-range missiles, such TMD systems could be viewed as supplementing an NMD system.

The U.S. is also developing two high-altitude systems, the U.S. Army's Theatre High Altitude Area Defence (THAAD) system and the Navy Theatre Wide system, intended to protect large areas from missiles with ranges of up to 3,500 km. Both of these systems operate in the same general way as the NMD system, and, if supported by the NMD sensor network may have significant capabilities against strategic missiles.

Over the past few years, there has been significant Congressional Republican support for deploying the Navy Theatre Wide system as a sea-based mid-course NMD system, either in place of or as a supplement to a land-based NMD system. Such a sea-based system could provide earlier and additional intercept attempts, and could be used to expand the coverage of the NMD system to anywhere in the world.

The Navy Theatre Wide system would use existing or modified launchers and radars on some or all of the many U.S. Navy cruisers and destroyers equipped with the Aegis weapons system. The interceptor for a sea-based NMD system could be a variant of the Navy Theatre Wide SM-3 interceptor that is currently under development, or it could be a larger and faster missile (which might require modifying the launchers on the ships). An infrared homing kill vehicle, likely a modification of either the Light-weight

Exo-Atmospheric Projectile (LEAP) developed by SDI or the land-based system's EKV, would attempt to destroy the missile warhead in a direct high-speed collision.

Advocates of naval NMD argue that such a system could be deployed more rapidly and more inexpensively than the currently planned land-based system, since it would be based on the already existing AEGIS infrastructure.11

Critics of sea-based NMD argue that it will take much longer and be much more difficult and expensive to build than its supporters argue.12 The Ballistic Missile Defence Organization recently reported that such a sea-based system would both cost more and take longer to deploy than the currently planned land-based system.13

More importantly, a sea-based NMD system would operate in essentially the same way as the land-based system (i.e., it would use infrared homing, above-the atmosphere, hit-to-kill interceptors, supported by radars and space-based infrared sensors), and thus would have all of the same vulnerabilities. In fact, the sea-based system would likely be even less effective because of the smaller size and more limited capabilities of its individual components.

However, the same BMDO report that concluded that a sea-based system would take longer and cost more than a land-based system also concluded that sea-based mid-course interceptors, such as the planned Block-II interceptors for the Navy Theatre Wide TMD system (currently scheduled for deployment sometime after 2010) could usefully supplement a land-based NMD system. As noted above, such interceptors could be used to make earlier intercept attempts and to expand the coverage of the NMD system overseas. In this approach, the sensors for the land-based system (including SBIRS-low) could be used to overcome one of the key weaknesses of the Navy Theatre Wide system – the relatively limited capabilities of its ship-borne radars.

The Army's THAAD system could similarly use information from the NMD sensor system to attempt to intercept strategic missile targets. However, because of its relatively slower interceptor speed (2.7 km/second compared to 4.5 km/second for NTW Block II), the size of the area it could attempt to defend is not as large, and there seems to be little interest in incorporating THAAD into the NMD program. The final group of U.S. TMD programs consists of those that attempt to intercept theatre missiles during their boost phase. The U.S. has one boost-phase TMD system, the Airborne Laser (ABL), under development and has studied (with Israel) boost-phase TMD systems using interceptor missiles on aircraft.

The primary program in this category is the Airborne Laser, which would put a megawatt-class laser aboard a Boeing 747 aircraft. Current plans call for the first test against a missile target in 2003 and for deployment of 7 ABL aircraft to begin in 2007. The technical feasibility of the ABL is not yet firmly established, and probably cannot be until it is actually tested. Even if it is feasible, there are significant engineering problems that could substantially delay its deployment.

If it works as expected, the ABL could have a range of about 300 to 500 km against short-range theatre missiles. However, it would likely have greater range against intercontinental-range missiles, because these have longer boost phases, burn out higher in the atmosphere (so the laser beam has to pass through less atmosphere), and usually have thinner walls. Thus the ABL could potentially be deployed against strategic missiles either as a free-standing system or as an add-on to a land-based or sea-based NMD system.

## *Potential Boost-Phase Approaches for NMD*

The inability of mid-course defences, such as Clinton's proposed NMD system, to defeat submunitions and the vulnerability of midcourse systems to countermeasures has increased interest in boost-phase defences, and a number of boost-phase approaches for NMD have been proposed. Boost-phase systems can destroy submunition-armed missiles before they can release their submunitions. In addition, boost-phase systems appear to be more resistant to countermeasures than mid-course systems, and thus could be more effective in the real world.

Although boost-phase systems are likely to be more effective than midcourse systems, a number of concerns remain. Most boost-phase systems have relatively short ranges and thus must be deployed close to the missile launch site if they are to be effective. This means both that the general location of the missile threat must be known in advance and that the boost-phase system may be vulnerable to attack. Most of the proposed boost-phase systems destroy the rocket booster and not the warhead, thus the question of where the warhead comes down and what happens when it does must be considered. Some types of boost-phase systems could also be overwhelmed if a number of missiles are launched within a short time interval. Most of the proposed types of boost phase systems cannot counter one of the NMD system's principal justifications – the possibility of an accidental or inadvertent Russian missile launch.

Finally, all boost-phase systems involve short decision time lines. A potentially significant advantage of boost-phase systems that use interceptor missiles is that these systems are inherently limited in range because the interceptors have only a few minutes to fly out to reach a missile target before its boost-phase ends. This raises the possibility that such a boost-phase system could be configured so it can cover a small country such as North Korea, but not a larger country such as Russia or China.

Such an approach may therefore be less threatening and more acceptable to Russia and/or China. However, although Russian President Putin's proposal for a European missile defence system is sometimes, and apparently incorrectly, said to involve a boost-phase approach, neither Russia nor China has given any indication it would find a U.S. boost-phase NMD system to be acceptable.

The U.S. Ballistic Missile Defence Organization is reportedly carrying out a preliminary study of boost-phase options for NMD. However, other than the Space-Based Laser, a holdover from the SDI Program that is two decades or more away from deployment, there are no NMD boost-phase programs underway.

Nevertheless, a number of potential approaches for boost-phase NMD have been proposed. Some have suggested adapting near-term or future planned missile defence interceptors and deploying these on ships near suspected launch points.14 However, the use of near-term terminal-phase interceptors such as Patriot PAC-3 or the Navy Area Defence does not appear to be feasible. These interceptors are too slow and cannot operate above the atmosphere, and could only hope to make an intercept under extremely favorable conditions – for example, against a missile launched from a site on a coast.

Longer-term, exo-atmospheric midcourse interceptors, such as those for the THAAD, Navy Theatre Wide and NMD systems, may have some capabilities if used as boost-phase systems. However, the kill vehicles used in these systems have not been designed to intercept accelerating targets such as missile boosters. This requires greater maneuvering capabilities than for midcourse targets, which travel on predictable trajectories. Thus it is at present unclear if any of these approaches could work. A boost-phase system could instead use interceptors specifically built for boost-phase use. Theodore Postol and Richard Garwin have developed proposals that would use large (ICBM-sized) interceptor missiles equipped with homing kill vehicles deployed on ships, submarines, or fixed sea platforms, or on land in cooperation with Russia.15 A system using such interceptors specifically designed for boost-phase use would almost certainly be more effective than a system that tried to adapt interceptors designed for mid-course or terminal intercepts. However no such mid-course interceptor is currently under development.

The use of small, high-speed interceptor missiles on unpiloted aircraft has also been suggested as a way of obtaining an NMD boost-phase capability. However, among other issues, it is unclear if the kill vehicle and missile can be made small enough to make this approach practical.

Finally, a boost-phase system could use lasers. As discussed above, the Airborne Laser, if it works as anticipated, would have a greater range against strategic missiles than against theatre missiles, and thus could potentially be used for NMD boost-phase purposes, since it could cover a launch area comparable to or larger than that of interceptor-based systems.

## George W. Bush on National Missile Defence

As a presidential candidate, George W. Bush has made a number of statements that indicate what his general approach to NMD would be. In a May 2000, op-ed, Bush said:

"First, America must build effective missile defences, based on the best available options, at the earliest possible date. Our missile defence must be designed to protect all 50 states-and our friends and allies and deployed forces overseas-from missile attacks by rogue nations or accidental launches."

"The Clinton administration at first denied the need for a national missile defence system. Then it delayed. Now the approach it proposes is flawed – a system initially based on a single site, when experts say that more is needed."16 He has also stated that he would not allow Russian objections to prevent NMD deployment:

"If elected president, I will offer Russia the necessary amendments to the ABM Treaty so as to make our deployment of effective missile defences consistent with the treaty." "If Russia refuses the changes we propose, I will give prompt notice, under the provisions of the treaty, that the United States can no longer be a party to it."

Bush reiterated his intention to rapidly deploy NMD following President Clinton's September 1 announcement that he would not deploy NMD:

"As President, I intend to develop and deploy an effective missile defence system at the earliest possible date to protect American citizens from accidental launches or blackmail by rogue nations." "...I welcome the opportunity to act where they [Clinton and Gore] have failed to lead by developing and deploying effective missile defences to protect all 50 states and our friends and allies." These statements, and other statements by Bush advisors, indicate that President Bush's approach to NMD will likely be built around the following propositions:

- NMD should be deployed as soon as possible;
- The NMD system should be larger (and presumably more effective) than the system proposed by Clinton, and should be effective against both emerging missile states and a Russian accidental launch;
- The NMD system should also protect not only U.S. territory but also U.S. allies and U.S. forces deployed overseas;
- Russia agreement to NMD deployment should be sought, but if such agreement is not forthcoming, the U.S. should withdraw from the ABM Treaty in order to deploy NMD.

## Administration Approach to NMD.

Assuming that, as now seems highly likely, the Bush administration decides to proceed with NMD deployment, what form will its NMD system take? It is argued here that a likely approach is a phased deployment of a significantly expanded and reconfigured version of Clinton's land-based system, supplemented with sea-based interceptors and/or a boost phase component. In this approach, the basic NMD components (X-band radars, Upgraded Early Warning Radars, EKVs on Ground-Based Interceptors, SBIRS-Low, etc.) developed for the Clinton system would be used as the basis of Bush's NMD system, but the system would be significantly expanded and restructured.

There are two ways such an expansion could be carried out, both of which seem likely to be adopted. First, more of the land-based system's basic components could be deployed. For example, more interceptors could be deployed at additional launch locations. Second, additional types of components, such as sea-based interceptors or the Airborne Laser could be added to the system.

From President Bush's perspective, such an approach could have a number of advantages. Because the first phase of its deployment would be similar in size, scope, and nature to Clinton's system, this approach could achieve an initial operational capability on about the same time scale as Clinton's system (2005 to 2007), which is probably faster than any other approach. Second, the greater size of Bush's initial and/or complete system could be presented as eliminating some of the vulnerabilities of Clinton's proposed system (although this might not actually be the case). Third, adding new components, such sea-based interceptors, would allow coverage to be extended to U.S. allies and forces overseas, a stated Bush objective. Finally, although the system would be built up from components developed during the Clinton Administration, it would be clearly different than Clinton's system, leaving no doubt that it was a Bush administration system.

This system would be deployed in phases in order to get an early initial operational capability. The first phase would likely be similar in scope to Clinton's first phase, although the component locations could be different, and there might be more than one interceptor site and/or more than one X-band radar deployed. This system might be operational by 2005-2007. It would subsequently be built up into a system with a sensor network resembling that of Clinton's final system (5-6 Upgraded Early Warning Radars, 8-10 X-band radars, and the SBIRS-Low space-based tracking system) but with a greater number of interceptor sites (perhaps 2 to 4) and interceptors (at least several hundred).

This system would be supplemented with one or more additional components that would be developed in parallel to it but which would not be ready in time to be part of the initial deployment.

The most likely such addition to the basic land-based system appears to be sea-based interceptors. As noted above, there is strong Republican support for sea-based NMD and BMDO has already stated that sea-based interceptors could be incorporated into a land-based NMD system. In this situation, naval ships would essentially become remote, mobile launch platforms for the land-based NMD system, extending its coverage over the entire globe.

Bush could additionally decide to formally incorporate the Airborne Laser into the NMD system, giving the system a boost-phase component. Perhaps somewhat less likely, a boost-phase supplement to the NMD system could also be obtained by deploying sea-based boost-phase interceptors.

### *Alternative NMD Options*

President Bush could, of course, decide to scrap entirely the technology developed during the Clinton Administration (and in some cases begun during his father's administration or earlier). However, a brief review of the possible NMD approaches shows why this is unlikely.

### *Sea-based NMD*

As noted above, there is support in some quarters of the Republican party for the deployment of a free-standing sea-based NMD system. However, taking this approach would significantly delay the date at which an NMD system could be operational. The Navy Theatre Wide Block-II interceptors that BMDO assess as having some capabilities against strategic missiles are not currently scheduled to be available until sometime after 2010. The Aegis radars on the ships are vastly inferior to the land-based X-band radars for NMD purposes. Either new ship-based radars would have to be developed and deployed or the sea-based system would have to rely on a network of land-based radars. (Although the

SBIRS-Low satellite system could be used for guiding sea-based interceptors, the discrimination capabilities of this system, which uses only passive sensors, are inferior to those of the X-band radars.)

Such a sea-based system would require many years of development and testing before construction could begin. In contrast, construction of a land-based system could begin essentially immediately. A purely sea-based system probably would not be operational even in the second term of a Bush presidency. Such a delay seems likely to be unacceptable both to Bush and to the Republican-controlled Congress.

A stand-alone sea-based NMD system would be also be very expensive, likely considerably more expensive than a ground-based system. It would also place a significant burden on the U.S. Navy unless a considerable number of additional Aegis cruisers or destroyers were purchased (and the Navy's operating budget increased correspondingly). In addition, given the limited sizes of the radars and interceptors that could be placed on a ship, the capabilities of a sea-based system are likely to be inferior to that of a ground-based system.

### *Boost-phase Defences*

As discussed above, boost-phase defences appear to offer significant advantages over mid-course systems. Moreover, at least one boost-phase system, the Airborne Laser, might be available on a time scale similar to that of a land-based system, by about 2007. However, the technology of the Airborne Laser is much less mature than those of the radars and interceptors making up the land-based system, and it is quite possible that an initial operational capability could be delayed many years beyond 2007. No other boost-phase approach is currently under development (except for the Space-Based Laser). Thus any other boost-phase approach would require starting a new development program and would thus almost certainly significantly delay an initial operational capability relative to a land-based system.

All boost-phase systems currently being discussed (except for space-based ones) also share the common problem that they must be deployed near the missile launch site, thus requiring this launch site be known in advance. While it is very unlikely that a missile attack could come from an unexpected country (although it could come from an unexpected location if the missile was launched from a ship), this situation may not appeal to many NMD supporters. Moreover, these systems cannot meet one of President Bush's stated requirements for his NMD system, that it be able to counter a Russian accidental launch, since a Russian ICBM launch could occur far inland, out of range of any of these systems. Similarly, such system could not counter a Chinese missile launch, which while not currently an official requirement, is certainly an important consideration for many NMD supporters. For these reasons, a stand-alone boost-phase system seems unlikely to be adopted by Bush, although a boost-phase system could be adopted as an eventual supplement to his NMD system.

### *Space-Based Weapons*

The only space-based weapon that the U.S. is currently developing is the Space-Based Laser, which is intended to provide a global boost-phase capability. The U.S. is currently spending about $140 million per year on this system, and current plans call for a possible in-orbit technology demonstration in 2012-2015, with deployment possible sometime after 2020. However neither of these dates are likely to be achieved, and recent BMDO cost estimates are as high as $75 billion for a deployed system (and this figure is almost certainly low).

Thus no space-based weapons will be available for well over a decade. A Bush decision to abandon other NMD approaches and proceed with space-based defences would in effect amount to a decision to indefinitely delay NMD deployment. However, there is still strong support for space weapons among some Republicans in Congress, so there could be a significant increase in spending on the Space-Based Laser, with the objective of accelerating its potential deployment and, less likely, that some development of space-based interceptors could begin.

## Theatre Missile Defences

In conjunction with an NMD deployment intended to protect U.S. territory, President Bush could choose to forward deploy TMD systems in order to satisfy his stated requirement of also defending U.S. forces deployed overseas and U.S. allies. Lower-tier defences, such as Patriot PAC-3 or Navy Area Defence, could be available before a land-based NMD system could be operational. However, such systems cannot be used to defend against intercontinental-range missiles and thus could only supplement, and not replace, an NMD system.

The THAAD upper-tier system, and possibly Navy Theatre Wide Block 1, could be available on a time scale comparable to the initial operational capability of a land-based NMD system. Such systems could also be deployed overseas to defend troops and allies. As noted above, such systems could also be used to defend U.S. territory, but only if supported by the NMD system's sensor infrastructure.

## Defence Issues for the Next Administration

In 2000, the incoming Bush administration assumed that the United States had entered a period of "strategic pause," during which the risks of war were low and would remain so for several decades. It therefore appeared prudent to contemplate a "military transformation," which meant accepting risks in the near-term to prepare for longer-term dangers. The corollary was that we might skip a generation of defence investments and maintain relatively small forces. With this in mind, the Defence Department gradually adopted a capabilities-based approach that measured the projected capabilities of future U.S. forces against those of current forces, rather than against those of potential adversaries. Developments in the international security environment during the Bush years, however, demanded a more traditional approach, derived from an evaluation of American strategic goals and an assessment of the corresponding threats and risks.

The grand strategy of the United States has remained remarkably consistent through the Cold War and post-Cold War eras, and none of the current presidential candidates of either party have offered more than a rhetorical departure. Americans are committed to continuing their position of international leadership and to preserving the favorable military balances that are at the core of this leadership role. The primary distinctions between the parties and candidates have been over ways and means, rather than strategic ends. Three major developments strike at the foundation of U.S. global leadership and threaten to tip the current balances of military power; these have been broadly recognized and were given formal expression in the 2006 *Quadrennial Defence Review*. The most immediate and pressing of these—what has been called the "Long War"—is the struggle to build a durable order in the Islamic world. It is a challenge of staggering scope, subject to many shifting variables, and it subsumes the ongoing operations in Iraq, Afghanistan, and the Horn of Africa.

The second and perhaps greater long-term challenge is the rise of the People's Republic of China, a state that is already a global power and perhaps will soon become a peer competitor—another superpower, but one quite different from the former Soviet Union. The third challenge—the accelerating spread of nuclear materials, knowledge, and weaponry—threatens to undermine the traditional ways in which military balances and international security are reckoned: the prospect of a weak and otherwise derelict state—or even terrorist or criminal organization—in possession of a nuclear weapon menaces the entire international state system. A final point is that these three challenges are not really distinct but intertwined. The energy resources of the Persian Gulf are as critical to China as they are to anyone. In an increasingly globalized world, how can it be otherwise? Yet as unsettling as these threats may be, they can be assessed with reasonable clarity, and they offer a sound basis for both short-and long-term U.S. defence planning.

### *Requirements for the Long War*

Obviously, the first demand of a long war is to build robust and sustainable forces. This tenet runs contrary to the recent enthusiasm among some defence policymakers for rapidly deployable, expeditionary forces, but there is now general agreement that in today's conflicts, how long we stay is more important than how fast we get there. U.S. military experiences in Iraq and Afghanistan have made it clear that sufficient land forces are essential for carrying out the missions that will characterize the Long War, but the massive size of the theatre and the diversity of operations within it (including maritime surveillance and sea-control operations from the Gulf of Guinea to the Straits of Malacca and many years' worth of air operations in support of no-fly zones) cannot be discounted. A sizeable portion of all U.S. military forces must therefore be designed with persistent presence in mind.

The first step toward establishing this kind of presence is having the ability to deploy and sustain an adequate number of forces in theatre. In order to do this, the size of U.S. active-duty land forces (Army and Marine Corps) must be increased from the current total of 750,000 to between 900,000 and 1 million – roughly 1990 strength. Even an initial U.S. Army expansion to 775,000 troops would yield valuable results. The expansion would optimize the force for its future missions; restore the unique value of the U.S. Marine Corps; and return the Army National Guard to its traditional status as a strategic rather than an operational reserve, as it functions now. (Indeed, recent overreliance on the National Guard has proven to be an expensive, ineffective, and socially disruptive tool for generating forces for the Long War.) The structure of U.S. land forces also needs to be rebalanced in order to make them more durable. This can be accomplished in part by trading firepower for diversity, persist-ence, and presence; improving situational awareness and sustainment; increasing headquarters and command nodes; and emphasizing operational and tactical mobility rather than strategic mobility.

Elements of U.S. naval and air power will need to be expanded and refined in order to meet the challenges of the Long War. The size of the U.S. Navy must be increased in ways that improve its surveillance of and presence in littoral areas, thereby denying terrorists and other adversaries both maritime and land sanctuary. Air support to Long War operations has been clearly defined and is well understood: the demands on strategic and theatre airlift are skyrocketing, as are the requirements for unmanned aircraft with reconnaissance, surveillance, and strike capabilities. And while the air defence environment is relatively benign, the need for responsive air support remains, particularly where land forces have sacrificed a measure of their organic firepower (often in areas where forces are widely dispersed, as in Afghanistan).

The newly introduced concept of building partnership capacity, which promotes an interagency model for delivering simultaneous military assistance and governance support to states susceptible to internal destabilization, should be expanded over time to include the prospect of creating some number of allied forces capable of deploying and fighting alongside U.S. forces in contingency operations.

### *Requirements for Hedging against China's Rise*

Responding to the rise of China as a global power with growing military strength presents an increasingly complex operational puzzle. The immediate focus is the balance of military power in maritime Northeast Asia—a problem set that engages not only naval and air power issues, but also space and cyberspace—but it is clear that the size of the potential "battlespace" will expand in fairly short order. Yet it is likely that, as the Fulda Gap defined the strategically and symbolically central front during the Cold War standoff with the Soviet Union, maritime Northeast Asia will occupy a central role in hedging against China's rise. This puts increasing demands on the ability of the United States to project elements of naval, air, and space power to the region, combining the problems of persistence and sustainment with those of lethality and firepower.

The size and posture of U.S. Navy surface fleets in the western Pacific and the Indian Ocean must therefore be increased to maintain a day-to-day presence of two carrier or surface action groups in the Pacific and, in time, a third in the Indian Ocean. Carrier air fleets must be modernized more rapidly to meet the requirement of projecting constant combat air patrols and strike missions at greater ranges and in an increasingly hostile air defence environment.

At the same time, the U.S. Navy must improve its ability to conduct antisubmarine warfare operations across this vast maritime expanse. The most immediate requirement for enabling such operations is to increase the size of the U.S. attack submarine fleet in theatre, but further demands—for airborne antisubmarine patrols, undersea sensors, unmanned undersea vehicles, satellite surveillance, and improved surface antisubmarine warfare—are emerging more rapidly than the supply of U.S. capacity.

Furthermore, the threat of nuclear ballistic and cruise missiles, either from a small rogue regime such as North Korea or from a larger and more modern Chinese arsenal—one that transforms China's nuclear stance from minimal deterrence to a more militarily significant counterforce posture—requires a more urgent response. This is not only a theatre threat, but one that extends to the U.S. homeland. This development has implications for the size and structure of U.S. nuclear forces as well.

China's military modernization now places U.S. military access to and exploitation of space and the electromagnetic spectrum at risk; the assumption of superiority on these "battlefields" can no longer be taken for granted. In addition to finding ways to protect current U.S. assets, a hedging strategy increasingly will demand the development of counteroffensive capabilities (the space and cyberspace equivalent of U.S. doctrine in the late Cold War) and an expanded ability to reconstitute satellite or information networks that have been attacked or partially destroyed.

To combat China's modernization efforts, more aggressive steps must be taken to increase the high-end military capabilities of U.S. allies and friendly nations in the region. While it is not yet necessary to assemble a NATO-like alliance, there should be an appropriate urgency about building partnership capacity for hedging as well as for the Long War. In particular, we must adopt a new approach to export licensing and defence transfers: it may be more important to put advanced and compatible technologies in the hands of our friends than to hide them from our enemies.

### *Requirements for Counterproliferation*

The spread of nuclear weapons, knowledge, and materials poses a profoundly different and more complex challenge than did the maintenance of nuclear deterrence during the Cold War. The emerging landscape involves an increasing number of actors—not just great powers, but smaller and weaker states, as well as so-called nonstate actors whose strategic goals may be uncertain, volatile, and even arguably irrational. These actors play out their roles in unfamiliar and distant theaters, and their weaknesses may be as important as their strengths: we must be as concerned with the failure to control nuclear devices as we are with their intentional or unintentional use. In response, the U.S. military must reshape its current nuclear forces and develop some useful capacity to respond to the nightmare of "loose nukes."

The size and structure of U.S. nuclear forces should be driven not by a bilateral assessment of the "balance of terror" with Russia, but by a more nuanced analysis that accounts also for the certainty of a growing array of small-state arsenals (most notably North Korea and Iran, but also Pakistan) and a diversity of midsize forces (particularly China and India) that will very likely number in the hundreds of warheads and include diverse delivery systems. There must be a counterforce element to this analysis as well as a countervalue element; indeed, the distinction between these two elements may be more opaque than in the past.

U.S. ballistic and cruise missile defences must take these new developments into account. In particular, it is important to explore the nature of deterrence in a multipolar nuclear-power context. The U.S. military must also develop, create, and hold in readiness distinct forces to respond to a variety of loose nuke scenarios with capabilities that run the gamut from long-range strikes to rendering safe nuclear materials, facilities, and personnel.

### *Programmatic Implications*

The demands of land force expansion extend well beyond simple personnel costs. Additional requirements include updates to the physical infrastructure; expanded educational and training needs; improved and increased command, control, communications, computers, intelligence, surveillance, and reconnaissance (known as C4ISR) capabilities; investments in new systems to maximize the effectiveness and survivability of individual soldiers and Marines; new crew-served, small-unit systems (such as unmanned aerial or ground vehicles); an acceleration of network capacity; more command nodes at higher ech-elons; and additional investments in ground combat and combat support vehicles. In short, the force must be better as well as bigger. Even if the pace of expansion is accelerated—which initially may be difficult—it must be framed as a ten-year project, continuing beyond the administration's term of office and indeed beyond the Future Years Defence Plan (the Pentagon's annual five-year spending forecast).

In the meantime, force modernization must continue apace: the U.S. Army's Future Combat Systems (FCS)—which is not a program per se, but a sophisticated full-force modernization initiative—needs to be funded at approximately one-and-a-half times the current annual rate; the goal is to accelerate, expand, and diversify the effort, "pulling forward" and fostering the development of a more capable and larger force. Sustaining and extending the life of the current helicopter fleet is also a crucial element of U.S. Army modernization and recapitalization; any investments in fixed-wing lift capabilities should be rationalized with U.S. Air Force efforts.

The U.S. Marine Corps would also benefit from increased investments dedicated to improving the tactical mobility, range, and responsiveness of Marine units during land operations. The V-22 Osprey program should be expanded and accelerated, and there should be greater Marine involvement in the FCS program, especially the networking capabilities it offers; in the interim, the Marines should consider buying a modest number of Stryker vehicles to replace the service's obsolescent and vulnerable amphibious assault vehicles and the versatile but aging Light Armored Vehicle. The planned number of Expeditionary Fighting Vehicles could also stand to be reduced.

Beyond land forces, the pressing priority lies with naval modernization efforts aimed at increasing mari-time surveillance and patrol in littoral waters. The U.S. Navy has made a mistake in reducing the size and scope of its Littoral Combat Ship program, which had been intended to produce a series of ships with antisubmarine and antimine capabilities, designed for unprecedented coastal access. In addition to pursuing increased inshore patrol missions, it would be wise to expand the number of long-range maritime surveillance aircraft, both manned and unmanned. An alternative would be to expand the Coast Guard's Deepwater program—an integrated system of naval and air platforms designed with the potential to capitalize on the Coast Guard's latent expeditionary capacity.

Finally, widely dispersed irregular warfare operations involving lightly armed ground forces require increased levels of air logistics support—both in theatre and at longer ranges. Both C-17 and C-130 cargo fleets are currently too small, however, and are being utilized more heavily than originally planned. Such land operations also require responsive and accurate air support, but the size and age of the F-16 and F-15E fleets are a concern, and the F-18 is a less suitable aircraft for such missions. It is unclear whether the F-35 Joint Strike Fighter will be available for such missions in a timely fashion or whether unmanned aircraft, or, alternatively, a reinvestment in artillery systems, can cover this mission set.

The immediate programmatic goal of a U.S. hedging strategy toward China is to reposture and retain—and slightly expand—current force structures to prevent the further aging and numerical collapse of the capacity of today's forces while preserving its technological edge. U.S. air and naval power are the decisive differences in the western Pacific and will be so in the Indian Ocean region, but U.S. Marine and Army land forces will be called on to play crucial roles as well.

The large swath of airspace from Japan to the Korean peninsula and southward over Taiwan is an arena in which the United States must maintain a favorable correlation of forces. This effort to maintain air superiority is already a challenging one and becomes more difficult every day as the People's Liberation Army increases the size and sophistication of its ballistic and cruise missile fleets, giving it a dangerous preemptive strike capability. Its growing strike aircraft fleet would allow China to capitalize on opportunities derived from initial missile attacks. Such scenarios deserve a more thorough and public treatment than they have thus far received. Beyond counterstrike operations involving cruise missiles and other standoff weapons (or the tiny B-2 bomber fleet), the ability of current generations of U.S. aircraft to survive and sustain operations in this hostile air defence environment is a troubling issue. The F-22 line, scheduled for termination after 2009, should be extended, and F-35 production accelerated; there are no other practical options at the moment.

The U.S. capacity to maintain sea control in greater Northeast Asia is tenuous. The limited range and survivability of the F-18E/F make aircraft carrier operations in these waters increasingly problematic. The F-35 will ameliorate this challenge but will do little to offset Chinese missile capabilities; surface fleet air defence is again a serious problem, and the expectation of unfettered access and an unlimited ability to strike land targets from the sea is becoming compromised. Further, the growth of Chinese submarine fleets requires a U.S. response. The recent U.S. trend toward building just one new attack submarine per year, which will soon reduce the total American fleet to just over thirty boats, is unacceptable. Additional investments need to be made in antisubmarine warfare, including undersea sensors, unmanned vehicles, and space surveillance, as well as the antisubmarine capabilities of surface fleets and mari-time patrol aircraft. The projected growth of China's naval power demands a U.S. response—namely, new deployments, basing, and infrastructure arrangements, and an adequate force structure to cover an expanding theatre of operations.

One of the central elements of any hedging posture for U.S. military forces will be the ability to retain access to and full utilization of space systems, especially surveillance and communications constellations. After years of controversy, the Spaced-Based Infrared System, which will give enhanced warning of missile launch, will begin operating its first satellite in 2009. Arguably more crucial will be the Transformational Communications Satellite Advanced Wideband System (TSAT). A five-satellite, laser-based communication network intended to supplement and replace the current Milstar system and provide faster and more secure communications, TSAT is the central nervous system for global military communications networks. As noted above, prudence argues for creating the capacity to reconfigure and reconstitute these systems quickly in a crisis or wartime situation, as well as to develop ways to defend them from simple antisatellite weapons.

With the development in 2003 of the *National Strategy to Secure Cyberspace* and the derivative but still classified *National Military Strategy for Cyberspace Operations*, the Bush administration has responded to the threats against critical civilian and governmental information networks. The sources of these threats range from terrorist groups and criminal organizations—which increasingly reap large profits from cyberspace operations—to cyberattacks by adversary governments. It is difficult to determine the level of spending associated with the various departments' and services' cyberspace initiatives, but they are critical investments for any hedging strategy.

Beyond preventive efforts such as the Proliferation Security Initiative—a multinational effort designed to curb the transport of weapons of mass destruction and related materials—U.S. forces must retain sufficient capacity, separate and distinct from other ongoing or likely operations, to mount a range of potential operations rapidly in response to the potential employment or spread of weapons of mass destruction and, most particularly, nuclear weapons. Further, force planning must take into account the larger geopolitical implications of such counterproliferation operations; they are likely to be first steps rather than decisive or last steps.

In the popular imagination, counterproliferation strikes are epitomized by the 1981 Israeli raid on the Osirak facility in Iraq, but any current or future analogous operation is likely to be much more demanding: the range, diversity, and "hardness" of targets is much greater. Penetrating enemy air defences will be more challenging, therefore, and success will require a sustained strike campaign rather than a single raid. Pentagon contingency planners are constantly assessing the demands of such operations, but force generation and availability questions are not often discussed or generally understood. This uncertainty may result in a kind of "unfunded requirement" for a variety of air and naval forces—those best tailored to execute a hedging strategy in greater Northeast Asia—from cruise-missile platforms to the most capable strike aircraft and associated support capabilities.

There is an emerging requirement for the employment of significant land forces, either as a follow-on to strike operations or perhaps in reaction to any one of a number of loose nuke scenarios. Such missions could call for the full gamut of special operations forces as well as other rapidly deployable forces such as U.S. Marines or Army airborne and light infantry units—that is, the kinds of units most heavily taxed by Long War missions.

### *Budgetary Implications*

As noted above, assessing the long-term defence needs of the United States is a different question from quantifying the short-term costs of wartime operations. The fiscal year 2009 defence budget request of $515 billion represents a baseline cost of raising, training, and initially equipping U.S. military forces. It also represents a mere 3.4 percent of U.S. GDP, a historically low figure. Defence Secretary Robert Gates has estimated that wartime costs for the 2009 budget year will be about $170 billion, a reasonably accurate assumption given the likely size and pace of military operations. It is unlikely that this figure will vary much—even if the incoming administration begins to withdraw combat forces from Iraq, the 2009 costs of withdrawal would be about the same as the costs of continued combat operations.

The Bush administration's Future Years Defence Plan has done little to address the underlying mismatch between the likely strategic requirements for U.S. military power and the institutional deficiencies that have resulted from the force reductions of the 1990s and the continuing lack of materiel recapitalization. Put simply, U.S. military forces are too small and their equipment is getting too old to sustain the three challenges defined by U.S. defence strategy. The new president must address the strategy-resources gap.

Despite the current slowdown, the American economy is more than able to sustain a modest increase in defence spending. The incoming administration should consider increasing baseline defence budgets to 4 percent of GDP, as recently recommended by Admiral Michael Mullen, chairman of the Joint Chiefs of Staff. This is still a very low figure compared to past spending: during fifty years of the Cold War—a period of relatively constant economic growth and increasing widespread prosperity—Pentagon budgets averaged more than 6 percent of GDP. And, in a $15 trillion annual U.S. economy, an additional one-half percent of GDP would translate into an additional $75 billion per year, certainly enough to begin to meet the long-term requirements outlined in this *Outlook*. In sum, the need to strengthen U.S. military forces is immediate, and the cost is modest.

# 13

# Defence Modernisation Challenges and Strategies

When we talk of defence modernisation, we normally focus on weapons systems and their procurement — in other words, the nuts and bolts issues. But the core issue for modernisation is the strategy that should guide it. For a country like ours, this assumes even greater importance since large sums of capital are involved and technology acquisition itself is a major challenge which, if tackled correctly, should support economic-industrial growth and also reduce the need to plough our export earnings substantively into import of weapons systems.

Military technological differential is the key to competitive advantage in wars of today and tomorrow. And whoever controls superior military technology in the 21st century would dominate in war and peace, on the battlefield and in the market. Force multiplication is no substitute for force where technological differential become low.

Defence modernisation is one area where trends in weapons manufacture and markets abroad have a major influence on not only costs and technology, but also access to them.

We had relied heavily on Soviet weapons and equipment since the mid-1960s, and the European industry provided an alternative, supplying one-fifth of our total needs. We have had negligible access to American weapons systems and military technology over the decades. But things are changing and it is necessary to look at them carefully to work out our defence modernisation strategies.

The end of the Cold War resulted in contraction of defence industry worldwide. Smaller production runs increased the unit costs of weapon systems; and rapid advances in technology have pushed costs further. Defence establishments worldwide have resorted to upgrades to enhance the operational capabilities as a via media to replacements. But this remains a partial solution in modernisation strategies. Meanwhile, collaborations and mergers became the norm in defence manufacturing, with an obvious strengthening of American hold over military industry worldwide. While some access to American weapons systems has opened with the sale of the artillery Firefinder radars to India, this process still could only amount to a marginal opening of a small window. The European option for weapons acquisitions remains. But the European defence industry is in a difficult situation for a variety of reasons that we need not go into detail here. Its consolidation has resulted in deeper linkages to US industry. We faced its implications after the 1998 sanctions, when naval aircraft and helicopters which we had purchased from the UK were held back while being overhauled at the manufacturers. It took a couple of years before the problem could be resolved, and the costs obviously went up. The disintegration and collapse of the Soviet Union, which has been our primary source of defence equipment since the mid-1960, resulted in serious disruption and decline in the output of the former Soviet defence industry. What Russia retained in reasonably good shape were the Soviet Union's outstanding design bureaus.

We must also note that the comprehensive self-reliance model put into place during Prime Minister Jawaharlal Nehru's time underwent change since the 1960s. This was based on three parallel tracks: Buy weapons, licence manufacture as much as possible, and undertake design and development (with foreign collaboration to build our own expertise). Unfortunately, as licence manufacture increased, providing significant indigenous capabilities and a degree of independence from imports, this also led to a sort of strategic complacency in that the key area of our needs for future modernisation, design and development of weapon systems, started to suffer. Notable examples are combat aircraft where the LCA design was started 30 years after we had undertaken the design and development of an excellent multi-role combat aircraft, the

HF-24 Marut, while technology galloped! Similarly, the design and development of the Mainbattle Tank, Arjun, started just after the 1971 War, has yet to enter operational service. Meanwhile techno-operational environment has changed substantively forcing us to buy the T-90 tanks.

The Indian Navy has fared better, although resource crunch delayed its shipbuilding programmes, forcing us to now buy the Gorshkov aircraft carrier when the indigenous Air Defence Ship should have been in service by now. Other examples abound. But the point that we need to note is that a comprehensive strategy for modernisation has been practically absent since the 1970s.

Our weakness since then actually lies in design and development of weapons systems. The DRDO has made valiant attempts, but seems to have shied away from collaborative projects. Scientific professional pride decried collaboration on grounds that it would hamper indigenous development; politically, foreign collaboration aroused negative passions; and the defence establishment was looking to immediate needs rather than long-term capacity building in defence industrial capability. Acquisition of military technology, therefore, has been localised to import of production technology rather than building design capabilities.

It is in this context that a unique historical opportunity opened up just at the time the most severe crisis for defence modernisation occurred with the collapse of the Soviet Union. The former Soviet Union looked for collaboration in design and development of military systems. The West plugged in where it suited them. But it was China, not India, which took advantage of the situation. By mid-1990s over 3,000 Russian engineers and engineers were reported to be working in Chinese defence industry, upgrading and working on design and development of numerous systems which China had not been able to achieve for decades. China is investing in military R&D programmes in Russian institutions and in collaborative programmes where our recent attempts at joint development of the Brahmos missile pale in comparison.

It is still not too late to plug into Russian design base and capabilities, although as it picks up economic strength it may seek to apply tougher terms. Similarly, we have been the largest customer of British Aerospace's weapons and equipment for five decades. But there is little in the country in the shape of joint production, leave alone joint design and development programmes. Regardless of the level of budget being allocated in any particular year, the backlog of modernisation and the needs of future high-technology weapons systems would require investment of the order of $20 billion over the next decade. And that is why most of the global arms manufacturers are setting up shop in India in the hope of selling arms. But this also provides us with a powerful bargaining chip to build indigenous design, development, manufacturing and export capabilities through joint collaborative programmes. What we need is to be clear on our strategy for modernisation that goes beyond mere procurement and licence production. This is also where the private sector can play a crucial role.

In a developing country like ours, there are additional complicating factors in the modernisation processes. First, a large proportion of our defence equipment is still purchased from abroad. Our traditional supplier, the former Soviet Union, disintegrated and landed up in serious socio-economic crisis. Bilateral trade also suffered heavily. The negative impact on supplies of weapons equipment and spares created additional complications for us. Also, many inefficiencies and complexities had crept into our procurement system and decision making for modernisation. Some of these have been sorted out by implementing the decisions of the Group of Ministers taken three years ago to improve the management of national security. But the result has been that with a system that allocates funds on an annual basis, with a review half-way down, large amounts of funds budgeted for defence and modernisation have been lapsing at the end of the financial year for the past few years.

For example, for the three-year period ending March 2003, a total of Rs 25,699 crore remained unspent out of the total budgeted figure of Rs 1,85,587 crore. The effect has been that while defence modernisation had suffered earlier due to lack of resources, now the inability to spend available resources within the stipulated financial year has adversely affected defence preparedness.

Establishing a DMF of Rs 25,000 crore would go a long way in assuring that modernisation processes do not suffer due to procedural delays and other unavoidable reasons. Both the National Security Advisory Board and the bipartisan Standing Committee on Defence of Parliament have been pressing the issue for years. The actual functioning of the DMF, of course, must be evaluated carefully over the coming years, since this is a deviation from the traditional budgetary approach. Its utility may remain less than optimal if the five year plans are not finalised well before the Plan period commences. Also, we need to redefine the budget heads to clearly indicate the resource allocation and utilisation under three functionally different heads of modernisation, maintenance and operating costs of the defence forces separately rather than the current system that does not indicate functional segments of a large amount of the tax-payers' money in an area so crucial to our security and defence.

## Blacklisting Foreign Vendors

India has a penchant for blacklisting foreign arms producers without considering negative effects it has on India's military preparedness. This is the reasons why recent reports of irregularities in the procurement of seven Barak anti-missile defence systems and 200 missiles from Israel Aircraft Industries Ltd (IAI) have caused serious concern to the Indian armed forces. They fear that the Government may get forced to blacklist IAI as per the provisions of defence procurement procedure. Should that happen, India's defence modernisation plan would suffer irretrievable damage. Having seen the adverse effects of banning Bofors, HDW and Denel, they dread a similar fate for a large number of ambitious plans under implementation. IAI is deeply involved in most of the major modernisation plans of the three services. In addition to the upgradation of fighter aircraft (Jaguar, MIG-21, MIG-29 and Mirage-2000), transport aircraft (AN-32) and all helicopters of MI series, it is supplying three Airborne Early Warning and Control System (AWACS) systems to India. It is also the prime supplier of unmanned aerial vehicles to the three services. Most importantly, IAI is involved in a number of developmental projects. India simply cannot afford to cut off all dealings with it. The saga of banning Bofors, HDW and Denel cannot be repeated.

### *Bofors*

After carrying out trials of various guns on offer, India opted for Bofors 155 mm FH-77B towed artillery system. A contract for

410 systems was signed with the Swedish firm in 1986 for Rs1437.72 crore. The contract included transfer of technology for subsequent manufacture of guns in India. India had planned to produce 1,840 pieces within the country to equip 92 artillery regiments. However, with the exposure of kickbacks, the Government banned Bofors for all future dealings. It had the following effect:-

- Although India had paid for transfer of technology, it failed to utilise it. India lost an opportunity to create a base for further development of artillery weapon systems. As a result, indigenous competence to manufacture and maintain guns remained stunted.
- As spares could not be procured from Bofors, middlemen thrived making huge profits. In the absence of adequate spares, the Army had to cannibalise parts from some guns to keep other guns functional. Essential maintenance also suffered.
- Without help from Bofors, India is struggling to carry out overhauling of guns in the stipulated time frame. It is feared that delay in overhaul will adversely affect extension of useful life of the gun systems. Indigenous capacity installed with a Base Repair Workshop is far too less and it will take unacceptably long to overhaul the complete inventory.
- The Navy was already using Bofors guns on some ships and they faced difficulties in ensuring regular supply of spares.
- Indian inventory of 84 mm Carl Gustav Rocket Launchers suffered as Carl Gustav subsequently became a subsidiary of Bofors and thus, came under the ban.

### *Denel*

Discussions were in final stages with Denel of South Africa for 155 mm howitzers (both towed and self-propelled) when it emerged that Denel had employed unacceptable means to grab contract for the supply of NTW-20 Anti-Material Rifle. It was alleged that Denel had engaged middlemen to offer bribes to obtain sensitive information about the internal proceedings of the Commercial Negotiation Committee. The Government decided to blacklist Denel in 2005 and cancel all orders placed on it. The development was highly unfortunate. Bhim project was almost concluded with Denel's T-6 155mm turret from the G-6 being mounted on Arjun hull. An initial order had also been placed on a public sector undertaking. With the blacklisting of Denel, Indian Army's Field Artillery Rationalisation Plan suffered a crippling blow. The total requirement envisaged by 2025 is 3600 artillery guns of 155mm/52 calibre. The current inventory is of 410 Bofors guns only. Therefore, India desperately wants to procure 400 additional gun systems (220 wheeled and 180 tracked) on priority to meet inescapable minimum requirement.

Field trials in respect of wheeled systems were carried out in 2003 to ascertain compliance of Services Qualitative Requirements. Three competitors participated-Denel, Soltam Atmos 2000 and FH77 of SWS Defence. All the three systems failed to meet specified standards. Retrials of duly improved versions were held in 2004. With the blacklisting of Denel, the choice got limited to Soltam and FH77. As per the press reports, FH77 emerged far superior to Soltam and was the choice of the Army. However, due to politically sensitive reasons, the Government incorrectly termed the case as a single vendor situation and decided to float fresh tender enquiries with reformulated Qualitative Requirements. Tender for wheeled guns was floated in March 2007 and the second tender for tracked guns followed soon thereafter. It is learnt that 12 producers of guns have been invited.

Nearly 20 years have passed since the induction of Bofor guns; no new gun system has been procured. Due to ban on Bofors and Denel, India has shut doors on two major producers of guns and thereby limited its choice. Continued shortage of suitable 155mm/ 52 calibre gun systems implies major gaps in India's defence preparedness. Additionally, India's quest for indigenous production of 155 mm ammunition also suffered a major blow. Work on a new ordnance factory in Nalanda to manufacture 155mm ammunition for Bofors guns has got stalled, as Denel was to provide technical know-how. Hundreds of crores of rupees have also gone down the drain.

### *HDW*

The case of HDW makes instructive reading. A contract was signed with the German firm in December 1981. India was to get two HDW 209 class fully built submarines and sub-assemblies and components for assembling two other submarines in India. HDW was also to provide required training to Indian personnel.

HDW delivered two submarines in 1987 and two more were assembled in India in due course. As allegations of bribery and kickbacks became public, the Government decided to blacklist the company. It was also decided not to build any more submarines of the same class. Marlog, a company jointly owned by HDW and Ferrostal, took over the responsibility to fulfill all contractual obligations.

There are just a handful of competent submarine manufacturers in the world. By blacklisting HDW, India antagonized one of the leading producers and thereby deprived itself of the benefits of latest technological advancements. HDW is the world leader with the most advanced air-independent propulsion system. Continued collaboration would have given a boost to indigenous submarine building competence. Additionally, India would have acquired wherewithal as regards maintenance, overhaul and repair support.

As India had not received the complete drawings and NATO identification numbers for all spare parts of the submarines, it faced immense problems in procuring them from other sources. Middlemen made huge profits. The Navy wanted to increase the offensive punch of the submarines by mounting Exocet missiles on it. As HDW could not be engaged, others laid unacceptably harsh conditions. Indian plans for the upgradation of the submarine entailed an increase in their length and that could be done only by HDW. To sum up, by blacklisting HDW India deprived itself of maintenance support, upgradation opportunities and development of indigenous skills.

## Probity Provisions of the Procurement Procedure

Defence Procurement Procedure-2008 (DPP-2008) has laid down clear guidelines for all foreign vendors. They are warned not to resort to any unethical practice to influence the decision makers. A 'Pre-Contract Integrity Pact' has been made mandatory for all schemes exceeding Rupees 100 crores. The vendors are required to sign and submit it separately along with the technical and commercial offers. It is a binding agreement in which the procurement agency promises that it will not accept bribes during the procurement process and bidders promise that they will not offer bribes. It also includes an undertaking by each bidder to disclose all payments made in connection with the contract in question to anybody (including agents and other middlemen as well as family members of officials).

The Government can enforce the following sanctions for any violation by a bidder of its commitments or undertakings:-

- Denial or loss of contract.
- Forfeiture of bid security and performance bond.
- Liability for damages to the principal and the competing bidders.
- Finally, debarment of the violator by the principal for an appropriate period of time.

While signing the final contract, every vendor (irrespective of the contract value) is required to give an undertaking that he has not given, offered or promised to give, directly or indirectly any gift, consideration, reward, commission, fees, brokerage or inducement to procure the contract. Any breach of the aforesaid undertaking by the seller or any one employed by him shall entitle the buyer to cancel the contract and all or any other contracts with the seller and recover the loss arising from such cancellation. Should the Government desire to ascertain if any unauthorized payments have been made, a vendor has to allow inspection of his account books. It will be seen that debarment of a vendor is the last resort and has to be taken only in extreme cases.

### *Appraisal of the Issue*

Before initiating any action against a company, the Government must weigh pros and cons of all alternatives open to it. While punishing a defaulting vendor, own interests must be fully safeguarded. India must consider the following points while taking decision on blacklisting foreign vendors:-

- There are limited manufacturers of major high-tech defence systems in the world. Additionally, world defence trade is circumscribed by embargoes on technology export. Thus, there are very few manufacturers who possess and are willing to offer advanced weaponry to India.

- To develop indigenous defence industry, India needs imported technology and reliable foreign partners with long term commitment. Blacklisting nullifies all transfer of technology agreements, even if paid for.
- India needs to modernize its armed forces expeditiously and its shopping list spans a vast canvas, including all major systems. As most major defence companies produce a large array of equipment, blacklisting in one contract will have a ripple effect on all other purchases as well.
- India possesses a huge inventory of weapon platforms which are in need of immediate upgradation to increase their useful life. This task can be undertaken by a handful of companies. Banning any will reduce own options.
- No company produces a complete defence system. Most major producers are in fact mere integrators. They outsource major assemblies from varied sources. Blacklisting of an assembly supplier can also jeopardize major acquisition proposals.
- One of the stated aims of DPP-2008 is to 'demonstrate the highest degree of probity and public accountability, transparency in operations, free competition and impartiality'. Blacklisting of vendors reduces competition and forces the Government to resort to single vendor procurements with related cost penalty. This is also contrary to Government's declared policy.
- Every time a finalised contract is suspended, the earmarked funds remain unexpended resulting in their surrender.
- Most importantly, the services get deprived of the essential equipment. It may have critical effect on nation's war preparedness. Fresh floating of tenders entails major delays and cost overruns.

In every irregular transaction, there are always two parties- the bribe giver and the bribe taker. Action must be taken against both and in equal proportion. It is unfair to apportion the entire blame to bribe givers and take no action against those who demand and extract bribes. It conveys an impression that the Government is reconciled to the fact that procurement functionaries are bound to fall prey to temptations, if offered to them. It amounts to a tacit admission by the Government of its inability to find officials with unimpeachable integrity and to exercise control over them. The Government thus, feels that the onus of keeping all transactions clean is entirely on the vendors-they should decline to pay bribes even if demanded by the decision makers. This is a strange logic. Instead of putting its own house in order, India holds foreign vendors accountable for all wrong-doings.

## *The Way Forward*

The Government must have conclusive proof that a major breach of probity provisions has taken place. Media reports and rumours cannot be the sole basis. As has been seen, a majority of media reports are subjective, biased and even planted to sabotage a deal. This could be done either by a losing vendor or even by entities inimical to India's interests. As has been seen earlier, every blacklisting of a foreign vendor puts back India's defence modernisation plans by decades. Undoubtedly, it is the most cost effective option available to adversaries to impede India's defence preparedness.

Retaliatory action must always be well considered and commensurate with the degree of misdemeanor. It does not have to be blacklisting at the outset. It is prudent to follow a phased and graduated approach for two reasons. One, the defaulting vendor gets unambiguous message that the Government means business and the vendor should exercise due caution in further dealings. Secondly, should blacklisting become inescapable, the Government can time it to suit own requirements. In the case of HDW, hasty action to ban the company deprived India of catalogues and drawings. India could have easily waited for a few months.

India must also remember that banning a major foreign vendor may have little effect on his business and India may suffer more. Thus the whole exercise of punishing a foreign vendor for his alleged misdemeanor may become counter productive and end up boomeranging on India. In fact this is exactly what has happened in all cases. We have ended up shooting in our own foot. There cannot be another example of immature and reckless decision making. While trying to fix a vendor for his misconduct, we put our own defence modernisation plans in disarray, with consequent critical capability gaps and cost overruns.

The Government seems to have realised the foolhardiness of its policy. It has decided to tread cautiously. Blacklisting of Bofors has been revoked as the company is now owned by SWS Defence with considerable equity being held by a US based company. The Government should similarly allow HDW to do business with India. Nearly 20 years have lapsed and India has not been able to collate conclusive proof of wrong-doings. It is time to close the old chapter and start afresh. Although Denel has been proscribed recently, the Government should offer a way out by asking it to make good financial loss with stiff penal deduction. For generating maximum competition to obtain best deals, the Government has to show maturity, practicality and adroit handling. Outright blacklisting is the easiest and the most imprudent way of managing a delicate and highly critical issue.

A sustained and inspired media campaign was carried out by a small section of press to sabotage Scorpene submarine deal. It is to the credit of the Government that it resisted all demands to reopen the case. It is similarly hoped that the current reports against IAI would be looked into judiciously and an objective view taken. In case any misdemeanor is proved, appropriate and balanced action should be taken against both the vendor and the functionaries involved. Blacklisting, however, must remain the last resort. Cutting off your nose to spite your face can never be considered a prudent policy.

## Implications for the Region

China has been steadily building up its strategic and conventional capabilities since the 1990s. Eighteen years ago, experts say, China had a "bare-bones" military: basic capabilities, but nothing sophisticated or top-of-the-line. But two decades of double-digit spending increases have changed that picture. China says its 2008 defence budget is $61 billion, though the Pentagon has historically challenged Beijing's reported figures.

In its annual report to Congress, the U.S. Defence Department estimated China's total military-related spending for 2007 to be between $97 billion and $139 billion, as compared to $52 billion reported by China. All that spending has gone to building a sophisticated, modern military: a large, increasingly capable submarine fleet, an air force stocked with Russian warplanes, and technical strides which have improved China's ballistic missile arsenal, as well as satellite surveillance, radar, and interception capabilities.

China continues to stress that its military modernization is in line with its peaceful rise in the world. Its latest White Paper on national defence emphasizes it will never seek hegemony or engage in military expansionism.

However, this has not alleviated concerns among its neighbours and regional rivals, say experts. A CFR Independent Task Force report (PDF) in 2007 on U.S.-China relations noted that many of China's neighbours and potential adversaries were making adjustments to their own defence plans and expenditures to balance China's growing military capabilities.

**Japan:** Japan and China compete over a host of issues, from regional security to international trade to access to energy. The two countries have a centuries-old history of conflict, including two Sino-Japanese wars that began in 1894 and 1931, and a bloody Japanese occupation of China during World War II. As this Backgrounder points out these animosities surface in recurring cycles, often involving Chinese anger over Japan's perceived lack of contrition for wartime crimes.

But concrete territorial and economic issues also aggravate the relationship, including Japan's close alliance with the United States, trade frictions, and ongoing disputes over ownership of various islands in the East China Sea. In 2007, China and Japan ranked third and fifth respectively in national defence expenditures (PBS), both spending only a small fraction of the U.S. budget even after adjusting for gross underreporting by Beijing.

China's military modernization fuels Japanese fears that China will use its growing economic leverage and military prowess to throw its weight around and dominate the region. Tanaka Akihiko of the University of Tokyo, speaking at a December 2008 CFR symposium on U.S.-Japan relations said China's growing military forces might change the balance of power in East Asia, which "would necessitate for Japan and the United States to readjust its force structure and other military management."

Japan has significantly upgraded capabilities over the past 15 years, deploying the Aegis radar and accompanying missile systems for its navy and warplanes armed with advanced air-to-air missiles for its air force. Since 1998, when a North Korean missile test violated Japanese airspace, Toyko has been working in partnership with the United States to develop theatre missile defences which have obvious application in the event of any conflict with China.

Over the past decade the U.S.-Japanese security alliance has been strengthened through revised defence guidelines, which expand Japan's noncombatant role in a regional contingency, allows for the deployment of an X-Band radar system in Japan as part of a missile defence system, expands bilateral cooperation in training and intelligence sharing, and allows a nuclear-powered U.S. aircraft carrier in the Yokosuka Naval Base. In September 2007 Japan joined a multinational naval exercise with the United States, Australia, Singapore, and India in the area west of the Malacca Straits.

The exercise reinforced the U.S.-led campaign of strengthening security ties among its democratic allies and "the strategic countering (PDF) of Chinese military power," argues a December 2008 U.S. Congressional Research Service report.

In 2005, a joint statement by U.S.-Japan Security Consultative Committee 2005 for the first time included Taiwan as a common strategic objective where the parties would "encourage the peaceful resolution of issues" through dialogue. Though Japan's foreign affairs ministry said this did not change the country's position on Taiwan, many experts believe the shift indicates that Japan is increasingly concerned with China's growing military capabilities.

**Taiwan:** It is the main driver for China's militarization drive and biggest concern for the United States as this Backgrounder points out. Taiwan is also pursuing modernization goals which include procurement of army attack helicopters, army utility helicopters, PAC-3 missile defence systems, fighter jets, and diesel-electric submarines, as well as transformation of the military.

Relations between China and Taiwan have improved dramatically under the administration of President Ma Ying-jeou, although U.S. arms sales to Taiwan remains contentious. In its white paper on national defence, China says the United States continues to sell arms to Taiwan "causing serious harm to Sino-US relations as well as peace and stability across the Taiwan

Strait." In October 2008, Beijing suspended military contacts with the United States in protest of the U.S. decision to sell $6.4 billion in defence equipment and services to Taiwan.

**South Korea:** It has undertaken a major modernization drive, replacing antiquated fighter aircraft, frigates, tanks, and artillery pieces with advanced systems, many of them purchased from the United States or developed in partnership with U.S. defence industries, notes the 2007 CFR report (PDF). However, most experts say South Korea's military initiatives are more in response to a possible conflict with a nuclear North Korea.A thorough look at the status of South Korea's military is contained in CFR's Crisis Guide: The Korean Peninsula.

**Russia:** The country is China's largest supplier of advanced military hardware as well as a potential great power rival. Moscow experienced a significant decline in its overall military capabilities during the 1990s, but buoyed by strong oil revenues in the past decade, it has been increasing its defence expenditure, in what most experts see as a sign to counter U.S. influence in the region.

The 2009 defence budget is expected to be $50 billion, a 25.7 percent increase from previous year. Fedor Lukyanov, chief editor of *Russia in Global Affairs,* told a January 2009 CFR meeting that there are limits to Russian military cooperation and arms sales to China. "We sold everything we could without making damage to Russian security," he said. CFR's Senior Fellow on Russian and Eurasian Studies, Stephen Sestanovich says Russia's relationship with China is based on the interests of some elites—those in the energy sector, the nuclear power sector, and the arms exports, that see China as an important market.

China and Russia also formed a security alliance to solve border disputes, which has grown into an important regional organization, the Shanghai Cooperation Organization (SCO), and includes Central Asian countries Kazakhstan, Kyrgyzstan, Tajikistan, and Uzbekistan.

China and Russia have held a number of joint military exercises under the SCO. In October 2007, the SCO also signed a memorandum of understanding with the Collective Security Treaty Organization, a military alliance of several former Soviet states.

Some analysts see the SCO as a vehicle for Russia and China to curb U.S. access to the region's vast energy supplies. But others say Russia and China have very different objectives in Central Asia. Russia wants to reassert its regional leadership there, while China seeks energy ties, note some analysts. In 2008, China and Russia resolved (BBC) their last remaining border dispute involving islands in the eastern part of the border which had seen armed clashes between the two sides during the Cold War.

**Southeast Asia:** Experts say Southeast Asian countries, including Indonesia, the Philippines, and Thailand, are currently calculating whether the political and economic benefits of closer ties with a strong China outweigh the military risks. Bilateral trade between China and all ten countries within the Association of Southeast Asian Nations (ASEAN) is expected to exceed $200 billion in 2008 up from $ 190 billion in 2007.

The region is now China's fourth-largest trading partner. Despite the economic windfall, ASEAN countries want the United States to pay more attention to the new security trends in the region, experts say. While these countries are not very vocal about their fears, experts say they are nervously looking over their shoulders at China's military buildup and wondering where it's headed.

Border disputes with some countries also complicate China's relations with its Southeast Asian neighbours. Vietnam and China each assert claims to the Spratly and Paracel Islands, archipelagos in a potentially oil-rich area of the South China Sea. Malaysia, the Philippines, and Taiwan also claim all or part of the South China Sea.

China's assertion of "indisputable sovereignty" over the Spratly Islands and the entire South China Sea has elicited concern from Vietnam and its Southeast Asia neighbours, according to the U.S. State Department. Vietnam has been pursuing closer military relations with the United States through joint military exercises, and sharing intelligence on terrorism, drugs, and other transnational threats. Vietnam has also hosted U.S. warships at its ports.

**India:** It has long-time rivalry with China over disputed borders and these two Asian giants also fought a war in 1962. New Delhi watches Beijing's military buildup closely and has undertaken military reforms of its own. It is currently building a nuclear submarine and is trying to acquire two more aircraft carriers in addition to the one it possesses.

It also launched its first unmanned moon mission in October 2008, another step in what many analysts see as a race with China in space. It has also been expanding its military cooperation with the United States. In June 2005, New Delhi and Washington agreed on a new framework for their defence relationship, including increases in defence trade, technology transfers, and joint exercises for the next ten years.

China's close military cooperation with Pakistan also concerns New Delhi. Each country helps the other to check India's power, say experts. China remains a key supplier of arms to Pakistan and in 2008, agreed to help Pakistan build two nuclear power plants. China also supplies Pakistan with nuclear technology and assistance, including what many experts suspect was the blueprint for Pakistan's nuclear bomb.

Pakistan's army has both short-and medium-range ballistic missiles that experts say came from China. According to Thomas C. Reed, a former U.S. Air Force secretary, China probably helped Pakistan test a nuclear weapon inside China in 1990. Reed adds that this weapon was most likely based on a Chinese design.

**Central Asia:** Several Central Asian countries— Kazakhstan, Kyrgyzstan, Tajikistan, and Uzbekistan —have forged closer relations with China as part of the Shanghai Cooperation Organization. Experts say tensions in China's western province of Xinjiang is one of the major reasons behind Beijing's eagerness to improve relations with the Central Asian states.

Xinjiang is largely made up of Uighurs, predominantly a Muslim community with ties to Central Asia, and China has been concerned that Central Asian states may back a separatist movement in Xinjiang. Beijing also seeks energy ties in the region. Under the SCO, the countries conduct joint military exercises. Problems with their own Muslim fundamentalist groups have led these countries to assist China in its struggle against separatists from Xinjiang, say experts. However, some experts say the Central Asian states still view China and Russia as possible hegemonic powers.

## Implications for the United States

China clearly complicates U.S. defence planning in Asia, says CFR's Senior Fellow for China Studies, Adam Segal. The Pentagon's 2008 report to Congress states: "Current trends in China's military capabilities are a major factor in changing East Asian military balances, and could provide China with a force capable of prosecuting a range of military operations in Asia-well beyond Taiwan." Most countries in the region have some degree of caution in their relationship with China, says James Mulvenon, director of Washington-based Centre for Intelligence Research and Analysis. However, none of them, he adds, want to engage in any form of containment policy with the United States. Meanwhile, though China is wary of U.S. military presence close to its border, its troubles with Uighurs has led it to support U.S. military actions inside Afghanistan, say experts.

The best way for the United States to ensure that its security interests in the region are not compromised by China's growing military capabilities is to strengthen security alliances with China's neighbours, notes the 2007 Council Task Force report. The report says the United States should better coordinate U.S.-South Korea-Japan security planning, give greater attention to ASEAN, work with ASEAN members to help draw China into constructive security relationships, and pursue a deeper military relationship with India.

## Democracy and Defence Policy

Democracy influences both the process and the content of defence policy. Thus, in a democratic setup, defence policy is based on a consultative process. Its goals and objectives, as well as many finer details, are often debated in Parliament, the media, by think-tanks and during election campaigns. This process ensures a more participative, inclusive and transparent defence policy. This indeed is the case in India and other democracies. An important outcome of this process is that democratic governments cannot concentrate on militarisation alone.

They have to balance the needs of other sectors like the economy, health and education, with the requirements of defence.

This ensures that there is no emphasis on militarisation and on an aggressive defence policy. It is well known that democracies do not go to war with each other.

The reason for this is that ordinary people want peace and prosperity and democratic governments have to reflect this aspiration in their defence policy. On the other hand, dictatorial regimes have compulsions to spend large amounts on military to take care of both domestic instability and regime survival against external intervention.

History is replete with such instances in the past and there are many contemporary examples today. This indeed is the case with democratic India's defence policy which has always focused on its own defence and has never contemplated aggression, even against its smallest neighbour. India's defence expenditure in early years of its independence was below two per cent of GDP.

Even now, it is less than 2.5 per cent, despite many real threats it has to face. Compare this to the amounts that some of our neighbours spend on military!

Another important outcome of defence policy making through a democratic process is that such a process enables nations to develop comprehensive national strength. The concept of comprehensive national strength includes economic strength, technological strength, infrastructure and other important aspects that help to build up a nation's power. A country cannot be defended by its military power alone. Recent history shows that even great powers with huge militaries can face serious difficulties in achieving their goals and can even disintegrate due to the weight of their own internal contradictions. In India, we have been able to develop comprehensive national strength and, today we are counted amongst the world's most important powers. This is not only on account of our military but also due to our economy, our science and technology, our knowledge power, our sunrise industries and our democracy. Given its vigilant citizens with a stake in the security of the nation, the genuine requirements of defence are taken care of in democracies.

Thus, despite the fact that India has been peace-loving, it has always made an effort to keep pace with the latest defence technologies. In its initial years, India had opposed nuclear weapons tooth and nail and favoured complete disarmament.

But, when the powerful nations of the world did not give up nuclear weapons and when our neighbours developed their own nuclear weapons, the Indian democracy showed enough dynamism and flexibility to change its policy and develop nuclear deterrence. However, our nuclear doctrine affirms that India will not resort to first strike and never use nuclear weapons against non-nuclear weapon states.

Thus, even India's nuclear doctrine has a purely defensive orientation. India's nuclear policy has evolved over time and is based on its essentially consensual approach in matters of national security. India's defence policy is flexible enough to respond to changes in the international strategic environment.

The primary task of the Indian Armed Forces has been to provide security for our citizens and to defend our vital interests at home and abroad. Democratic India also wishes to play a friendly and responsible role in the international arena. India has always been in the forefront of UN peace-keeping missions. It has been an important actor in international fora, particularly the United Nations.

In accordance with its growing profile and role, it deserves a place in the United Nations Security Council. India also seeks to provide an adequate military capability for operations to promote international stability, and humanitarian missions after natural or other disasters, providing assistance to the civil authorities at home, and maintenance of essential national services. India has worked for regional peace and stability and rendered exemplary service to provide relief in times of disaster. A recent example is that of relief operations following the Tsunami disaster. We are also ready to cooperate with the nations of the region to provide maritime security and participate in disaster management and disaster forecasting mechanisms.

In its external dimension, India has always sought a cooperative relationship with all nations. It has also made continuous efforts towards peace at the international level. It was in this background that in the Cold War era, India had refused to side with one bloc or another. India led the Non-Aligned Movement to mitigate tensions at the international level and to play a positive role in resolving conflicts. However, its proximity to the Soviet bloc for defence supplies was misinterpreted.

Due to the configuration of the Cold War era, India and some western nations were unable to come together and form a strong partnership. Now that the Cold War has ended and India is rapidly integrating with a globalising world, it has entered into either a strategic partnership or a strategic dialogue with all important powers of the world.

Our growing friendship with United States, Russia, European Union and Japan is a testimony to this positive development. India and China have set aside their boundary dispute to come together in the area of economic cooperation. Earnest efforts are also being made by the two sides to resolve the boundary issue but this does not allow our growing cooperation to be affected. We are trying to develop close and cooperative relationship with all our neighbours, including Pakistan. Our future vision of South Asia is a region which is stable, at peace with each other and cooperating to accelerate economic growth and prosperity of its people. We want our neighbours to take full advantage of our growing market and a rapidly globalising economy.

India has suffered from terrorism for many decades and has been able to cope with the problem effectively. In doing so, it has respected human rights. It is an important player in the war against terrorism which is seen as an assault on our secular, inclusive and democratic polity.

Countries which are undemocratic in their orientation are often a heaven for terrorists and even pursue terrorism as a part of state policy. This is an important distinction between the defence and security policies of democracies and autocratic rulers. Because democracies do not favour draconian measures and respect the rule of law, they are some times perceived to be soft or weak. The process of debate and consultation also can be a stretched out process at time. However, democracies are inherently strong and tend to promote defence policies which are conducive to the welfare of their own people and to peace and stability in the world.

## *India's Defence Industrial Policy*

Defence industrial policy in the initial years after independence was guided by the simple phrase called 'self sufficiency'. This was subsequently modified to 'self reliance' in defence production and has become a matter of varied interpretation. While for some it means the ultimate objective of complete non-dependence on imports for defence hardware, for others it means selective self-sufficiency in certain critical technologies.

And for some others it is a simple reduction in the ratio of imports to indigenous sources of supply to the armed forces. However, one can say that India's defence industrial policy broadly consists of three components: (i) maximisation of indigenous manufacturing and production (ii) License production of what could be obtained from abroad and (iii) direct purchase of those equipment not covered by the other two categories but considered essential for ensuring security.

Another important unspoken element was that everything, whether indigenous production, license production or direct purchase, was done within the government setup in line with the general industrial policy. The recent policy change, of course, demonstrates the intention to involve the private sector in defence R&D and production through licensing and the indirect opening of the defence industrial sector to foreign companies through equity participation and the offset arrangement.

The moot question is: was there something wrong with the past policy objectives? On the face of it, the policy components and objectives appear quite sound and logical for a country like India. In simple terms, it means that indigenous production should be maximised; what could not be produced indigenously should be produced under license arrangement; and those that could not be obtained through these two routes should be acquired by direct purchase.

A sound policy indeed. But the soundness of a policy has to be judged from tangible outcomes. Arguably, the problems might not have been in the contents of the policy per se. It is due to the nature defence technology and limitations of vision as embedded in the policy.

The policy objective was essentially to substitute imported equipment with indigenous production in the hope of attaining 'self-sufficiency' or 'self reliance'. Unfortunately, the security imperatives of a country translated into defence equipment are like 'moving targets'. Neither the technological capability of the defence sector nor its policy instrument as highlighted above was able to catch up with the targets.

The increasing quantum of defence imports from year to year, the country's inability to upgrade the imported equipment held for significant period under license production, and, indirectly, insignificant defence exports amply testify to this situation. The general industrial policy wherein defence items and their productions were kept strictly within the government setup further compounded the problem.

In this context, two aspects of the policy - indigenous production and license production, merit detailed analysis. Maximising indigenous production would imply more than one thing. It would mean meeting the quantitative requirements in terms of the existing demands of the Armed Forces for equipment or items at any point of time.

It would also mean increasing the varieties of items and equipment required by them. Most importantly, it would mean the ability to meet the challenges of supplying their ever-changing demands of technology specific equipment and items. India's defence industrial policy has conspicuously failed in this respect. In fact, the implication of this policy is that the country should be able to indigenously produce the challenging demands made by the Armed Forces.

Its logical extension is that defence research and development efforts have to be strengthened through policy focused research and development and adequate resources allocations thereto. It is a known fact that the defence research and development organisation has 50-odd laboratories and establishments. However, its lack of focused research and development is equally well known, though of late it has been able to achieve break-throughs in certain strategic technologies. Moreover, its budgetary allocation has been quite modest even within the overall defence budget and until recently it was part of 'Army Demand'. In fact, the Parliamentary

Standing committee on Defence recommended that defence R&D budgetary allocation should be at least 14 to 15 per cent of the total defence budget so that indigenous production to imports in the ratio of 70:30 could be achieved.

This recommendation was in line with the projected target of the report of the self-reliance committee entitled '10 year plan for self reliance in Defence systems'. But the fact remains that there is no evidence of adequate policy back-up to attain this desirable but difficult goal. The DRDO does not seem to be suffering from lack of funds per se since only 8 to 10 per cent of its total budget is reported to be spent on fundamental research. Perhaps, the solution to this issue lies somewhere else.

How about production under license, another important pillar of the policy? The normal assumption is that production under license would enable the country not only to acquire the capability to produce a particular equipment or product but also help it gain the technical know-how for subsequent upgradation and further technological innovations.

For the last fifty-odd years, India has been producing a number of defence equipment under license. Good examples in this regard are the Vijayanta tank and the MIG series of fighter aircraft. But this does not seem to have helped in the development of the Arjun Main Battle Tank and the Light Combat Aircraft. Moreover, India has not even been able to upgrade certain fighter aircraft held and operated for a long time by its Armed Forces. Thus, the above assumption is definitely not correct.

A closer examination of license production arrangements reveals certain interesting features. License production arrangements are more of an 'institutional framework' under which various types of contractual agreements could be entered into between the supplier and the buyer.

It is not necessarily a proven mechanism of technology transfer as such. It may envisage the setting up of a simple production line or facilities in the buyer country for assembly of the finished parts and components for the final finished product. In such cases, hardly any technology transfer takes place and the supplier does not part with any technical know-how. In fact, the supplier agrees to sacrifice only a small portion of his economic interest. It is also not possible to discern under these circumstances whether the supplier has compensated itself for this marginal loss by way of increasing the cost of the technology or equipment and components thereof.

On the other hand, there could be a situation where license production involves an intensive process of technology transfer within and beyond the physical production of the equipment in the host county. This is rare rather than routine. The truth of the matter is that since technology is know-how, it is the function of human understanding.

The focus of active mechanisms, implicitly or explicitly, is people. However, the truth is that no foolproof prescription could be given for the effectiveness of technology transfer. It all depends on the nature of technology to be acquired. Perhaps, India has learnt it by the hard way the limitations of licence production for attaining the objective of self-sufficiency or self-reliance in defence production.

The fact that defence technology needs long term investment, its obsolescence is high and economies of scale are difficult to attain unlike in other areas of civilian technology are well known. This is essentially because higher capability tends to drive downward the scales of production.

In the context of a limited number of customers, this trend is more regressive. On top of this, contrary to logical expectation, the production of the next generation of an equipment or of a different variant does not bring down the cost of the equipment.

It has been the British experience that a new generation could cost between one and a half times to four times of the previous variant. This is due to the fact that production of the next generation is not a simple straight line trajectory work but involves the integration of various systems, which sometimes may involve a number of companies and agencies, that were not partners earlier.

This leads to the conclusion that the policy of maximising indigenous production without a strong R&D policy back-up would not bring tangible results. License production is more of an economic compromise between the supplier and the buyer, and it does not and cannot bring about significant technology transfer without an inbuilt specific and suitable mechanism.

Every country at one point of time or the other will attain a saturation level when it comes to supplying certain categories of equipment for its armed forces. Therefore, the ultimate defence industrial policy goal must be to foster defence exports without which it is difficult to sustain the economic base of a country's defence industry.

India's defence industrial policy seems to be lacking in all these important ingredients. Since the industrial base has to be sustained for technological and economic reasons, exports are an essential element of defence industrial policy.

This is why many countries and their companies are aggressively competing in the global defence market for exports under different arrangements including license production. It is reported that way back in 1995, the United States government spent more than $7.6 billion in subsidy to help export defence equipment to sustain the economic base of its defence industry.

It is a matter of fact that strategic depth in defence production can be increased only by aiming at being 'internationally competitive' through the policy objective of defence exports. In the absence of such an approach, India's defence industrial policy is unlikely to take off in the foreseeable future.

### *Vibrant Defence Industry*

Every major power aspires to build a vibrant defence industrial base. This status is however not easily attainable. Apart from the United States and to some extent Russia and France, all other countries are in the state of struggling to arrive at such a defence industrial position.

Certain countries like the United Kingdom may be able to attain this, but due to strategic or economic preferences may deliberately choose not to consider the enormous costs involved as against the perceived security requirements. India's aspiration for this is well documented wherein it has publicly pronounced its goal of 'self sufficiency' soon after political independence and now graduating it to 'self-reliance'. The unfortunate part is that

India is still far from nearing that level even after fifty years of this laudable policy. One of the identified ongoing policy drawbacks is its weak linkage with the civilian sector of industry.

The thrust of the new policy initiative therefore is participation of the private sector in defence industry for both research and development as well as production purposes.

It has also opened up the defence sector to foreign equity participation up to 26 per cent, with the government recently expressing its willingness to consider even up to 49 per cent on case-to-case basis. Together with this is the initiation of the 'offset policy' for major foreign procurement of defence equipment of Rs.300 crores and above. The big question is: will all these initiatives contribute to the growth of a vibrant defence industry in India?

The immediate effect of these initiatives is that significant numbers of licenses have been applied for and issued to major Indian companies for production of varied components and systems. In fact, according to CII sources alone, as of date, more than 140 companies are involved in about 345 defence items/products.

Complete systems/platforms/weapons systems constitute the majority of the licenses issued, which demands higher financial investments and technical capability. This reflects the ambition and confidence of the private sector in their new ventures. On the other hand, there is a flurry of partnership agreements/collaborative ventures by these industrial companies with major global defence industrial giants from the United States, Western Europe and Israel.

This is, of course, not to ignore the existing and ongoing collaborative projects of Defence Public Sector Undertakings (DPSUs) and Ordnance Factories (OFs) with companies from these countries at the governmental level. An analysis would reveal that India's defence industrial scene now is moving on two distinct parallel lines.

The first is equipment and technology emanating from Russia and Eastern Europe, which represent approximately 70 per cent of the country's defence industrial setup. The new addition is Western technology or modified/upgraded technology through private sector companies that are poised to enter India's defence market. The moot question is: Will these different technologies eventually strengthen India's defence industrial base or add further complexities through highly mixed inventories?

In this emerging situation, a few logical things are bound to happen. First, due to the emerging competition from Western technology largely through the private sector, the Russians or other traditional suppliers are likely to at least scale down their often-repeated business behaviour of project delays, delay in supply of spares and parts, and unwillingness to transfer technology. Moreover, the tendency to jack up costs midway while implementing agreements may also get tempered with the arrival of new competitors.

However, the fact remains that the domination of Russian origin technologies and their grip on the Indian military establishment will sustain for quite some years to come particularly given that they are largely embedded through the defence public sector undertakings and other government agencies. The major positive impact of the new situation is, however, that the government agencies/DPSUs are likely to wake up from their slumber at least in those areas where they are producing items of common use, which can be easily produced at a competitive level by the private sector. This will be the immediate benefit brought in by the private sector.

While the above may be the likely positive impact, it is unlikely that western technology will be able to easily challenge the existing market structure through the private sector. This is due to the peculiarity of defence technology and its market structure. First, given that control of technology is the essence of the growth and expansion of MNCs, the global western defence giants may not easily part with high-end technology, whereas the Indian establishment would be looking for sophisticated weapons and equipment to supplement what has already been acquired from existing sources.

The private sector's ability to enter the market will depend on its capability to supply the components, parts and subsystems of the new equipment in the initial period. Secondly, opportunities for the private sector would largely depend on the government decision to opt for higher and complete major systems of western origin technologies such as the MMRCA. If such a decision goes in favour of any of the fighter aircraft of western origin, the private sector would definitely have significant scope to capture the market through the offset channel or through normal business dealings. Thirdly, the ability and willingness of western technology to supplement the defence technology requirements of the Armed Forces would be the decisive factor. As of now, the Armed Forces are already in possession of a certain level of defence technology. What they are looking for is conceptually of a higher level, which would be supplementary in nature to bridge perceived security gaps. Will the western powers through their MNCs be willing to part with this level of technology to fill the gap, which, though may be lower than the high-end strategic technology that they possess? If the answer is in the affirmative, the prospects of their capturing the Indian market are very bright. So is also the market potential for the myriad private domestic defence companies in the next five to ten years.

The challenge for Indian industry as a whole would be the will and ability to integrate the two major technology streams in the coming years. This demands the need for dedicated and focused research leading to the capability to integrate existing systems with incoming systems. While the major platforms may continue to be of Russian/Soviet origin, the genius of Indian industry would be tested in its capability to build armaments and other subsystems and integrating them at higher levels. This is the core challenge and the capability to do it would eventually make the defence industry genuinely vibrant. This will usher in the 'Indian brand of defence technology' even for export purposes free from possible objections on accounts of violations of intellectual property rights. The role of the Government of India as patron and principal customer shall be very crucial for success in achieving the above objective.

## Indian Defence Policy in Major Transition

Recently the US journal Defence News reported that the Indian government is working on a program whereby Israel would replace Russia as India's largest supplier of weapons and defence equipment by 2008. Since Russia now supplies some 70 percent of India's weapons imports, this report, if true, would mark a major transformation in Indian defence policy. Under the terms of the program, India would identify the products it wants and ask the Israeli government to negotiate with domestic firms on its behalf as Jerusalem does with regard to its own weapons.

Israel is already the second-largest supplier of military systems to India, so this program could affect a major transformation in India's security relationships. The potential repercussions of this project, which would clearly show a serious break with Moscow's arms salesmen, are immense. Given the deep ties between the US and Israeli defence industries, if this program does materialize it will also probably enhance the United States' competitive position in the Indian defence market and result in further substantial increases in the already rising amount of US arms sales and security cooperation with India. Those sales could either be bilateral or brokered through Israel, such as weapons made jointly by Israel and the United States, including missile defence systems that India reportedly is interested in acquiring.

This program would then also strengthen the developing tripartite relationship among Israel, India, and the US in regard to defence sales. We can see this already occurring, because the United States has brushed aside Pakistan's objections to India's receiving the Israeli Phalcon radar, made with US technology and thus subject to US veto on its transfer to a third party.

Realization of the projected Indo-Israeli project would also simultaneously symbolize and express India's rising continental Asian status as a great power with interests and capabilities across the continent, allowing it to break free of its confining chains as merely a major South Asian power if not the regional leader, something that both Indian and foreign observers have labeled as a prerequisite for a full partnership with the United States.

Not only would those trends strengthen Indo-Israeli ties, they would provide fuel to the oft-reported desire on the part of at least some US elites to create a tripartite alliance with India and Israel against terrorism (if not for other, broader objectives that would emerge later). Joint Indo-Israeli defence collaboration on a scale envisaged above would also, or so these advocates hope, tie into the US alliance and Israeli partnership with Turkey, creating a kind of pan-Asian bloc. The new program grows out of India's difficulty in negotiating a US$10 billion multi-year defence acquisition program with Russia. Three areas in particular seem to have caused some anxiety in New Delhi.

In March 2002, The Times of India reported that the Parliamentary Standing Committee had urged the government to avoid overdependence on Russia for armaments and spare parts. The committee reportedly acknowledged Russia's previous contributions and reliability as a provider of defence equipment to India but cautioned that the current dependence on Moscow for almost 80 percent of its arms imports is unhealthy. It also observed that Russia was not providing military hardware on the same beneficial financial terms that it had during the Soviet era. Therefore the committee also urged the Indian government to cease making advance payments for weapons acquisitions from Russia, and that in the future it seek to put more defence contracts up for competitive tender. Russia also has come under criticism because of India's difficulty in obtaining and negotiating speedy delivery of spare parts for these weapons systems. At the same time it became clear that given its worsening relations with Pakistan, India is seeking to diversify its foreign purchases and use foreign partners to develop its own defence industrial capability, eg by conditioning purchases on obtaining offsets from the sellers to develop its own indigenous capability.

The alliance, if it were to materialize, would build on the already greatly improved Indo-Israeli relationship that has led to large-scale military sales from Israel and to India's rapprochement with the United States as well. As the Phalcon deal suggests, it could become possible to envisage tripartite collaboration among these states on missile defence, especially if India's great goal of securing the end to all US sanctions on the transfer of both civil and military technology is realized.

Moreover, the broadening of India's ties and reach in political-military terms through the acquisition of top-quality defence systems would enable it to play the kind of role that analysts in both India and the US postulate as being essential to any serious strategic partnership with the United States. And that role also accords very much with some of the deepest aspirations of India's foreign and defence policy elites, thus highlighting a congruence of visions concerning India's future international position.

In effect India's aspiration to play a major role "from Socotra to Sumatra" would have been both realized and blessed by the United States, as Secretary of State Colin Powell implicitly suggested in 2001. India would then become not just a South or even Central Asian power but a major player in the Persian Gulf, the Middle East, and Southeast Asia.

At the same time, India's search for new vistas in defence acquisition and production relates very much to its rising economic, technological, and military-industrial capabilities as well as to its desire to strengthen existing long-standing partnerships, eg with Russia. For example, beyond the existing $10 billion weapons sales from Russia to India, India is collaborating with Russia on joint production of a fifth-generation fighter that Russia feels vital to its military future. Both are also collaborating on research that is probably tied to missile defence and nuclear systems as well. More broadly, India is the only country with whom Russia is collaborating on joint production of sophisticated and futuristic weapons systems. Likewise India, not China, gets the best weapons currently being produced in Russia, systems that not even Russia's armed forces can obtain. Moscow offers offsets in the form of technology transfer of production skills and know-how to India, one of its largest customers. Although India obviously seeks to diversify its sources of foreign procurement, Russian producers have until now been confident of their ability to obtain the bulk of Indian defence contracts.

Whether or not this confidence is misplaced, time will tell, but diversification and strengthening of India's own capabilities surely would increase India's scientific-technological and manufacturing capabilities for weapons production. This objective also appears to be a major goal of the deals now being made with Russia, Israel, and presumably the United States. We see similar deals with Italian and French firms for joint manufacture of weapons systems.

India's leading defence firm, Hindustan Aeronautics Ltd (HAL), is also pressing an outsourcing program whereby it would help private Indian companies find and choose foreign partners to undertake such high-tech projects as avionics integration, weapons-system integration, and other related efforts to "lay the foundation for a credible domestic aerospace industry base that could meet the majority of India's military aerospace requirements in the next 10 years". And it is no less logical to assume that India would be thrilled to duplicate this particular kind of relationship with Washington, especially as India already has a large space program with military applications and very much wants US conventional-weapons systems and technology transfer.

Indeed, a Pentagon-commissioned study of Indo-American perceptions reported that on the basis of many interviews, a uniform conclusion was reached that "for Indians, technology transfer from the United States is military cooperation's touchstone". Other Indian assessments confirm the great importance that India attaches to transfer of both civil and defence technology as a critical and essential element in any partnership with the US. While India's aspirations in the defence industry are common to other countries that seek the capability for indigenous production of most, if not all of their weapons, it is nevertheless clear that this deal, if it materializes, would utterly transform defence relationships among major players in the defence business: India, the US, Israel, and Russia. The major transformations in Asian security that accelerated after September 11, 2001, have clearly not yet run their course. Nor is it clear when the overall Asian situation will stabilize or when also the rising tide of weapons sales will abate.

But there can be no doubt that major changes are in the offing and that the future holds many more surprises and jolts for all of those who seek to play a key role in the security and defence of Asia.

# Bibliography


*Alperovitz, Gar. The Decision to Use the Atomic Bomb. New York: Vintage Books, 1996.*

*Arend, A.: International Law and the Use of Military, London, Routledge, 1993.*

*Damrosch, L.F.: Law and Force in the New International Order, Boulder, Westview Press, 1991.*

*Friedman, G.: The Future of War: Power, Technology and American World Dominance in the 21st Century, N.Y., Random House, 1996.*

*Huntington, S.P.: The China Modernisation Military and the State, N.Y., Vintage Books, 1964.*

*Jones, W.H.: The Government and Politics of Indian Military, London, Hutchinson, 1971.*

*Mary, W.: Military Space Force: the Cultural Dimensions of Authority, Cambridge, Belknap Press, 1985.*

*Posen, B.R.: The Sources of Modernization Military, Ithaca, 1984, Cornell Univ. Press.*

*Rhodes, Richard, The Making of the Atomic Bomb, New York: Simon and Schuster, 1988.*

*Rosen, P.: Societies and Military Power: India and its Armies, Ithaca, Cornell University Press, 1996.*

# Index



♦♦♦